Ray Chesterton was *The Daily Telegr*...
rugby league writer for 15 years, winni...
way. He lives on Sydney's North Sho...
children Katey, Lucy and Andrew a... ...ondering if
Balmain will win a premiership before he dies.

By the same author

DOING MY BLOCK

RAY CHESTERTON

Pan Macmillan Australia

First published 1996 in Ironbark by Pan Macmillan Australia Pty Limited
St Martins Tower, 31 Market Street, Sydney

Copyright © Ray Chesterton 1996

All rights reserved. No part of this book may be reproduced or transmitted in any form or by any means, electronic or mechanical, including photocopying, recording or by any information storage and retrieval system, without prior permission in writing from the publisher.

National Library of Australia
cataloguing-in-publication data:

Chesterton, Ray.
Good as Gould: Phil Gould's stormy life in football.

ISBN 0 330 35873 1.

1. Gould, Phil. 2. Rugby League football—Australia—Biography. 3. Rugby League football—Australia—Coaching.
I. Title.

796.3338

Typeset in 11½/14 pt Times New Roman by Post Typesetters, Brisbane
Printed in Australia by McPherson's Printing Group

*This book is dedicated to
my parents Bruce and Nancy,
and my brother John.
– Phil Gould*

CONTENTS

Foreword by Brad Fittler — ix
Preface — xiii

The Long and Winding Road
FROM PLAYER TO COACH

Ben — 3
The Day the Game Stood Still — 34
When You're a Jet — 63
Bulldogs and Bullfrogs — 80
The Phantom Coach — 100
The Smooth-As-Silk Premiership — 118
The Feudin' Fightin' Family — 139
Putting Pride into The Panthers — 168
Penrith's Greatest Day — 185
From The Mountains to The Sea — 201

State against State, Mate against Mate
THE ORIGIN EXPERIENCE

Call to Arms: Origin Coach — 225
Re-inventing the Blues — 234
The Brotherhood — 252
MG's Crash — 258
Magic Night at the MCG — 270
The Fatty Vautin Miracle — 287

The Super League Wars
TALES FROM THE PHILLIP STREET BUNKER
    The April Fool's Day Massacre   299
    The Lolly Shop   324
    Down For the Count   358

Short Passes   376

Epilogue   390

FOREWORD

The first time I met Phil Gould I was 17-years-of-age and he had just taken over as first grade coach at Penrith in 1990.

I had played half a dozen first grade games the year before and thought my career was on the way up. The first thing Phil Gould did was drop me back to reserve grade for the opening five rounds of the season.

I thought I was a first grader. He thought I needed more time to develop. He won that argument. At least it taught me a lesson. Never argue with the coach.

Looking back I feel Phil might have been right. I spent the first five rounds in reserve grade and came back into first grade against Balmain. I've been there ever since.

I consider it an absolute bonus to have been under Phil's tuition for the greater part of my career. He was my coach at Penrith, he was my State of Origin coach and now we're both at Easts.

Being coached by Phil is more than just learning about rugby league. It's a lesson in learning about life. His tuition extends well beyond the training and playing fields. He has been around enough himself as a footballer and as a man to have learnt about the game and about how to live the right way.

His guidance and support have been vital in any success I've had. I don't want to pour the honey on too thick. Gus will think I'm sending him up. But I think he knows how much respect and admiration he commands both in and out of the rugby league community.

If Phil Gould had not been around in 1992 when Penrith was undergoing so much trauma following the tragic death of my friend—and a friend of everyone at Penrith—Ben

Alexander, the havoc wreaked on the club would have been much worse.

Phil was the binding agent most responsible for keeping the club together during those dark hours. He carried a lot of pain within himself but somehow managed to keep everyone else focused on the future while allowing time for mourning.

Although he has won premierships with Penrith and Canterbury and State of Origin series with NSW, dealing with a shattered Penrith in 1992 may have been his finest hour.

Putting the pieces back together and rekindling Penrith's ambitions required patience, diplomacy, foresight and courage. Phil was equal to the challenge.

It was during that disruptive period that I actually moved in with Phil for a while to try and come to grips with the ever-changing situation. Sharing a unit with Phil Gould is not something I would recommend for anyone looking for a conventional lifestyle. He's an insomniac at times, staying up for what seem to be hours at a time while he studies videos and playing patterns of rival teams.

I have never known anyone as thorough as Phil Gould when it comes to preparing a football team for a match. I think if you asked him, he would be able to tell you what size boots the opposition players wear. He certainly always knows every other characteristic of their playing style. He knows whether they step off their left or right foot, whether they're lazy in defence or have weaknesses in attack.

State of Origin under Gus was a culture shock for both the players and Phil. When he joined the NSW team he was the youngest coach ever to have won a first grade premiership. He was too old to be a player and too young to fit comfortably into the stereotype age bracket of the usual representative coach.

The first time he saw the NSW players in action at the team

hotel having a drink, being laid back and seemingly unconcerned about the seriousness of the situation, he said nothing. But he pulled me aside and asked if this was the way the NSW team usually behaved in camp.

I told him it was—and waited for the reaction I knew would come.

It was only hours later that Phil sat us down and started getting us re-aligned with the reality of what we were trying to achieve. He made us admit that playing for NSW was important to us and to our pride. From then on we were a NSW team focused on success.

Three consecutive State of Origin series wins shows how effective his approach was to our performance. Those Queenslanders never had a chance.

No-one who knows Phil Gould would ever suggest he is a wowser. Someone who doesn't know the importance of having a drink, having a bet, having fun. If the circumstances are right and the piano player is banging out some familiar songs, he can be as big a party animal as anyone else. Well, perhaps a quieter party animal than a lot of us.

But he sets rules and parameters. There is a time for fun and games and a time for embracing the work ethos and the seriousness of what we are all about when we pull on the sky blue jumper of NSW. Gus allows us just the right blend of fun and focus when we are in camp.

Although Phil has an encyclopedic knowledge of rugby league and tactics he is not a walking computer. There is a human side to his approach as well. There are team talks and there is time for individual consultation as well if a player thinks it's needed.

When I first met Phil at Penrith as a 17-year-old neither of us knew where we were headed. We were both Penrith boys looking for an opportunity.

Phil had already taken the chances that had come his way and played for Newtown, Souths and Canterbury before turning to coaching and winning the first grade premiership with Canterbury. Now he was back home in Penrith country looking to take his old club to its first premiership. And he did in 1991.

My chances came as well. I was in that 1991 premiership winning team. I've played for NSW and I've captained Australia to a World Cup win. I'm proud of that record and I'm realistic enough to know that perhaps it might not have happened if Phil Gould had not been around to point me in the right direction at crucial times.

We were two Penrith boys who made good and hopefully opened the way for a lot more players and coaches from that district to go on to bigger things in rugby league, the way Greg Alexander, Mark Geyer, John Cartwright and a host of others have done.

I'm glad Phil's story is being told and I'm pleased that Ray Chesterton is the author because I know they have been close mates for years as well.

Brad Fittler
May 1996

PREFACE

The gestation period for female elephants is around 18 months. According to Greek mythology, Helen of Troy was born from an egg. The Romans say that Rome was founded by Romulus and Remus, two brothers who were suckled by a she-wolf.

All of those transformations and deliveries were nowhere near as difficult as the genesis of this book.

It has been a project that seems to have stretched back almost to Gutenberg inventing the printing press.

Phil Gould and I first talked about the book after he won the 1991 premiership with Penrith, without us quite getting the momentum to make it happen. It has been an on and off project ever since, until it finally started becoming a serious discussion around 1994.

If you hold this book to your nose you will catch the faint odour of Chinese food. Much of the note-taking was in Chinese restaurants from Rozelle to Redfern to the City of Sydney.

The pages will also have a touch of the briny about them as well because we also compiled notes in the Clovelly Hotel beer garden. With hindsight that was probably not such a good idea.

If you ask me I will tell you that Phil Gould is the most unreliable, inconsistent, unmanageable, mind-changing and difficult man to work with in the entire world.

Trouble is, he will tell you the same thing about me, so we would break even.

My knowledge of Phil Gould goes back to when he was a player at Penrith. I wrote the first feature story about him being one of the youngest first grade captains in the history of Australian rugby league.

The yarn's had some sort of immortality imposed on it by being incorporated as part of a 'Hall of Fame' in Penrith Leagues Club.

Come to think of it, I don't think any royalties changed hands for that either. Another one I'll put down to experience.

I can clearly remember going to Prince Alfred Hospital as a young sportswriter on the *Daily Telegraph* to check on Phil's condition after one of his eye injuries—the first I think.

For some reason, like one of those fragmented memories that become indelibly etched in your mind, I can still see Phil coming down the hospital corridor, a bandage over his eye like an old-time pirate, to have a chat.

Researching this book, I discovered I'd been writing about Phil as a player, coach, premiership winner and three times State of Origin winner, for more than a quarter of a century.

Probably his most successful high-profile achievement was his courageous stand against the planned intrusion of Super League.

At the moment he stands on the crest of a never-ending wave of success. His media involvement grows with each passing year and now involves pay-TV, Channel 9, radio with 2UE and newspaper columns.

He has gone from the modesty of playing at Penrith to become a giant of the coaching scene, a visionary about rugby league's future, a strategist without peer and widely-respected authority.

His status has risen so sharply that he is now on first name terms with Kerry and James Packer and a host of other celebrities. He's something of a celebrity himself as an after-dinner speaker.

I used to wonder how he found time to fit it all in every day, until I realised he saves time by not returning my phone calls.

In his time, Phil has been with Penrith, Newtown, Canterbury and Souths as a player and Penrith, Canterbury and now Easts as a coach.

I will not say it was impossible to find someone who was critical of Phil after all those years in the game, but the overwhelming feeling towards him was one of friendship and memories of good and successful times.

Anyway, their opinions are all in this book.

The vast majority of interviews in this book were conducted over a period of time and Wests' Paul Langmack and Penrith's Steve Carter and the club former chief executive Don Feltis were especially helpful.

To capture the accurate ambiance of the circumstances surrounding Phil at earlier stages of his career we used some quotes from the Penrith club history book and Mario Fenech's biography about his time at Souths.

Ray Chesterton
May 1996

The Long and Winding Road

FROM PLAYER TO COACH

Ben

At 11 pm on June 21, 1992, Phil Gould was playing the poker machines at Penrith Leagues Club when the paging system summoned him to the front foyer. The shocking news that waited there was to detonate the greatest explosion of headlines and controversy over a single incident the Sydney rugby league scene had ever known.

Thinking the call might be from a disgruntled supporter or merely from someone wanting to be signed into the club, Gould's pal Ross Seymour offered to answer the page.

Seymour was gone for 10 minutes, then returned, ashenfaced. 'That was the police,' he said. 'There's been an accident. Players are involved and at least one is dead.'

It was the tragic beginning to the saddest, most disruptive and bitter episode to confront any club. Its ramifications were widespread and poisonous. By the time it was all over, a star player would have been sacked, another emotionally wrecked, a chasm would have opened between sections of the team, and animosity would have erupted. Players would take part in matches side by side while refusing to talk to one another. A year after winning the first grade premiership Penrith would disintegrate into a million fragments. Sorrow would flow as freely as the nearby Nepean River, without being able to carry away the pain as floodwaters do with debris.

Death is no stranger to rugby league. Players of great reputation held in the warmest regard have obviously died of natural causes since the game started in Australia in 1908. Death has also come shockingly and unexpectedly to young players. St George forward Geoff Selby was killed in a car smash in 1989. Easts centre James Matthews, 24, died on December 24, 1992, in a head-on collision on the Hume Highway in southern NSW, while driving home to spend Christmas with his parents at their home in Wagga.

On those occasions rugby league's grief was genuine and heartfelt. But life eventually returned to normal within the accepted parameters of conventional mourning periods. The death of 20-year-old Penrith player Ben Alexander transcended everything that had gone before. Ben's death that terrible night served to simultaneously unite and divide the local community, confirming for many people that, despite its classification as a city, Penrith was still at heart a big country town where tragedy had widespread repercussions and everyone was affected.

Alexander was one of the most popular players in the club. He had grown up with most of the local first grade side, including internationals John Cartwright, Mark Geyer and Brad Fittler as well as his older brother and first grade star Greg.

Greg and Ben were looked upon as young sporting princes, part of the premiership-winning achievement of 1991. The winning of the first grade competition had given Penrith distinct stature, recognition and pride, and defined community achievement. It seemed to be the beginning of a golden period.

But it only took a few moments of madness, ill-fate and alcohol on a quiet Sunday night in Penrith to end that dream and plummet Gould, his players, administrators and supporters into an abyss from which none would return unscathed.

The day had started innocently enough. Penrith played Eastern Suburbs at Penrith Park and won first grade 23–10.

FROM PLAYER TO COACH

Ben Alexander earlier had played reserve grade, kicking a field goal in a 25–6 win.

Scheduled after the matches was a get-together of the players at the Leagues club across the road from Penrith Park. There they would receive their blazers for winning the previous year's grand final.

The combination of youthful exuberance at receiving the blazer that all players dream about, coupled with the disenchantment at the way his career had stalled in 1992, made it a night of mixed emotions for Ben. The blazer was a reminder of the promise and potential he possessed but had not been able to fulfil at that stage. Behind the scenes of that 1992 season there had been bickering with Gould about Ben's failure to harness his considerable skills and buckle down.

The retirement of skipper Royce Simmons after the 1991 grand final had left the first grade hooking job vacant. Coach Gould, in a move that would be adopted more and more by other clubs as the 1990s evolved, chose to put half-back Ben Alexander into the hooking role. North Sydney would take the same step with Mark Soden in 1994. Bob Fulton would take Manly to the 1995 grand final with ex-half-back Des Hasler as hooker. The positional switch made sense at Penrith. There was no room for another half-back in first grade while Greg was healthy. Even so, it was a move that did not sit all that easily on Ben's shoulders, although he was coming round more and more to the idea. Compounding the stress was the fact that his brother Greg was out injured for the match against Easts, but Gould had overlooked Ben as a replacement.

Ben left Penrith Leagues club that night after drinks with fellow players—climbing into his car with Glenn Liddiard, Luke Goodwin and Scott Murray. There were reports that Ben had insisted on driving to another nightspot in Penrith after being asked to surrender his keys.

Good as GOULD

Minutes later his life ended when his car crashed into another vehicle and ricocheted into a steel pole. The driver's seat where Ben was sitting took the full brunt of the impact. An eyewitness described how he had rushed to the scene and pulled Liddiard out through the window of the wrecked Honda. Rescue workers cut the other passengers from the wreckage. Murray broke his leg and jaw. An elderly couple in the other car escaped injury.

Goodwin had desperately tried to alert Alexander to the dangers in the final fatal second—calling: 'Look out for the pole!' as the car skidded.

The accident site on the corner of Desborough and Bennett Roads was a known danger spot in Penrith. However a coroner's report handed down a month after the accident by Coroner John Hiatt revealed that Alexander had gone through a red light and that his blood alcohol reading of .148 was almost three times the legal limit.

The immediate effect of news of Ben Alexander's death triggered initial shock, then bewilderment and finally an extraordinary outpouring of grief and pain that shook the entire city.

Gould was one of the first on the scene of the accident. So was Greg Alexander. His grief was overwhelming. Out of his mind with the agony of losing his beloved brother, he attacked one of the players who had been in the car, forgetting that Ben had been driving. Alexander kicked and punched the ambulance carrying his brother's body.

The funeral at St Nicholas' Catholic Church in Penrith attracted 5000 mourners, the excess congregation flowing out of the crowded aisles and filling the garden outside. The emptiness on the tear-stained faces of Greg Alexander and Brad Fittler as they carried the coffin were enough to break a city's heart.

FROM PLAYER TO COACH

Police closed off streets around the church because of the congestion and senior players formed a guard of honour. The club called in John Merrick, the leading grief counsellor from the NSW Coroner's Office, to talk to the players for more than an hour at a gathering called in lieu of training.

'He did a wonderful job. His words were firm but reassuring. He urged everyone to deal with their grief by ripping into training in the next few days,' said chief executive Don Feltis.

The pain would fragment into many different directions and pull down stanchions that had taken 25 years to erect. Greg Alexander played barely at all for the rest of the season. Close friend and eventual brother-in-law, a grieving Mark Geyer, was sacked by Penrith for refusing to take a drug test and life became a swirling tangle of accusations, innuendo, headlines, lies and feuding.

Gould was portrayed by some as the catalyst of the tragedy because he had dropped Ben to reserve grade, a decision based on the player's poor form. Some members of the Alexander family and their supporters viewed Gould as a heartless villain who might have averted the tragedy if he had left Ben in first grade.

'It was a pointless and idiotic argument. The fact was that as painful as it might be to accept, Ben was to blame for the accident. No-one else,' said one Penrith official, who preferred not to be named. Even at this late stage, the issue is still sensitive.

'He's dead, and that is a tragedy. But he was well over the legal limit from drinking, he was speeding, he went through a red light and he wasn't wearing a seat belt. Those are the facts of it.

'As coach, Gould had sat down with Ben and showed him video of his performances in his last couple of matches. Ben agreed that he didn't deserve to be in the side, and accepted being dropped. When he was dropped, all hell broke loose. He was killed a week later. Ben was one of five players dropped after Penrith were beaten 20–0 by lowly placed Parramatta.

Good as GOULD

'Some members of the family claimed that if Gould had not dropped Ben, he would have stayed at the leagues club that night and would still be alive today. They say he only left the club because he could not stand to be in the same place as Gould. That's just bullshit. Ben came to the club, got his blazer and drank from 6pm to around 9.30pm when he left. He was in no hurry to rush away.'

Emotions were at white heat.

One night a woman walked up the driveway to Gould's house, screaming that he was a 'murderer, murderer'. Then radio talkback host on 2KY's breakfast show and former grand final-winning forward with Manly, Peter Peters, received constant telephone calls from Mrs Leonie Alexander.

'She wanted to go on air, giving a different side to it. Off air she told me what she thought. I had Mark Geyer, who is a mate of mine, ringing every day. It was a very traumatic story. I was going to put Mrs Alexander to air. It would have been terrific radio but it was too emotional,' said Peters.

Gould became a man under siege from the media, with newspapers devoting pages to the Alexander saga. He was also under considerable pressure to hold his team together as it splintered under the unrelenting strain.

Stories were told of the $30,000 Gould provided so the Alexander family could buy a trophy-manufacturing business that would be run by Greg's step-father, Gerard Hughes.

It was not the only time Gould reached into his pocket to help the family.

The money was not extended for any other reason than love and respect.

The Alexander brood of boys, headed by Greg and Ben, awakened paternal instincts in Gould.

The Alexanders became his extended family. He

FROM PLAYER TO COACH

socialised with them and helped whenever he could with finance and encouragement as a mentor and, in time, a football coach to Greg and Ben.

Greg's sister Linda attended business college at Gould's expense, and at one stage he was paying Ben's wages out of his own pocket at the trophy shop.

He also paid for Ben to holiday in Hawaii and helped when family bills became a problem.

The business was a recurring nightmare, Gould recalls. The telephone and electricity had to be continually re-connected after being disconnected because bills were not paid.

Gould was single and being paid as a first grade coach as well as having outside interests.

Gould's $30,000 contribution to the trophy shop was not repaid, although he had not pressed for compensation.

Gould's only concern was that the already failing business would continue to lose money to such an extent his liability could balloon to $100,000 or more.

He wanted out.

Forsaking $30,000 was a worry. Remaining in the business could be ruinous.

Eventually club boss Feltis intervened and organised Greg Alexander to legally replace Gould as an investor in the business.

It was not an amicable agreement with Hughes and there was rancour on both sides.

It was the start of the toxins that would, for a while, rupture the relationship between Gould and the Alexanders.

Greg Alexander and the emotional Geyer were devastated by Ben's death—but in many ways the rhythm of a successful side was already rupturing well before the accident.

Geyer was angry at Gould's treatment of Ben in selecting Penrith teams. Other problems were developing as cliques formed among the players. Penrith's management stepped in at one stage to voice its concern about a 'family' of players that included Geyer, Greg Alexander and others.

Then Geyer fell out with Gould over representative selection. He claimed he had been assured by Gould that he would still be in the NSW squad if he dropped out of the 1992 City side with injury. He dropped out of the City side but missed NSW selection.

Gould was appointed City and NSW coach in 1992 for the first time and Geyer put his non-selection down to victimisation. His omission, coupled with what he viewed as ill-treatment of Ben Alexander, meant he and Gould did not speak for a month leading up to Ben's death—and rarely after that.

NSW utility back Steve Carter counselled Geyer, trying to convince him not to blame Gould for Ben's accident. 'I told him, mate, you can't blame him for that,' said Carter. 'It's just life. You can't put that sort of thing on someone's conscience. A lot of other players felt the same way as I did. I don't think anyone blamed Gus. He had at least half the club on his side.'

Geyer would in time reassess his evaluation of Gould. 'I confess that during the darkest hours of it all, I thought about going around to Gus' house to seek some vengeance,' Geyer said two years later about his immediate reaction during those troubled times.

'In my bitterness the more bad things I heard about him back then, the better I felt. With a clearer head I realise it was a less emotional way to think. I apologise wholeheartedly to Gus for what I even thought. I was unfair. I know now that he was just as much affected by Ben's death as all of us who knew him.'

No club could hope to function in such a volatile and disjointed environment as 1992 produced. Gould and Cartwright and to a lesser degree Fittler bore the brunt of it. To assuage their grief, Geyer, Greg Alexander and some friends spent nearly two weeks after the funeral sleeping under a giant tarpaulin in a field, washing away their sorrows with alcohol and other pacifiers, the centrepiece a giant bonfire that blazed away night after night.

Concerned neighbours, not happy with the flames and the noise, lodged complaints with the police. Morning suits hired from a local shop for the funeral were thrown into the flames as the hirers vowed that the suits would never be worn by anyone else again. It is rumoured that because the hired suits were never returned, the players were sued and the football club eventually had to pick up the bill and deduct the costs from the appropriate contracts.

In an effort to offer his own condolences and establish bridges of communication between bitterly divided groups of people, many of whom had grown up together as friends and acquaintances, Gould took the step of going to the Alexander home. There, he was so badly rocked by the abusive language hurled at him by a member of the Alexander family that he wandered aimlessly for a couple of hours.

John Cartwright was a rock through it all. He and his family were subjected to considerable torment via a smear campaign because he was seen as siding with Gould. Relations between the Alexander and Cartwright families had been shaky since the late 1980s when Greg and John had fallen out over a girl. They went through a period of nearly 12 months of not speaking until the feud was ended by the arrival of Gould in 1990 as coach. Cartwright contemplated retiring as the pressure refused to abate. Even Brad Fittler, a friend of the Alexanders since childhood but also a friend of Gould's, was viewed with suspicion. Fittler, trying to be even-handed, stayed at Gould's house during the State of Origin campaign to get some respite from the pressure. He also pulled out of the Australian squad to take on Great Britain in the second Test of 1992, citing the upheaval caused by Ben's death as his reason.

Trying to remain civil to both the Gould and Alexander cliques, Fittler was caught in an emotional crossfire.

There were also anonymous and hateful letters sent to Penrith club about Gould, to Fittler and to Gould himself. Geyer was also a target for sick minds and received abusive letters, especially when he walked out on his contract.

Brett Boyd, named as the new hooker in the side, was also a target.

Such pressure had to take its toll. Steve Carter walked from the field during a match against the Gold Coast one afternoon and declared to Gould: 'I'm going to retire. I can't play any more.' Gould pacified him and Carter returned to the match. Gould several times approached Feltis, wanting to resign, saying he believed it was the best result for everyone.

'I'd go into his office to tell him and he'd say: "If you go, so do I",' Gould remembered. 'In the end we'd say to each other: "Let's stick it out."

'A lot of things were making our life very difficult but at the end of the day, the future of the club lay in our hands.'

Mark Geyer seemed constantly in the spotlight. A devastating performer at club, State and Test level when he was focused, Geyer was also one of the most volatile players in the premiership with a hair-trigger temper. Often he would act first and consider the consequences later. One night at a team meeting at Penrith Park in 1991, Gould reviewed the team's losing performance in a match the previous week, pointing out that lost possession had been costly. Geyer, who had spilled a couple of balls in the match, jumped to his feet and stormed out of the dressing room shouting: 'So it's all my fault we lost, is it?'

FROM PLAYER TO COACH

He returned at the next training session and apologised. At the next team meeting Gould told the team that he was going to discuss errors in the previous game. With a wink and a grin he turned to Greg Alexander: 'Will you just check and see if that's all right with Mr Geyer?'

Geyer made a late start to the 1992 season because of an eight-week suspension imposed after a NSWRL drug check at Penrith. There had been a humorous side to a previous appearance at Penrith by the NSWRL's drug agency. The night the check was to be made, the first grade players were training at a nearby oval and Gould drove down to tell them to come back to Penrith Park.

Geyer took exception to Gould's inquiry about his readiness for a urine check. 'Why are you asking me?' Geyer said. 'Do you think I won't pass?'

Gould: 'No, MG. I'm just telling you it's on.'

As he drove back to Penrith Park Gould glanced in the rear-vision mirror to check that all of the cars were following. They were, except one. It was going in the opposite direction.

For all of his volatility, Geyer was a proven and exceptional performer. But his long-term absences from training and matches after Ben's death were harmful to team morale. The club, having extended sympathy, was looking for a return to normality, despite Geyer's claims of a knee injury and the knowledge of his distress over Ben's death.

Weeks of speculation ended with Geyer being called to a meeting with club boss Don Feltis and asked to submit to a full medical check which would have revealed any substances in his system that were outside the NSWRL's drug guidelines. Geyer refused and, in a sometimes heated confrontation, quit the club, throwing away an extended contract worth around $350,000.

Feltis had tried repeatedly to contact Geyer and get him to

a meeting but appointments were constantly broken or ignored. Eventually Geyer, having been told it was his last chance to attend a meeting, arrived at Penrith Park on Saturday morning, July 4, with Greg Alexander as a passenger in his car. Penrith by then had decided to sack Geyer and had been in communication with NSWRL general manager John Quayle to inform him of their intentions.

Geyer sat in the front seat of Feltis' car—Alexander in the back—while details of Penrith's dissatisfaction with his commitment were detailed. Feltis told Geyer that unless he submitted to a drug test on the following Monday and began to comply with his contract conditions, serious action would be taken.

Geyer's response to quit would prove the most expensive decision he has ever made. Had he sat quietly and let Penrith sack him, Geyer would have received most, if not all, of his contract money. Instead all he received was pro-rata contract payments for 1992 and winning and losing bonuses for games the club had played.

When Geyer said he was quitting, Feltis seized the moment to produce the contract and ask Geyer to tear it up. He did. Friends say Feltis still has the eight pieces of the contract.

'It had got to the stage where Geyer was ignoring directions from our head coach Phil Gould to come to training and to matches,' Feltis said. 'When Geyer did attend training he was not doing the right thing. It just got to the point where Phil recommended that Geyer go. It got down to one of them having to go. There was never any doubt that I would stick to the club's head coach. The board did as well.'

To signal the unity of the decision, three club directors were at Penrith Park as observers for Geyer's meeting with Feltis to ensure there was no misunderstanding of the club's decision.

With Geyer gone, Feltis and Gould would continue

Penrith's spring-cleaning of the club's playing strength. Three more players departed before the end of the season; the likes of Glenn Liddiard and Luke Goodwin were associated with Geyer and the Alexander family. But others were part of a general restructuring process as Gould and Penrith looked for a new direction.

At the end of 1992, Geyer, Paul Dunn, Col Bentley, Andrew Leeds, Glenn Liddiard, David Greene, Shayne Boyd, Mark Lyons, Graham Lyons, Luke Goodwin, Paul Smith, Grant Izzard, Tulsen Tollett and Keith Leyshon were gone.

It was as if Penrith and Gould were straddling two different worlds in 1992. In one there was disharmony, vindictiveness and spite. In the other, astonishingly, there was success on the football field.

The weekend after Ben Alexander's funeral, Penrith were drawn to play Wests at Campbelltown and given little chance of winning after such a week. Instead they did win, somehow, 18–10, going into the match on a preparation of doing almost nothing.

'We didn't do much training that week. In fact we just sat around mostly, looking at videos of comedy shows,' remembered Cartwright.

In the dressing room Cartwright told the players in a pre-match speech: 'You remember some wins more than others but if you win today, you will remember it for the rest of your lives.' Steve Carter, who like prop Barry Walker, Cartwright, Fittler, and Colin Van Der Voort was loyal to Gould, said: 'You could see the emotion on the players' faces. Everyone was saying the same thing. I don't know if it was for Ben, but it was for the club and it was for his memory of what Ben was all about. He was a friend of everyone's.'

After beating Wests the impetus faded and Penrith lost five of its last six games.

Good as GOULD

Penrith quashed speculation that the match against Wests could have been forfeited because of the special circumstances. 'Forfeiting was never really on and I don't think the NSWRL would have let us do it anyway,' Feltis said.

'We understood that Wests had responsibilities to their players, their sponsors and their supporters and they wanted to play. If the circumstances were reversed, Penrith would have wanted to play.' Gould included Greg Alexander and Mark Geyer in the side to play Wests, pending their confirmation of selection on the morning of the match.

'I included them in the side because of the respect with which they were held in this club,' Gould said. 'That was all. It was up to the players. If they woke up on Sunday morning and wanted to play, there was a place for them. If they woke up on Sunday and didn't want to play, their jumpers would be rested.'

A 1992 season that had started with Penrith being hailed as a potential 'team of the decade' because of the youth and talent of its premiership-winning side in 1991 would end in fragmentation and severe public scrutiny. It was a season that devastated Gould personally while bringing him the glory of a winning series with NSW in the State of Origin—and a far more credible performance with Penrith than many remember.

'We lost the first two games of the season and then we put three in a row together, culminating in us belting Brisbane 24–10 at Lang Park,' Gould said.

'Greg Alexander was excellent. I remember taking a video of the match to the NSWRL to show the State selectors. At that stage Brisbane's Allan Langer was a dominant force but Greg controlled him in this match and so we controlled Brisbane. I had been appointed State of Origin coach and liked the idea of Greg being in the NSW team and doing the same thing again to Langer when he played for Queensland.

'But the following week against Illawarra he ruptured a

medial ligament which ended his chances of representative football. While he was recovering, Ben died and Greg didn't play again apart from some token appearances.

'At the time of Ben's death we were still in semi-final contention,' Gould recalled. 'After his death I think we won four or five, including an astonishing 10–8 win against Canberra at Penrith Park when we only had three or four first graders in the side. It was one of the best wins I've ever seen. We put some terrible sides on the field in 1992 mostly because we had up to 12 injured players a week.

'We moved into equal third place but we had to play Newcastle at Newcastle, Manly at Manly, Illawarra at Wollongong and Brisbane at home. We lost all four games but all four of those sides made the semi-finals. In the first match we lost lock Colin Van Der Voort suspended for four weeks, and that was the last straw. We missed the five by two points.'

Although Penrith failed to make the five in 1992, the performance, viewed in the correct perspective against a season of unprecedented emotional upheaval and injuries was a meritorious one. Coach Gould had done his best to change an arrogant attitude that emerged after the 1991 grand final win.

'I think we celebrated too long,' says Carter. 'We took things for granted. I don't think we worked as well as we should have during the off-season. We lost the plot. For the first three months after the grand final, while other clubs were planning what they were going to do, we were still celebrating. We didn't get ourselves ready for the next year.'

The stabilising influence of Royce Simmons was missing because he had retired; then Geyer walked out; Greg Alexander was seriously handicapped by a knee injury and his brother's death; Fittler was sidelined for weeks with a suspected hernia; Brad Izzard missed the season with a neck injury and eventually retired; winger Graham Lyons and hooker Brett Boyd both

Good as GOULD

missed 12 games; Paul Dunn missed eight, Paul Clarke four, Steve Carter seven, Paul Smith five, Graham Mackay four and Barry Walker three matches. Penrith finished the year in equal seventh place. John Cartwright was rightly rewarded for his courage and leadership in holding the trauma-struck side together. He was selected in Australia's World Cup team to play in England. He also won Penrith's best and fairest player award and was named Dally M second-rower of the year. Brad Fittler was centre of the year.

In the midst of it all the 1992 season marked Gould's successful debut as a representative coach. His City team became the first to lose to Country since 1975 but NSW, under his tuition, regained the State of Origin trophy from Queensland 2–1.

After winning the State of Origin series Gould announced he was stepping down from the job, leading to speculation that he was upset by criticism from ARL general manager John Quayle about the playing standard and tactics of NSW. Gould said constantly that Quayle's remarks had not been a consideration, he just wanted more time to spend with Penrith. It sounded a lightweight excuse, even allowing for Ben Alexander's death. No-one outside the club realised Penrith was disintegrating.

Feltis said Gould suspected early that his players had lost the hunger to chase back-to-back premierships in 1992.

'Before Ben's death the team looked to be simmering. Phil was desperately trying to get them interested in winning another premiership but they seemed to think they had done it all by winning one. We told them they could win more than one. Phil would say to me: "They can't do it. You're wasting your time." I believed they could but he was with them all the time. He knew the mood.'

Penrith's failure to retain the premiership disillusioned the prophets who had been seeking a consistent champion for the decade. Canberra was hailed as the team most likely after they won in 1989 and 1990 and looked set to dominate before losing to Penrith in 1991. Then Penrith, with its secure financial backing and talented team, toppled after just one year. Brisbane (winners in 1992 and 1993) missed out in 1994. And so the search went on. Parramatta in 1981–82–83 remains the only side since St George in the 1950s and 1960s to win three in a row.

Although there were genuine reasons for Penrith's failures in 1992, there was still a feeling of disappointment. The dream had come true in 1991 after 25 years of waiting. But it could not be maintained. Things had to get better in 1993. They did not.

Carter says the buying policies as Penrith tried to rebuild were questionable. 'In some cases we just bought deadwood,' he says.

'We needed a stabilising force at that stage to get us back on the right road. Instead we bought in blokes who were half first graders and half reserve graders. Our recruiting was not as good as it could have been. "Sparkles" (Mark McGaw) was a terrific bloke but he wasn't the answer. In 1993 we lost a heap of games early. We got six or eight players from Parramatta and they'd finished 15th the previous year. By 1994 when "Whiz" (Gary Freeman) came to the club and Trevor Gillmeister there was a better feeling. We had success here and there but our consistency was hopeless.'

A run of serious injuries that would have stretched the facilities of a private hospital ended Penrith's challenge in '93 before it even began. Penrith won only one of its first 10 matches (26–10 against Balmain). It was a devastating statistic that left no-one in any doubt that the confidence and expectation built up in the off-season had been quickly dissipated.

Former international centre Mark McGaw had been part of a busy recruiting drive in the lead-up to 1993 that had also included the promising Adamson brothers Matt and Phil from neighbouring Parramatta. Ryan Girdler was signed from Illawarra and winger Ashley Gordon from Newcastle. Penrith hoped to turn the corner. But it was just another dead end. Cartwright played only five matches before a recurring rotator-cuff problem in his shoulder ended the season. Greg Alexander, Steve Carter, Col Van Der Voort, Barry Walker, Graham Mackay and Paul Clarke were all out for long periods. Gordon managed only five games in first grade.

'Injuries killed us from the opening round. We were relying on those senior players like Cartwright and Carter to stay on their feet in 1993 but they were just part of a massive injury toll,' Gould remembered. 'There were times when I genuinely couldn't believe we had so many players unavailable. That year we used a total of 46 players in first grade.' In 1992 with all of its attendant troubles, Penrith only used 38 players in first grade.

And for Gould there was still one problem that could not be overcome—Greg Alexander. His relationship with the club continued to be fragile and uncertain. It was at that stage that Cartwright and Alexander were not talking on the field in matches. There are suggestions that after Ben's death, the two players did not speak again. There was at least a public patching-up of the relationship between Gould and Greg Alexander, who confirmed in a newspaper interview that there had been ill-feeling in the past between the two high-profile personalities.

'Phil and I have both got our careers at stake and we both want to get Penrith back on top again,' Alexander said. 'I'd like to think we have put our differences behind us and we are starting afresh. If things had kept going the way they were between us, the club would have suffered again this season. The place would have fallen apart.'

There was also the problem of a small group of sponsors who started trying to apply pressure because of on-field performances, blaming Gould for the failures. The same group had also been vocal about Gould dropping Royce Simmons in 1991. When Gould felt sponsors were acting against him at the club, he simply stopped going to functions they attended. The decision was not well received by Penrith, who realised the importance of the corporate dollar and knew what a sponsorship attraction the club was with Gould as its figurehead.

The only consoling result for Gould in 1993, a year in which Penrith finished equal twelfth with Wests on 14 points, was another series win against Queensland in the State of Origin. At the end of the season there was another clean-out at Penrith with Mark McGaw, Ashley Gordon, Shane Vincent, Ian McCann and Paul Clarke among the dozen or so departees. The idea was in Gould's mind to start from the bottom again and restock.

But it was hard going. There were still plenty of reminders around the club of what had happened over the past few years. One memory-jogger was Alexander. Although he produced moments of good form, Alexander's career continued to be below the standard he had previously produced. At this stage even though it would be regarded as heresy by club officials and supporters Gould was close to being convinced that Alexander had to leave Penrith for both his own sake and the sake of the club. The coach opened negotiations with then Western Suburbs half-back Jason Taylor with every intention of signing him to play first grade and letting the Alexander situation just work itself out. Out of loyalty he told Alexander of his plans, saying he considered paying a lot of money for a new half-back to be wasteful because the club already had the best player in that position in the world. It was just a matter of Alexander applying himself.

At that early stage it was believed that Alexander had signed with the new club Auckland for their debut season in 1995 and

Good as GOULD

he was only filling in with Penrith because he had a testimonial year with the club in 1994. Gould suggested that Alexander have 12 months playing in England before heading for New Zealand. Alexander asked for two days to make up his mind then came back and said he would prefer to stay at Penrith and lift his playing performance. Gould resigned himself to the situation. Taylor opened talks with Norths and joined the Bears.

During 1993, as the club slumped to just seven wins from 22 games, Gould made the historic decision that Alexander's vacillating form offered no alternative but to drop him and choose a new half-back. Although given autonomous powers as head coach on the selection of the first grade side, he contacted Feltis to discuss dropping Alexander.

A telephone call soon afterwards from Feltis, who had spoken to leagues club boss Roger Cowan and one other director, said Alexander could not be dropped. The potential for more damaging headlines and a reopening of old wounds was too much of a gamble.

'I was surprised he took it so easily,' Feltis said. 'It was the first time it had ever happened. The first time we had ever interfered in selections. Generally when Gus did not get his way, he would be a very difficult man to handle. This time he and I laughed about it. Our thoughts were that Alexander even on one leg was a better proposition than the player Gus had in mind to play fullback.'

Penrith might have missed the significance of the bid to drop Alexander. It was not to find a better player but to keep faith with the other first grade players who were looking for some sort of disciplinary action over the way Alexander was playing. Players had seen the club get rid of Geyer and several other players and could not understand the more lenient treatment of Alexander.

'The club was just sick of the drama. They thought we

FROM PLAYER TO COACH

would be portrayed as cruel for sacking Alexander from first grade after all that had happened,' Gould said. 'I thought they should have been stronger.'

At the end of 1993 Alexander dropped another bombshell. He no longer wanted to play half-back. The pressure was too much. He was forgetting calls in games and, according to Gould, just catching and passing the ball and missing tackles.

So in 1994 Alexander moved to fullback where he might enjoy the greater freedom and room to move. Penrith acted quickly and signed New Zealand Test captain Gary Freeman from Easts to be half-back. The results were no better. Season 1994 was one of only moderate success bringing an associated group of new problems as Penrith again struggled to make an impression. 'Greg went back to playing fullback but obviously he still hadn't come to terms with playing football, because his displays were poor,' Gould said. 'We tried positional switches to centre, five-eighth and fullback—anything to accommodate the switch from half.'

Eventually Penrith settled on Alexander at five-eighth and Freeman at half—but it was not successful. The 'family' of supporters backing Alexander saw his switch from half-back as another Gould plot and directed their venom towards the new half-back Freeman as well.

'It was starting to wear on Gary Freeman,' Gould said. 'We even got to a situation where Gary wouldn't pass the ball to Greg and Greg wouldn't pass it to Gary.

'Freeman, who was such a competitor, had never experienced anything like it before and would come and tell me of his frustration. I felt inadequate in my explanations because I knew the best thing I could do would be to drop Greg from the side—but that it couldn't be done.'

'There had been complaints to management from players

Good as GOULD

that Alexander was not playing to his full potential in matches,' Feltis conceded. Gould was also familiar with the players' complaints. 'Three or four times in a row the opposition scored tries off kicks they made down-field. Greg either didn't get across the field in time to cover or he ran into touch a metre from his own line or the ball went over the sideline,' he said. 'We had a side that was reasonably competitive but not functioning on all eight cylinders. We eventually sat Greg down and talked to him about it but nothing changed. It was more frustrating than you can possibly imagine.'

Gould had never walked away from tough decisions as a first grade coach. Dropping Royce Simmons was one. So was limiting Steve Mortimer to run-on appearances at Canterbury in 1988. But Penrith in 1994 was an emotional battlefield and the scars were too fresh to risk reopening.

'Players like Gary Freeman and Trevor Gillmeister, who had played against Penrith so often in the past, now had a greater understanding of what was going on,' Gould said.

Freeman, who has signed with Parramatta after being released from Penrith to join Super League, remembers clearly what happened but is reluctant to get too involved.

'I tried not to be affected by it all,' he said. 'It was between the club and whoever else was involved. We (Greg and I) both liked to command a lot of ball. Players at Penrith knew what Brandy could do. They were still getting used to me. In some cases, it made it easier and in some cases it made it more difficult.'

Was there a refusal to pass the ball?

'I never really looked at it like that. He always had more pace than me. There were times I wished I'd got the ball but whatever happens on the field happens. It's done. I don't worry about it. I did have a couple of talks with Gus about the frustrations. He certainly ironed them out. Gee, mate, I really don't want to talk about it. I know they had some problems when I was there but I just wanted to stay out of it. That's the God's honest truth. I'd say to Gus: "What's happening?"

'He'd tell me, and I'd say: "Whatever".'

Eventually it was considered easier to structure Penrith's plans in the expectation of Alexander eventually not being available. 'We virtually went on with life without Greg even though he was still at the club,' Gould said. 'If he didn't come to training no-one batted an eyelid. We just had to play with him on Sundays. I tried to justify Greg's position to the rest of the team but it was very hard. I think it would have been better if Greg had given the game away at that stage but he possibly couldn't afford to financially. He had not been all that well managed in that area in the early stages of his career. As long as Greg was at Penrith, it was unsatisfactory for him and for the club. As much as I am a friend of Greg's and have admired his play, I believe the club would have recovered much quicker if it had cut him and let him go somewhere else.'

The on-field dramas did not affect the relationship between Gould and Alexander socially. Committed to the cause of reviving Alexander's career, Gould would have long talks, a couple stretching until dawn, over a few beers. Nothing worked. Alexander continued to flounder.

'Our relationship was always fine despite reports that it was in turmoil,' Gould said. 'The drama was between me and Greg's family, and Greg's family and the club. Greg was caught in the middle of what he was told about me at home and what he learned from me personally.'

Over a beer, Alexander would admit he just did not want to play football any more. Gould would reply that the decision was Greg's to make.

'Certainly the pressure he was putting us under strained the relationship a couple of times,' said Gould. 'I was willing to accept that Greg would never again be the footballer he had

Good as GOULD

been before Ben died but I always felt he could have given more. That he could have got over the tragedy earlier. But he wasn't helped by those people around him who would not help him put it behind him and get on with his life.'

Midway through 1994 Gould decided to step down as first grade coach at Penrith at the end of the season. At that stage the initial intention was to have at least 12 months away from the game to recharge his batteries. Since 1992 Gould had been working to try as best he could to put things back together at Penrith and to his mind there was more stability and competitiveness in the side than at any time since 1991. The job that Gould and Feltis had vowed to do of reviving Penrith had been achieved.

An unexpected meeting with Mark Geyer in the Penrith Leagues Club foyer early in 1994 had led to a long and intimate talk that resolved a lot of misunderstandings and perceived ill-feeling. Geyer had been walking through the leagues club when he saw Gould. The coach simply said: 'Hello, MG,' and the years of bitterness peeled away. Gould from then on tried hard to convince Penrith to bring Geyer back to the fold because he was without a club at that stage although he was signed to the Western Reds in Perth from 1995. Geyer eventually spent 1994 on the sidelines but his relationship with Gould was back in place.

'Leaving Penrith had been on my mind for a couple of years—ever since Ben's death, in fact,' Gould said. 'I had agreed to a new four-year deal after we won the premiership in 1991 but even at that stage Don Feltis said that any time I felt like going, I could. So, leaving had been on my mind for a while. It was just a matter of when. In 1994 the club was once again healthy. We'd restored ourselves. Probably for a month before I actually resigned, I had it in my mind that this was to be my last year. Feltis himself had already resigned as chief executive, saying his quality of life and the time available to

FROM PLAYER TO COACH

spend with his family was being affected by life as a football administrator.'

The decisive moment in Gould's plans to step down came in the 12th round when Penrith beat Canberra in all grades, including 30–16 in first grade, at Penrith Park. When it was obvious Penrith had the match won, Gould went down to the sideline to wait for the players to walk to the tunnel. While waiting, Gould spontaneously turned to the crowd in the grandstand and started clapping them as they had been clapping him. It was meant as a tribute to their forbearance and patience during the past three years while their team wandered in the wilderness.

The crowd started clapping and cheering in reply, acknowledging Gould's own devotion to a difficult task in staying in charge of the side during the problems. He woke up the next morning and realised that there was never going to be a better time to make it official that he was quitting.

He told Feltis the following Tuesday morning, telling him he was quite prepared to stay on until the end of the season or he would leave immediately if the club had someone else in mind to take over as coach. He recommended Royce Simmons as his successor after inviting him to join the coaching staff earlier that year when he came back from coaching in England. The club appointed Simmons caretaker coach for the rest of 1994 and he was subsequently appointed to the job on a full-time basis from 1995.

'Beating Canberra in all three grades was probably our best day in three years,' said Gould. 'I was prepared to stay on if that was what was wanted but I didn't like the idea of staying on and having to keep lying to the players about my future plans when I knew I wouldn't be there.'

Gould gathered the players together on that Tuesday morning on the pretext of a team golf day. He arrived at Penrith Park

Good as GOULD

and immediately the players suspected that golf was not the principal item on the agenda. 'He was at his car and he just sort of walked over towards us,' said Steve Carter. 'You could see he was upset. I thought to myself, "what's happened now?"'

Of the players Brad Fittler was quickest to recover. Gould had promised Fittler that he could drive the team bus to the golf course. When Gould made his quiet announcement that he was quitting, Fittler chimed in with: 'Does that mean I don't get to drive the bus?'

The players say they had no real hint that Gould was leaving mid-season although they had followed media speculation that he would be going to Easts in 1995. 'We got a big shock,' Carter remembered. 'He said, 'I'm moving on. I'm finishing up now.'

'At that stage there was a lot of anger directed his way because we were only a couple of points outside the five and we considered ourselves a good chance of getting there. A lot of players took it as though he was leaving a sinking ship.'

The players climbed aboard the bus but the proposed golf day petered out as soon as they reached the course. With a few dozen cans of beer, the players came back to the bus and sat, drinking, talking and reminiscing . . . and wondering where it had all gone wrong.

Gould had been expected to turn up for the golf day but had not arrived. 'That's typical Gus,' said Steve Carter. 'To organise a golf day and then not turn up.'

Simmons had an immediate effect on straightening things out. The team was still disillusioned by Gould's departure and the lost prospects of the previous two years until one night at training.

The new coach spoke out.

'You blokes better start waking up to yourselves. It's over. The past is gone. Get on with the job and with the present,' he said.

Penrith waited 25 years for a premiership and then let it all evaporate. Alexander joined Auckland and made a fresh start. Geyer settled down in Perth and played some inspiring football and Gould laid down the seeds of success with Easts and then became a prized defender of the ARL against Super League.

The common ground all shared in securing Penrith's first premiership had blown away. 'When Brandy (Alexander) came and said he was going to Auckland my first reaction was relief,' said Feltis. 'I have enormous respect for Phil Gould as a coach and that has not changed but I felt a similar sense of relief when Phil said he was resigning.'

Feltis, a former policeman who took over as chief executive at the request of Penrith boss Roger Cowan, blamed his own inexperience in the job for the way things got out of control but his reliability and strength more than compensated for any imagined shortcomings he might have had.

It was simply a horrendous and fragmented period that knows no equal in the history of any rugby league club. Individual and widely diverse personalities and ambitions, that perhaps were never meant to blend, miraculously did so in a single season before spinning wildly out of control.

When Roger Cowan presented Feltis with a life membership in 1995, with Penrith then in Super League ranks, he joked about the circumstances. 'Don must have looked into his crystal ball when he stepped down as chief executive because he handed me all of the difficulties of Super League.

'But I used the same crystal ball when I stepped down and Don became chief executive, because he experienced the worst three years in the history of the club.'

Gould preferred to remember only the good times at Penrith.

'In all the trauma, a lot of relationships were broken. There were a lot of scars,' he recalled. 'But time heals. My relationship with Greg's mother Leonie has been mended and all of us worked hard at getting a lot of bridges rebuilt.'

Good as GOULD

As the players sat in their bus at the golf course on the day Gould stepped down, there was a recurring theme in their discussions. How did it happen?

'My memories are of winning the grand final in 1991. Losing the 1990 one too. The club was so close at that stage and yet so disjointed and antisocial just a couple of years later,' Carter said.

'The most bewildering thing to me is how it could have happened.

'But it did. I just don't think any of us handled it as well as we could have.'

Many nights during that painful time Gould lay awake, thinking of earlier, playing days when life was simpler at Penrith. Although it wasn't always so . . .

PHIL GOULD'S Reflections on
BITTERSWEET DAYS WITH THE PANTHERS

This was a period I would have preferred to have been omitted totally from the book. Of course, it couldn't have been.

The events surrounding Ben's death, the anger, the frustration and the rage that built up were like cancer. They are things I do not like talking about. I would prefer that Ben's life and untimely death be allowed to slip permanently into a warm cavern in the hearts of those who knew and loved him.

But since the story is here, there are some aspects that bear reflection.

Ben and I were very, very close, as I was to the family.

My relationship with the Alexander family extended well past just being a coach to Greg and Ben.

The things that I have been reported as doing for the family, I did out of love and respect. They were never seen by me to be simply benevolent or charitable. They had much to do with Ben and Greg's mother Leonie. I had watched her single-handedly raise her five boys and found her maternal nature and loving dedication inspiring.

All of the children were outstanding young Australians. I always tried to do whatever I could to help along the way. The family itself gave me a great deal of enjoyment and I loved the times I was in their company.

In the aftermath of Ben's death and in the face of the accusations that were levelled at me, a lot of rumours developed. The media had a field day with the tragedy, constantly speculating on

Good as GOULD

the events, or supposed events leading up to Ben's tragic crash. The media added fuel to what was already a tragic situation.

Leonie was a grieving mother who had lost a son in terrible circumstances. Anything she said and did at that time, I completely understood and accepted.

Sometime later when Greg Alexander and I talked about what had happened, I told him that the day Leonie decided to come and talk to me about the situation, things would improve for her and him.

Eventually that occurred. Leonie and I spent long hours talking about what had happened. Eventually bridges were rebuilt and she offered apologies although none were necessary.

What has always angered me was the way certain individuals in Penrith used the tragic situation to try and settle old scores. Leonie's husband and Greg's step-father, Gerard Hughes, was a focal point of a lot of the problems we all faced at that time.

The club itself—the board of directors and the management—did everything they could. Our chief executive Don Feltis, through his experience in the police service, was a rock and a great supporter of me and the Alexander family. Without him, things would have been immeasurably worse. There was no manual for us to consult about how to handle the situation. We just did the best we could from day to day. The hardest part was biting our tongues and closing our ears to the things that went on around us, while all the time wanting to tell the truth about the situation. It just seemed more important to keep silent and reduce the pressure on the families involved.

Rebuilding the club was a slow process and a painful one. We cut the place to the bone at the end of 1992 and decided to start again. Injuries did not help our situation and some poor player purchases only added to the problem. It would have been nice to enjoy instant success, but we were realistic enough to know it would take time. By the middle of 1994 we were again a competitive football club.

Greg Alexander is one of the most naturally gifted and talented footballers I have ever seen. He is also a close personal friend. Contrary to many reports—and I am sure it will disappoint a lot of people to know—we have never had a cross word in all the time we have known each other. Only recently Greg and I agreed that he should come and work with me in coaching once his playing career was over. And again contrary to a lot of reports, Mark Geyer and I did not exchange a single harsh word during the 1992 season. In fact from the time of Ben's death until the day at Leichhardt Oval when he stormed out of the City–Country dressing rooms, we had not spoken a word to each other. When you know Mark, you realise that what happened in the dressing room at Balmain that day was more 'show' than anything else.

Sometime later when Mark was cut from Balmain, I worked very hard to get him back to Penrith. He and I and our manager Wayne Beavis went to lunch at one stage and it was one of the funniest afternoons I've ever had. Mark and I swapped stories and recollections of all the lies and excuses he had used on me to get out of training sessions. Mark is a difficult person for people to understand. I have formed the opinion that Mark enjoys living the life of a footballer but he does not want to be one. He's a great bloke. This whole episode was just a very difficult time for the whole club.

The Day the Game Stood Still

The most shattering on-field moment in Penrith's founding years as a first grade club came on a quiet Sunday afternoon during a match against Newtown at dilapidated Henson Park, Marrickville, on May 28, 1978.

In a tragic and frightening few seconds, one of the club's most popular players was crippled for life, the Panthers' young team was mentally scarred, and the club as a whole experienced a brutal introduction to the realities of how cruel a game rugby league could be in extreme circumstances.

Prop John Farragher was young, promising, well liked and talented. He had joined Penrith from Gilgandra at the start of the season in a second attempt to prove his worth. Farragher had tried his luck with Penrith the previous year but had realised very quickly his limitations because of insufficient physical fitness. Rather than retreat back to the country and settle for lesser rugby league standards, Farragher had spent the previous season and off-season improving his physical strength and endurance and then returned to Sydney for another chance to test his talent against the best players in the world.

The newly developed strength, added to Farragher's natural ball skills and ability to off-load, made the strapping 21-year-old an eye-catching commodity.

In a split second of unparalleled and freakish ill-timing, that potential was to be cruelly snuffed. A scrum collapsed in the familiar fashion of those times. There was a greater emphasis on ball-winning and competitive scrums then as opposed to the current method of the team that feeds the ball being virtually assured of retaining possession. This one scrum went horrifically wrong. As the players peeled off each other and regained their feet to repack the scrum, one player, Farragher, remained prostrate. In the collapsing of the scrum his spine had been permanently damaged and in those awful moments he was already a quadriplegic.

For all of the perceived violence and sometimes brutish behaviour associated with rugby league there have been few serious injuries bringing permanent problems. Broken arms, jaws and legs do occur in 80 minutes of fierce physical confrontation. Sometimes it's deliberate. Sometimes accidental. But an injury as grievous as the one suffered by Farragher was a rarity in 70 years of rugby league in Australia.

Phil Gould was playing lock forward and was the Penrith captain on that fateful day.

'I stood out of that particular scrum,' he recalled. 'It was Newtown's feed and I was out of the pack to defend if we lost the ball.'

'There had been about 10 minutes' play without a break which was unusual in those days. No penalties, no knock-ons or anything. We'd been going flat out and it was about 15 minutes before half-time. The referee had just awarded a penalty and I was walking away with my back turned. I looked back just as the scrum collapsed and John cried out: 'I can't move! I can't move!'

'He just lay on the ground. There was no scream of pain. There did not seem to be any pain.'

Farragher later told Gould that his experience as the scrum collapsed was like watching a television set turning off and the picture telescoping into a pinpoint . . . to nothing.

'He could feel everything shrinking inside him and then

Good as GOULD

going out like a light. He felt his whole body collapsing,' Gould said. 'At first we didn't realise the enormity of the situation. We were going to pick him up and carry him to the sideline but the Newtown trainers raced onto the field and stopped us.'

The small crowd watched in shocked silence as the on-field drama unfolded, not fully realising the magnitude of the problem but aware that something was dramatically amiss. The game was halted for more than 35 minutes.

The Penrith players did not need to be told the seriousness of the situation. They had sensed tragedy in the confused air. 'We sort of knew straightaway and when we went into the dressing room at half-time the doctor told us the worst,' Gould recalled.

'He sat us down and said: "John has badly injured himself. We suspect that he has really serious spinal damage and the odds are that he will never walk again."

'How he came to that diagnosis so quickly was something we didn't even think about at the time. But he was 100 per cent correct.'

There was an eerie pause in the normal run of match day. Outside, mystified supporters waited for the second half to be played. Newtown players in the other dressing room were equally uncertain about what should happen.

'It was a confusing scene,' Gould recalled. 'We wanted to call the game off and get in the ambulance with John. I think Newtown wanted to abandon the game too when they realised what had happened.'

Penrith's coach Don Parish made the decision, ordering his players to go back for the second half. Parish, a former Kangaroo and Test fullback, had been one of the first to reach Farragher's side after the scrum collapsed.

'Don,' Farragher said to him, 'don't tell me I'm going to be a cripple.'

Parish's reply carried the confidence of decades: 'Don't worry, John. That sort of thing doesn't happen in rugby league.'

Gould said playing the second half was the last thing on the players' minds. But they were footballers and they returned to the field.

'Don had told us: "We can't just call it off. We've got to play and get things finished off and then find out after the game what has happened".'

Penrith went on to win 21–5 but the result was irrelevant. Concerned and uncertain, the Penrith players gathered at the Newtown Leagues Club to wait for news of Farragher, who had been rushed to the Royal North Shore Hospital for treatment.

The players moved on to the hospital around midnight after doctors had completed checks on Farragher and they virtually took up residence there in small groups around the clock.

Despite their heartfelt concern, all found the situation daunting. The sight of Farragher immobile was a chilling reminder to each player of his own mortality and vulnerability as a professional footballer.

'We were only allowed in to see him two at a time,' Gould recalled. 'It was hard to talk really. He had bolts in his head and was in traction. I hate hospitals anyway. Just the smell of a hospital is enough to put me off. I found it really difficult to go in and talk. I remember saying to my girl at the time that I was going to give football away. It was all just too much. Later came the shock of seeing a mate in a wheelchair and knowing he would be there for life. It was a very difficult time.'

The stabilising influence in the entire painful episode was Farragher himself. He converted the courage he had shown so often on a football field into a stoic acceptance of his own misfortune.

Good as GOULD

'John seemed to know as soon as it happened that he would never walk again,' remembered Penrith's then chief executive Ian Maurice.

'He said to me in the ambulance taking him to hospital from Henson Park that he knew how serious the injury was. He was very brave.'

Farragher's injury touched the hearts of the Sydney rugby league public and there were numerous fund-raising functions organised by Penrith officials, headed by club bosses Ian Maurice and Roger Cowan and all of them wholeheartedly supported by the players.

In the end a trust fund was established to give Farragher the financial independence he needed to supplement his wages as a doorman at Penrith Leagues Club.

'Through it all John remained as bright as a button. His sunny nature never altered despite all he had been through,' Gould said. 'You'd like to think that you would handle it as well as John did if it should happen to you. In the years I spent with Penrith, Johnny was as familiar as some of the furniture. He was always in the dressing room after games.

'What happened was shattering for everyone. One minute I was captain of a first grade side and the next one of my mates had a broken neck and would never walk again.

'It was something we all took a long time to get over.'

It was on Farragher's insistence that Penrith tried to put the tragedy behind them and pick up the pieces of the 1978 season.

For a time the momentum of the win against Newtown and Farragher's injury would combine to fuel the first grade side. Parish had called the players together at training the week after Farragher was injured and said they would have to continue playing despite the difficult circumstances.

Penrith played a 7-all draw with Canterbury the week after beating Newtown and then beat Balmain but the tragedy had

FROM PLAYER TO COACH

taken deep roots in the players' psyche. The constant involvement in fund-raising—including a telethon—and visits to the hospital had drastically reduced their enthusiasm for football.

Farragher's girl friend at the time was also subjected to unnecessary media speculation and pressure about her thoughts and plans for the future. Her relationship with Farragher was in fact in the very early stages. Being portrayed as his long-term girl friend, or almost fiancée, was unfortunate.

'It was a very heavy ask on her,' Gould remembered. 'It was really only a "walk in the park romance" at the time but the media wanted to emphasise the girl friend aspect. Johnny (a keen greyhound follower and owner) was probably more in love with his dogs. It was difficult for her. She did not want to be seen as the one who walked away from the relationship and she stuck for a long time.'

She eventually married another player and they moved away from Sydney.

For Gould the resultant publicity, giant newspaper headlines and presence of intrusive media anxious for any scrap of information about Farragher and the club's future plans represented a big test for the maturity of a 20-year-old captain in his first season as a leader.

Similar headlines and drama would recur to haunt and torment Gould more than a decade later when he was Penrith's first grade coach.

Phil Gould became a footballer with Penrith as a matter of choice. He was living with his parents in Merrylands in Parramatta territory but the family's geographical roots were centred further west. His parents, grandparents and other relatives all lived at Penrith. His father had grown up at Wallacia.

Although keen on all sport, soccer and cricket were Gould's main interests until he was 14. He played for Wentworthville Leagues until he was 17 and then quit—on the

Good as GOULD

insistence of his parents—to concentrate on schoolwork and the HSC. At the time he was on the verge of selection in Penrith's Jersey Flegg team.

Football had interfered with his studies in fifth form and Gould's parents insisted there would be no similar disruption in sixth year. Their firmness paid off and Gould won a place at the University of NSW in Kensington, where he studied law for two years before dropping out.

In 1976 he trialled with Penrith, one of the scores of eager hopefuls, all of them desperate to catch the eye of a selector and make the graded lists.

'I played in about five different games on the one day,' Gould recalled. 'They kept pulling me off in one trial and putting me on in the next one. The first trial started in about 40 degree heat in long-sleeved black jumpers. By about 4pm I'd graduated to the brown and white strip Penrith wore in those days and I thought I must be getting close to the money.'

He was selected in a 20-man squad to go to Blaxland in the Blue Mountains and play a trial against Western Division, the country side that had snuffed out Penrith's eager ambitions two years earlier in the final of the breakthrough weekly televised series, the Amco Cup. Western Division's line-up for the trial included TV Ted Ellery whose distinctive bald head and rugged play had captured the imagination of television viewers during the Amco Cup series. 'Getting to play against Ellery was my main claim to fame at that stage,' Gould laughs.

Penrith Club was entering its 10th year in the premiership when Gould trialled in 1976. They had nine seasons of frustration, lack of success, controversy and headlines. Penrith were generally closer to the bottom of the competition table than the top but they often generated more headlines than the premiers.

FROM PLAYER TO COACH

Penrith was a relatively quiet rural spot in the shadow of the Blue Mountains that had grown as a satellite city as young families pushed further west from the established metropolitan boundaries in search of a lifestyle they could afford.

When promotion to first grade came for the club in 1967 it was tinged with the controversy that would hallmark Penrith's record for years to come. Penrith won a first grade place on the strength of the club winning the second division competition in 1966, winning 9-7 against Wentworthville, the club which had dominated that premiership for years leading up to the grand final. Wentworthville had made loud and frequent calls for inclusion in first grade but had been continually overlooked. A motivating factor was the stern opposition from the then powerful Parramatta delegates to the NSWRL. Parramatta knew that having nearby Wentworthville as a competing first-grade side instead of being a conveyor belt of junior talent for Parramatta's sides would be a disaster.

As the first decade of Penrith's life in first division came to an end there was little to show for the efforts of the players, coaches and officials. The wooden spoon and disappointment seemed constant companions.

If talent was light, enthusiasm was not. Penrith went to South Africa to sign Springboks Keith Howie and Peter Swanson. In 1973 Swanson, a Springbok centre would adapt to rugby league and play 21 games in two years as a first grade fullback, centre and winger. Howie, a prop, would struggle with the change of codes and play one first grade in his only season after a torn cruciate ligament in a knee ended his career. From New Zealand in 1978 came All Black prop Kent Lambert. The most significant buys were Great Britain Test hooker Mick Stephenson, who cost $39,000 in transfer fees, and his Test team-mate Bill Ashurst, who cost $27,000. It was phenomenal money at a time when many established first

Good as GOULD

graders were getting around $10,000 a season.

Stephenson's introduction to Penrith emphasised the rural atmosphere. Standing with his wife in the kitchen of the new home provided by Penrith, Stephenson turned around to find himself face to face with a horse that had wandered in from a nearby paddock.

Stephenson and Ashurst were two of the most talented, if contrasting, players ever seen in the premiership. Stephenson, strong, reliable, clever and a born leader, gave great value. Ashurst, enormously talented with stunning individual skills, was much less reliable. His erratic behaviour eventually culminated in him quitting the club in secret and returning to England. The only clue to an imminent departure was his offer to sell his team-mates his furniture at a training session days before his plane left.

'Mick was the club captain and he was a complete professional,' Gould recalled. 'He got on well with everyone and was very big on fitness, training and never giving up. Bill had heaps of ability. He could make a football talk.'

The recruitment was part of a developing process at Penrith, with the various personalities, skills and experience of a diversified gathering of players all contributing to an emerging club that was also producing its own future stars.

'Out of the group of kids that started with me in 1976, a number went on to be first graders and stayed on with the club for a long time,' Gould said. 'Players like Brad Waugh, Mick Kelly, Cliff Cartwright, Pat Roderick and Tim Sheens. Tas Baiteri was there as well. He's now heavily involved in French rugby league and is their former Test coach.'

Gould began 1976 in the under-23s, an unknown making his way—but finished the season in encouraging fashion and tagged as a player of the future. 'In those days I was more of a ball runner and a five-eighth or centre,' he said. 'I had a

FROM PLAYER TO COACH

kicking game and I could use the ball but that wasn't such a big thing in those days. You just passed it out.

'At that stage the game had moved to six tackles (1971) after the introduction of four-tackle football (1967) and a definite pattern was starting to emerge. At Penrith it was a year of transition. The club had been to America looking for ideas. They'd been to South Africa and England for players.'

Gould found the initial weeks of graded football taxing. He played in the opening two or three games before being relegated to the bench for the next six weeks. The inactivity, combined with travelling from Parramatta to university in Sydney and then back to Penrith for training and then home to Parramatta, took its toll and he decided to give the game away.

His father rang the club to inform them of his son's decision—only to be told that reserve grade coach Bobby Moses and first grade coach Barry Harris were among his fans, but had been under the impression he was out injured.

Recalled to the under-23s Gould played fullback with such success that he emerged as the club's under-23 player-of-the-year as well as getting his first chance in first grade.

'I went on for half a game in first grade against Balmain as fullback, mainly because they didn't have a goal-kicker on the day,' Gould remembered. 'I was the goal-kicker in the under-23s and was kicking pretty well. At half-time in first grade Barry Harris sent me on. It was a strange experience because I had never ever expected to go into the game. I was very nervous. I reached into the pocket of my tracksuit to take out my mouthguard but it wouldn't fit into my mouth. In my excitement I had picked up someone else's tracksuit and was using someone else's mouthguard.

'I frantically grabbed a pair of scissors and tried to cut the shape of the guard to fit my mouth. The scissors slipped and I

Good as GOULD

cut off the top of two fingers. I took the field with blood running down my hand.'

Although Penrith lost that first grade match 12–5, Gould was happy with his contribution of a goal and two kicks that hit the upright. A couple of smart runs off the clever passes of Great Britain Test five-eighth David Topliss, who was with Penrith at the time but would later return to Australia and play with Balmain, confirmed Gould was not overawed by playing first grade.

In 1977 Parish took over as first grade coach and Buck Rogers, whose relationship with Gould would rise and fall in dramatic circumstances in the next decade, was in charge of the under-23s.

Gould was in reserve grade as five-eighth after four rounds under coach Stan Bottles, a friend of coaching authority Jack Gibson.

'Bottles was a little flamboyant and outlandish for us but he brought some good ideas to the club. He was a very, very wealthy man and there were not a lot of those in Penrith at that time. He used to drive to training at Penrith Park from Cronulla. He would bring us all our own vitamin tablets and make us drink junket before the games and take us out to eat lobster during the week.

'He gave the most inspiring half-time talk I'd ever heard. We were playing Parramatta and I think we were equal leaders of the reserve grade premiership at the time. It was 5-all and a very tough game. He must have been scratching for inspiration because he took off his Rolex in the dressing room and said: "All I can say is that the best player in the second half will get this gold watch." It must have been worth a fortune. We all just looked at the watch. It was mesmerising. We went out for the second half and we lost. So no-one got the watch.'

Bottles also introduced the idea of a 'game ball' to the

FROM PLAYER TO COACH

Penrith club, a motivational ploy used subsequently at other clubs whereby players voted for the best player on the day. The winner would be presented with a football signed by all the players.

'Stan would then slip around and give the next best four or five players fifty dollars each for drinks. We all used to vote for the one bloke to get the game ball and then stand there for the handout of fifties.'

For Gould there was also more first grade in 1977, as a winger. He played his initial first grade game on the wing in an Amco Cup match against Easts, marking international Ian Schubert and against a side that also featured superstars Arthur Beetson, Russell Fairfax and Bobby Fulton.

'Schubert scored three tries down my wing so it was obviously time I moved closer to the action,' Gould laughed.

'We gave some cheek for three of the four quarters then Easts got us. It was the first time I had been chosen in first grade although by then I'd come on a few times as a second half replacement.'

It was a continuing and colourful introduction to grade football. Penrith had a good reserve grade side in 1977, and made the top three only to lose to a strong Manly side featuring established stars such as Ray Branighan, Lindsay Drake and Ian Martin. A loss to Easts the next week meant the end of an eventful season—but greater shocks were ahead for Gould.

In 1978 he was named as first grade lock forward for the trials and was still there for the preseason series. But for the opening premiership round Parish put Gould back in reserve grade, saying he needed more time to mature. Five weeks later with the first grade side yet to win a game and the reserve grade side with four wins from five games, it was time for changes. Five reserve grade players were named in first grade, with

Good as GOULD

Gould lock. It was his first selected game in a first grade premiership side.

'Dropping back to reserve grade was not all that disappointing even though I had started the year in first grade,' he said. 'The game was a lot different in those days to what it is now. It was very spiteful. It was considered essential for young players to cut their teeth in the lower grades before they got a chance in first grade. You learnt self-preservation in the lower grades. The one thing that we don't teach young players nowadays is how to protect themselves because it is not necessary. That's why some tackles look a lot nastier than they are. It's more because players have taken no evasive or protective action in the tackle. In those days a tackle across the chest would end up hitting you in the chin because your elbow was carried in a position to lessen the impact or ward off the blow. Nowadays all players run with both hands around the ball.

'I wasn't much of a ball player then although I could catch and pass. I was more of a worker. A terrier. I was heavily involved with high workrate, lots of tackles, take the ball up, run the ball and kick it. I was never seen as this bloke who could set up the play.'

Gould's first premiership game in first grade was against North Sydney and for the bunch of former Penrith reserve graders making their debut it was a day to remember.

Gould remembers Mick Kelly, Tas Baiteri, Pat Roderick and Brad Waugh being in the Penrith side for that match at Penrith Park.

'Midway through the second half we were down 16–7 then Mick Stephenson, our captain, lifted us,' Gould said. 'He revved us up and kept us going. Three minutes from the end I had to kick a penalty goal for a one-point win—and it went through the posts for 17–16.'

For young players in first grade together for the first time to have snatched a dramatic last-minute win was the stuff of dreams. First grade had been conquered and the future looked bright with promise.

'We were all in first grade. We were all going to stay in first grade. Everything was great. We were going to be great forever,' Gould remembered ruefully. 'We jumped on a plane the following week and went to the Riverina to play Riverina in the Amco Cup.

'We were going to do this to them and that to them. They beat us 36–2.'

With hindsight a Riverina side featuring future Test players Ray Brown, Greg Brentnall and Les Boyd along with champion half Steve Hewson, whose career was cut short by a chronic knee injury, was always going to be hard to beat. But the initial embarrassment of losing to a side of then little-known country players punctured the smugness of the young Penrith players with a bang that could be heard all the way from Wagga to the Blue Mountains.

Penrith limped back into Sydney by plane, the players too embarrassed to immediately make the trip home for fear of confronting club supporters and being quizzed about the loss. Instead Stephenson took the players to the late-closing Musicians' Club in Surry Hills to drown their sorrows.

'We met up with Peter Cook and Dudley Moore at the club. They were on tour in Australia at the time and we all had a great time telling jokes over a few drinks and trying to forget the loss to Riverina,' said Gould.

Stephenson, whose leadership skills were so valuable to Penrith, would provide the initial impetus for Gould's career. A violent, late head-high tackle from a Balmain player near the end of 1977 caused Stephenson to contemplate retirement on medical advice after a series of brain scans. A broken jaw against Manly in the second round of 1978 convinced him to retire.

Good as GOULD

His recommendation as Penrith's new captain was 20-year-old Phil Gould. Coach Don Parish agreed with Stephenson—and Gould became one of the youngest first grade captains in the history of the game in Australia and the youngest since the great centre Dave Brown had been in charge of Easts more than 40 years before.

Gould's captaincy experience in grade football was restricted to a reserve grade semi-final the previous year. After Manly had beaten Penrith by 20 points in the first semi-final first grade coach Don Parish took charge of the side. Among the changes he made was moving Gould from five-eighth to lock and making him captain.

On Stephenson's retirement, Gould was the captain in his second first grade premiership as a selected player. It proved a decisive judgement by Parish and Stephenson.

'Because of injuries and the disaster of the Amco Cup loss, Don Parish brought up another four or five reserve grade players,' Gould recalled. 'It was virtually our reserve grade side of a few weeks back. I was captain of that side so it probably seemed logical to keep me as captain.'

Gould's first match as captain was against a very strong Easts side at the Sports Ground, Moore Park, where the Sydney Football Stadium now stands.

To expect a Penrith side that had been flogged by Riverina just days earlier and had been reinforced by more unknown young players and was led by a 20-year-old captain playing his second first grade game to topple an Easts side headed by 'Immortal' Bobby Fulton was like expecting the sun to rise in the west.

Bookmakers bet 40 and a half points start about Penrith.

'In those days at the Sports Ground if you won the toss, you always chose to run into the sun because it would then be setting behind you in the second half and shining in the eyes of the opposition,' Gould said.

FROM PLAYER TO COACH

It was a meteorological truism that was not exactly unknown to Easts' wily captain Fulton either. Fulton, an experienced campaigner, lived up to his reputation for quick thinking and opportunism against a tyro captain.

The coin went up for the toss. Gould called heads and that's the way it fell. Fulton had already walked from the field, feigning ignorance of the toss and advising the referee that his team would play into the sun.

Gould stood firm: 'We won the toss and that's the way we want to run.'

Fulton indicated that his team would be running that way and no argument would be entertained.

'They were the home team and they ran out first and Bozo ran his players down to the eastern end,' Gould said. 'He was hoping we would come out and automatically go to the other end. I came out and thought: What are those blokes doing down our end of the field? So I took my blokes behind the eastern goal posts and we suddenly had both teams down at the same end of the field.

'We were saying: "Get up the other end."

'They were telling us the same thing in less complimentary terms.'

Easts fullback Russell Fairfax settled the impasse by saying: 'What does it matter. We're going to smash you anyway,' and Easts headed off down the paddock.

In an unthinkable turn-up Penrith led 15–10 until the final minute when Easts prop Bob O'Reilly crashed over in the corner for 15–13.

As O'Reilly got to his feet to walk back, leaving it to Easts goal-kicker to line up the conversion attempt that would force a draw, the faces on the Penrith players were as long and dark as the shadows falling on the Sports Ground from the setting sun.

Good as GOULD

O'Reilly, a familiar face to Penrith players (he had spent the previous two years with the club) lightened the mood of his former team-mates.

'Bob turned around and winked at us,' Gould related. 'He said, "Don't worry, boys. This bloke can't kick".' The shot at goal, from a goal-kicker whose name Gould has forgotten, fell short and Penrith under Gould's captaincy had brought off a bewildering triumph.

'I'm not a great one for photos, but one of my favourites is one taken that day of me with Mick Stephenson and our coach Don Parish. It was a great day,' Gould said.

'But Easts got square. They flogged us in the second round.'

The jubilation of the remarkable win against Easts evaporated quickly just a few weeks later when Farragher was injured against Newtown, bringing home to the players that there was a lot more to life than winning football matches.

Gould himself did not escape season 1978 unscathed either. He suffered a serious eye injury that threatened not only his sight but his playing future. His retina became detached in half a dozen places after a series of high tackles in different matches. The continual knocks to the head caused further damage.

The vision in his right eye was deteriorating. There was no pain, no suffering. Just increasingly limited vision. There were initial parental fears of a brain tumour. Eventually Gould headed to the Sydney Eye Hospital for a check-up, on his way to Randwick races. He passed the reading checks applied by the hospital's interns, but continued to complain of no peripheral vision.

A specialist was called and her words were icy. 'You've got a detached retina,' she said.

Gould, his eyes full of drops and his pupils dilated to the extent that he was almost blind, was speechless.

FROM PLAYER TO COACH

'The retina has come off the back of your eye,' said the doctor. 'Where it has peeled off is where you have lost your vision. We'll operate and staple it back down again.'

It sounded good until the punchline came.

'Do you play sport? Do you do boxing?' she asked.

Gould: 'No, I don't box, but I play football.'

Specialist: 'Oh. Well, you'll never play football again. You won't play sport ever again.'

Only someone completely insensitive to how important sport can be to young men could have spoken so coldly to a 20-year-old blinded by eye drops and confronted with words he could not comprehend.

Adding to the drama was the specialist's insistence that the eye operation be performed immediately to comply with a direction that once patients were admitted to the hospital their condition had to be rectified before they could be discharged.

Gould demanded a telephone and rang his father, a police officer at the nearby Police Academy in Redfern. Gould senior was on the spot in minutes. Flashing his police badge he had his son out of the hospital immediately. Coincidentally, a policeman's son had not long before suffered a serious eye injury caused by a toy arrow. The problem had been corrected by an international eye specialist who happened to be in Australia at the time. The same surgeon was now in Australia again. Calls were made and some days later he repeated the operation on Phil Gould's eye with great success.

'He was leading the way in the area of detached retina problems,' said Gould. 'In the past it would mean no more touching your toes for six months, no heavy exercise, no sport, no football and all that. But he did warn that if I suffered a similar injury again, it would mean no more sport.'

A heavy tackle and a punch on May 4, 1979, in a match against North Sydney revived fears for Gould's sight. This time he was admitted to Royal Prince Alfred Hospital for an operation on a different part of his retina. Again he was stabilised and his sight saved but the incident led to a prolonged outcry about the growing thuggery in the game and public disillusionment with the tactics of some teams.

Gould, as a leading ball player and distributor, was an easy mark for thugs. If Gould was stopped, Penrith's attack short-circuited.

'Phil needed an operation to save his sight from that game but he had also been hit in late tackles in the previous four games,' said Penrith's boss Ian Maurice, now a sports commentator on Channel 9. 'The retina was detached in about eight places the previous year. Now he had been hit again.

'Gould's skill with the ball made him an automatic target.'

Gould recalled how an elbow to the cheekbone just under the right eye had caused the second problem.

'My vision went blurry immediately. Everything was still fuzzy when I got up to take the penalty kick after the incident. I finished the game but I didn't mention the fuzziness. I was just hoping it would go away.

'It just got worse. I nearly died the next morning when I woke up and my sight had deteriorated. It was like someone putting a hand across my face.' Other prominent players suffered similar attention from the roughnecks who were involved in rugby league in those days. They inflicted enormous damage not only on opposition players but also on the game's image.

Violence in matches of that era and the inability of the NSWRL's judiciary panels and referees to cope with the situation caused widespread criticism from the public, the media and in some cases schools, who said their involvement with the game would be under review unless immediate changes were made and firmer penalties imposed.

It took the appointment of solicitor and former first grader with Sydney University club, Jim Comans, as judiciary panel chairman and a succession of penalties of 12 months, and longer, before the balance was corrected and skill again became the focus of the game.

For Gould the eye injury had taken much of the good from the 1978 season. Earlier in the year Test second-rower Rod Reddy of St George, who would go away with the Kangaroos that year, tipped Gould as a future international.

'Gould has the rugby league world at his feet and needs only a little more experience and polish to go right to the top,' Reddy wrote in a newspaper column after a match against Penrith. 'There were times when he toyed with the St George defence.'

Gould's time at Penrith was coming to an end but there were still good times and days he could laugh about.

One day while walking into Penrith Park he fell into step with leading referee Greg Hartley who was in charge of the afternoon match. Hoping to get the day off to as good a start as possible, Gould attempted to make conversation. But Hartley had only one thing on his mind.

'I hear you blokes have a good disco at your leagues club after matches,' he said to Gould.

A little taken aback, Gould said yes, that was true.

Hartley: 'Any chance of you arranging tickets for me and two mates?'

Gould: 'Not a problem.'

During the match a wild melee developed involving several players from both sides and Hartley had his whistle blowing shrilly as he tried to regain control. Eventually in his most theatrical manner, he cautioned the players involved.

Unexpectedly he called over Gould, who had not been involved. Thinking he was being told as captain to keep his Penrith team in order, Gould instead heard a different story.

'Listen, all of this mob in the grandstand think I'm giving

Good as GOULD

you a caution and a warning,' said Hartley. 'I'm not. I just want to tell you that another mate of mine has turned up and we'll need four tickets to the disco tonight.'

Eye operations of 1978 and again 1979 forced Gould out of the game for long periods and dramatically affected his chances of making the representative teams despite his obvious talents. A late start to the 1980 season because of injury and further setbacks made that season a write-off as well and there was a growing feeling in Gould that a change was necessary to get his football career back on track.

So it was that at the end of 1980 he was given a release from the final year of his contract with Penrith and moved across to join Newtown for the 1981 season.

'I'd had offers from Warren Ryan at Newtown and Roy Masters at Wests. I don't know if Roy knew whether I could play or not. He just wanted me because Warren did. At that time they were pretty fierce rivals,' Gould says. 'I'd had a pretty good game against Newtown in 1979 and I'd spoken to Warren Ryan over a beer afterwards. We had beaten Newtown comprehensively and I had been named man of the match. Not long after that I suffered my eye injury and when I came back after nine months off in 1980 I struggled for fitness and with injury after two consecutive lay-offs. I played mostly reserve grade in 1980. At the end of the season I still had a couple of years to run and I intended to play in the country. Penrith had a secretary named Tom Ellis and he was leaving. I did a deal with him. I said if you're going, let me go too. We can both find greener pastures. In the end I went to Newtown.'

The Penrith experience was the beginning of Gould's transformation from hardworking back-rower to skilled ball-player. It was a transformation that developed slowly, finding its creation in changed circumstances. 'I first got into reserve grade as a five-eighth because I could make 30 tackles a game and kick the ball a little bit. I was a workhorse in first grade, just taking the ball up,' said Gould.

'But following my eye injuries, with increasing size and increasing awareness of injury and that sort of thing, I slowly changed my game. The captaincy changed my attitude as well. I started to have to call a lot of things on the field and point out the direction. So it all worked hand in hand. The eye injuries meant that if I was to survive in the game, I would probably have to find a different way of playing it to what I had been. That all helped change the way I played in the latter half of my career.'

Gould gradually asserted himself, calling players through moves at training and in matches, looking to set up play and acting as a ball distributor. His team-mates progressively became more confident in his skills.

Ryan was also to provide encouragement at Newtown. He was happy to have a ball player in the side to create something in attack among the pillars of muscle he used to carry out his defensive tactics.

'He always worked his game plan around having one or two ball players in his unit and the rest working hard,' said Gould. 'Even at Canterbury when it got to tough games that were going to be close, he would always have a Darrell Brohman or myself around because we might be the ones who would prise open a half chance in attack. He was always mindful of the need for that quality in a side.'

It was the need for change—not money—that took Gould to Newtown, a feeling that there had to be more to first grade rugby league than what he had experienced at Penrith. 'There was also the chance to be coached by Warren and to play with someone like Tommy Raudonikis,' said Gould. 'Ken Wilson I knew very well. He had recommended me to Warren. Kenny became my reserve grade coach when I took over at

Good as GOULD

Canterbury. Warren asked me if there were any more good players at Penrith and I told him about Ray Blacklock. Blacklock came down and ended up a sensation on the wing.'

Gould's departure from Penrith had widespread repercussions. Tim Sheens, who in 1979 had become the first Penrith player to play 200 games, moved into coaching, first with Penrith and then with Canberra. He and Gould would have a rocky relationship as rival coaches in the future. As he walked out of Penrith Park for the last time it was not a one way street. It was a cul de sac that would eventually lead him back to Penrith to lead the club to its most glorious triumph.

PHIL GOULD'S Reflections on
PENRITH

In my early days at Penrith professionalism had a softer sound than it has now. Professionalism meant simple things like wearing your boots at training or maybe having a coach who called a Saturday morning training session.

Those Saturday morning sessions were extremely inconvenient because a lot of blokes worked or were recovering from giant hangovers from a Friday night drink.

I'll give you an idea of how things were: My favourite memories of training nights on Tuesday and Thursday at Penrith are of going to the pub after the sessions and watching the likes of Bob O'Reilly and Ken Wilson impersonating Bugs Bunny cartoon characters in the bar until all hours of the morning.

Our reserve grade coach Bob Moses, who was a renowned gambler, would be playing cards at a table nearby and telling us his life story.

We'd drink on Tuesday nights until the pub shut. And on Thursday night until the pub shut and we'd play games in the pub. Penrith was an extremely social club.

On Friday night we'd train.

The coach and the players would go to the pub for a couple of glasses of squash.

As soon as the coach left, you'd peel off your tracksuit and underneath would be your disco gear for the night club and away you'd go again. It was little wonder we could only compete for 40 or 50 minutes every week.

Good as GOULD

Our idea of professional football was obviously a little different to every other club in the premiership. We were certainly on the outside looking in at professional rugby league. We were new to the premiership and we were a long, long way from the centre of rugby league happenings in Sydney.

In my early days at Penrith I was going to NSW University at Kensington, working at Ryde Ex-Servicemen's Club as a barman for casual money and playing football for the Panthers.

In those days of peak hour traffic and limited highway access, that schedule represented an horrendous amount of travelling.

It was a matter of getting to University by 8 o'clock each morning, back out to Penrith to train by 5pm, then back to Ryde to work. I'd crawl into bed by 2am and be up the next morning at 6 o'clock to start all over again. Something had to suffer and I had already decided it was not going to be the football. Some days I would get up to go to university and end up at Wyong races, then be back in time to start training at Penrith.

After three years of trying to fit in all the pieces, I gave university away to concentrate on football.

I had been passing the exams. My only failures were in the exams I had not attended.

I think I had passed something like 15 of the 23 subjects but the travel was really getting to me. Adding to the pressure was the improvement in my rugby league status.

The first three years I played I didn't have an injury and things looked promising. I'd been under-23's player of the year in 1976 and reserve grade player of the year in 1977 and first grade captain in 1978.

The progression was fairly rapid. Then, I broke my collarbone and got my first eye injury in the same tackle in the last match of 1978.

From that I had impaired vision. I had an operation in the off season, then came back and played the first six or seven rounds in 1979. The week before the City sides were announced the eye went again—when I was punched in a tackle. This time I was out for nine months.

During that period of uncertainty and the time off to recuperate, enthusiasm for study and the long trek to university suffered and that helped my decision.

There was also a feeling I had at Penrith that somewhere, somehow there had to be a better way.

In those days the image of rugby league footballers generally was disgraceful on and off the field—especially off the field. They were mostly hooligans. Certainly the ones that I associated with were not the type you would take to a church social.

We were all having a good time but it was basically hooliganism—getting drunk in discos, in pubs, lewd behaviour. There were almost contests to outdo each other in gross behaviour. In group situations there were also occasions when the fairer sex were not treated with the dignity they deserved.

As a young bloke I was naturally impressionable. If the older players were doing things and behaving in a certain way, then you were going to be doing it too. I was certainly behaving in a way that was different to the way I had been brought up but it was a matter of peer pressure I suppose.

It is credit to the work of the New South Wales and Australian Rugby League that behaviour like that is now just a memory—apart from a few isolated incidents. Hard work from a lot of people has polished the image of the game and players to a bright sheen. Irresponsible behaviour has been eradicated and players now have modelling and advertising contracts that reflect their improved status. The game is also a lot cleaner and a lot safer to play.

In those early days, football was just another name for thuggery. At least until everyone in games tired a little. It was just mayhem and very spiteful.

Good as GOULD

Gouging, biting, stiff arms, punching, grabbing testicles and other foul acts were accepted behaviour, at least by the players. The physical danger was so great in first grade that players were required to serve an apprenticeship in second and third grade to get them ready.

Promoting a young promising player too early into first grade could see him simply bashed out of the game. You would never take the ball up without getting belted and punched. Everyone in my era finished up with broken noses and missing teeth.

Nowadays they are models. That says it all about the improvement in playing standards and the emergence of skill ahead of skulduggery.

At Penrith in my day, it was a unique rugby league situation. Basically we had no idea what was required for first grade and what preparation was needed.

By 1978 the club had only been in first grade for a decade and the lack of experience, which was worsened by the distance we were from other first grade clubs, made improving difficult.

With hindsight I can see now that we really had no idea of how to train and how to play.

I think now of our coach Don Parish. He was better than we realised. He was better than he realised I think. He expressed a lot to us about the game, about where to position ourselves, the way to play, manoeuvres, what we should be doing. I found him very good but he was constantly trying to motivate us. In those days it was all motivation. That is just emotion—and emotion lasts about ten minutes once a game starts. So once the bashing and thumping was over and you had to get down to playing football, we had nothing.

Don knew a lot about football but the football was not emphasised enough in what we were doing.

There was a lot of talent around Penrith at the time and

over the next few years, as well as potential administrators. Tim Sheens came through the era. So did Jim Jones, who is now the club's development officer, Mick Kelly, who was a lower grade coach, Royce Simmons. Ken Wilson played out there in those days. So did English players Mick Stephenson and Bill Ashurst. Mick was the ultimate professional. Bill probably had more influence on the younger players than he should have had. I've heard from England that Ashurst has since found God. He would have a lot to tell him about. If we had taken after Mick we might all have been better off.

Although Penrith's results were not much to talk about, there was a growing awareness of the talent being produced and increasing confidence among the players that they could hold their own with other first grade sides. Unfortunately this awareness was coming from the fact that players were leaving Penrith and succeeding with other teams.

Paul Merlo left and played first grade at Wests and Cronulla in a semi-final series. Glenn West left and played with Parramatta in a semi-final series. Then Des Hasler left and joined Manly and became an instant sensation. Ken Wilson went and played with Newtown in a grand final. Bob O'Reilly left and they told him he was washed up. He played in a winning grand final team with Parramatta. It became obvious that players who had never aspired to any great heights at Penrith were going to other clubs and having great success. It made Penrith more aware that they had to be looking after their own players, both juniors and the ones they were recruiting. And that their development process had to be better. It was probably the start of Penrith's maturity as a first grade club.

The trouble in the early days was that the only players the club could attract when it went into the international rugby league and rugby union markets were those who were a bit past their best. There was no real thought to developing the

Good as GOULD

guidelines that would later prove so successful. It was only in the 1980s when the club changed policy and concentrated more on local talent and juniors, that Penrith started producing internationals like Greg Alexander, Mark Geyer, Brad Fittler and John Cartwright as well as highly regarded first graders like Brad Izzard and Colin Van Der Voort.

Looking back it is easy to see our shortcomings. We simply did not understand what professional rugby league was all about and what you had to do to succeed. Penrith was a long way, both mentally and geographically from the heart of Australian Rugby League in Sydney.

I think Penrith had the talent to be a force much earlier than it did. It was only when locals like Tim Sheens became coach that the club started heading in the right direction.

I got the shock of my life when I moved from Penrith to Newtown. I'd had offers from Roy Masters at Wests and Warren Ryan at Newtown. I don't think Roy had even seen me play. He just wanted me because Warren had made an offer.

My father Bruce influenced my decision. He said I needed a coach like Warren, so I went to Newtown. If I had not chosen Newtown I wonder how much longer my career might have lasted. I don't think I would have survived as long as I did. Coming to Newtown was like going into another world. Newtown, Canterbury and then Souths gave me a completely new look at rugby league and the way you should train and prepare for matches. Those clubs gave me a chance to develop an attitude towards sport and professionalism that I have never forgotten.

When You're a Jet

Newtown has claims to being Sydney's unluckiest rugby league area. For years Newtown basked in the glory of being the game's oldest club until a more comprehensive check by sports historians showed that Glebe had usurped them by a few days back in 1908. Things like that always seemed to be happening to Newtown. The area, an average inner-city suburb, somehow failed to capture the imagination of young upwardly-inclined professional couples as other similar areas had done. Newtown houses did not undergo the same gentrification as those in similar areas like Glebe, Paddington and Balmain. By the late 1970s, there were grave fears for Newtown's rugby league future.

Crowds were down. Junior league numbers were fading. Money was in short supply to sustain the side and the home ground of Henson Park needed extensive renovations just to be rated poor.

Newtown football club, once the 'Bluebags', now the 'Jets', was playing in a time warp. Its only three premierships had come in 1910, 1933 and 1943. The club had been premiership runner-up in 1913, 1914, 1929, 1954 and 1955.

By the 1960s the Blues were starting to struggle and with each succeeding season the situation worsened. There was talk of Newtown becoming the first club since Glebe in 1929 to be cut from the premiership after joining in 1908 (although Sydney University quit of its own accord in 1937) and the

Good as GOULD

deeds of famous players like Frank Bumper Farrell and Len Smith, the Australian Test captain whose omission from the 1948 Kangaroos had caused such a storm, were no more than ancient memories. Smith had captained Australia to a Test series win against New Zealand in the afternoon. Hours later selectors met to pick the Kangaroos and Smith was omitted. The captaincy went to Wests Col Maxwell in a side that lost the Ashes Tests to Great Britain 23–21, 7–16 and 9–23. To this day mystery surrounds the reasons behind the selection decision but there are strong pointers indicating that Smith, a Catholic, was a victim of religious bias. It was the way of things in earlier decades of rugby league as Catholics and Masons formed cliques.

By the 1970s pallbearers were dressing in black as they prepared for the body of Newtown's historic presence in the premiership to be presented at the parlour for the final rituals.

Years of poor results in the 1970s had culminated in Newtown's almost permanent tenure at the bottom of the premiership table. A shortage of money made improvement unlikely and the picture was bleak.

Between 1970 and 1980 Newtown would finish eighth in 1970, tenth in 1971, fifth in 1972, third in 1973. Under Jack Gibson, seventh in 1974, tenth in 1975, and last in a 12-team competition in 1976–7–8 before lifting to fifth in 1979 and then dropping to eighth in 1980.

Then came, unexpectedly and almost miraculously, a saviour in the prickly form of a new coach, Warren Ryan. A former Commonwealth Games shot-putter for Australia in 1962 in Perth, Ryan finished seventh with an effort of 15.75 metres. Ryan had been a St George lower grader and Cronulla first grader as a player. He finished his playing career in Wollongong as a player–coach with the local side Wests with instant and remarkable success. Confirming his appreciation of

FROM PLAYER TO COACH

young talent and a sharp eye, it was Ryan who went knocking on the door of a 17-year-old in Wollongong to convince the boy's parents that their son was big enough, talented enough and mature enough to play in the first grade grand final. Ryan's side won and it was the start of a sensational club and international career for John Dorahy. Ryan played under coach Don Parish the former Test fullback at Wests Wollongong, winning premierships in 1969 and 1970. He took over as Wests captain-coach and won the 1971 and 1972 titles. He was non-playing coach but quit over a dispute about the quality of players.

An effort like that could not escape the attention of Sydney clubs ever on the lookout for coaching talent and Ryan was appointed coach of the Wests under-23s in 1977 under first grade and head coach Roy Masters.

It was not a marriage made in heaven. Ryan and Masters fell out quickly, beginning a feud that would not be repaired—at least cosmetically—until after the 1985 grand final at the SCG when Ryan's Canterbury side prevented Masters' St George teams making a clean sweep of all three grades by winning the first grade match 7–6.

Ryan that day walked across to the crestfallen Masters and offered his hand. Before both men released the white doves of peace before 44,569 spectators they had exchanged enough venom to make half a dozen cobras cast an envious glance in the previous six years.

One cause of the trouble centred around allegations that Masters had wanted to borrow a move he had noticed Ryan using in the lower grades with Wests and was met with a less than enthusiastic response. The situation did not get any better when Ryan left at the end of that year after a remarkable effort to take the under-23s into the semi-finals in fifth place and then guide them into the grand final. Had Wests won, Ryan would have been the first man ever to coach a side from fifth place to a premiership. Instead that singular honour would go to Brisbane's Wayne Bennett in 1993. Brisbane finished on 32 points in equal fourth place with Manly, but in fifth place on percentages. On the way to the premiership Brisbane beat Manly 36–10, Canberra 30–12, Canterbury 23–16 and finally St George 14–6 in the grand final.

Even at that stage coach Ryan was showing a remarkable intolerance of anything he ran across in rugby league that did not correspond with his way of thinking. After one season with Wests he left but not before the acrimony was deeply established between him and Masters. The two men had not been on speaking terms for some time.

Years after being recruited to Western Suburbs in Sydney, Dorahy would repay the favour by trumpeting Ryan's ability to club officials and helping him secure the under-23's coaching job under Masters and second grade coach Fred Nelson.

Masters says the scenario between him and Ryan over a coaching move has strayed a little off the track with time—although he concedes the animosity was very real.

'He was nearly sacked after two weeks because he was confrontational and abrasive,' Masters revealed of that year at Wests.

'I had been down to Griffith with Les Boyd (a former Test second-rower) and Tommy Raudonikis for a preseason game. We came back to this dreadful confrontation going on, with the committee wanting to sack Ryan. I held a meeting with the under-23 players—I knew them well because I was their coach the previous year when we won the under-23 grand final.

'I said to Alan Neil and Peter Walsh and some of the others: "What are we going to do with this bloke? Are we going to sack him or not? It's all on my say-so."

'They said no. We'll stick with him.'

FROM PLAYER TO COACH

Masters smoothed the situation over with Wests' president, the former Test forward Billy Carson, and Ryan remained. However, tension and drama were never far away. Masters remains certain that a perceived plot to depose him from the first grade job at Wests coincided with Ryan's arrival at the club.

Legend has it that the final falling out between the two coaches came about because Ryan refused to let one of his moves be 'borrowed' by Masters for use by the first grade side.

'I said to him: "It's a good move. Go through it with me",' Masters revealed. 'Most of the coaching fraternity in such a situation would sit down at a bar and map it out on a beer coaster. Then you would go to training and make it work yourself as I would do with Jack Gibson when he and I swapped moves. But Warren wanted to coach the entire move himself with the first grade side. He was adamant that any move he made available to the first grade side was conditional on him coaching them in its execution.'

Masters says he raised no objections to Ryan's demand, saying it was probably a more beneficial method. 'It does seem stupid to me that you can have A explaining it to B and then B explaining it to the players. You lose something in the translation,' he said. 'That's all it was about. It has gone into the history books a little wrongly that he wouldn't let me use his move. He showed the move to the first grade side and we used it.'

Masters says Ryan ran a campaign to try and get the reserve grade job for 1979 but failed. 'When the appointments were made I was still the first grade coach, Freddie Nelson was the reserve grade coach and we had a new under-23s coach. Ryan had gone to Newtown.'

Wests point out that while getting the under-23 side to the grand final was commendable, the team's experience and proven skill as defending premiers were also significant factors.

The pattern established at Wests in his first premiership coaching job in Sydney would prove a true guide to Ryan's career. There would be incredible success mixed with animosity, tirades against the Phillip Street administration, his own club's officials—and often bitter exchanges with his own star players such as Tom Raudonikis at Newtown, Steve Mortimer at Canterbury and Steve Roach at Balmain.

When Ryan arrived at Newtown as coach Gould was a year away from joining him from Penrith. There was no hint then that two of the most significant coaching identities of Australian rugby league were coming face to face for the first time. To an outsider it was just another coach, with some success in a one-year stint in the under-23's, trying to lift Newtown and a skilled second rower who was trying to make a fresh start after some injury-ridden years at Penrith.

For the next decade Ryan and Gould would find their careers intertwined repeatedly as their careers expanded dramatically. They would be together at Newtown, opposed when Gould went to Souths, re-united as coaches at Canterbury and then opposed when Ryan went to Balmain and again when Gould moved on to coach Penrith.

'At Newtown there was a feeling with Warren that if the team won it was regarded as Tommy's answer. If the side lost, it was called Warren's problem,' Phil Gould remembered.

There was also a seemingly special place in Ryan's armoury for the media. He fell out with several rugby league writers in his debut year with Newtown, opening wounds that were not healed for years. Initially the media was unconcerned with Ryan's uppityness, thinking he would be just part of the cannon fodder that would be involved with lower-placed clubs and that he would quickly disappear after a couple of dismal seasons. Instead Ryan's astonishing success and emergence as a premier coach took them by surprise but made peace options more difficult to achieve. Eventually one journalist after a lengthy feud with Ryan, swallowed his pride and approached NSWRL chief executive John Quayle to act as mediator to sue for peace.

Ryan coached Newtown to a grand final in 1981, won premierships in 1983 and 1984 with Canterbury, took Balmain to back-to-back grand finals in 1988 and 1989 and won a coach-of-the-year award. Along the way he generated constant headlines, controversy and bitterness with his outspokenness and the siege mentality he was seen to adopt with his teams. His style was adversarial in almost every aspect of rugby league and his 'scorched earth' policy required balm and bandages whenever he left a club.

On the credit side Ryan was a crafty, innovative and far-sighted coach who dramatically lifted the performance of his teams. He devised, developed and executed a philosophy of defence so ferocious it bordered on assault. Under Ryan, teams were given a new and penetrating insight into rugby league tactics and what could be achieved by absolute and fearless discipline. The sum of the total parts playing in unison to their total team potential was his aim and always superseded the skills and flamboyance of individual players in the team. He would take five first grade sides into grand finals as well as Wests' under-23 side.

'He was revolutionary at the time,' Gould remembered of his time with Ryan. 'There was nothing ad hoc about what we did. We knew where we would be in two tackles' time, where we would be in four tackles and where we would be in six tackles' time.

'He was by far and away the best coach in the game. Jack Gibson (who steered Parramatta to premierships in 1981–82–83 and Easts to wins in the 1972 and 1973 grand finals) had given coaches an identity but Ryan really made many of the coaching advances that have occurred in rugby league in recent years.'

To Ryan rugby league was as structured as a concerto. Every section from the tubas to the flutes, to the piano and the violins, had to combine in total unity.

But back in 1979 Ryan was unknown as a conductor. The three years to 1981 would be ones of consolidation and quiet improvement. With hindsight, Newtown's rise through the ranks in its burgeoning years is quite obvious. But at the time Newtown's improvement was seen as an aberration. They were too deeply installed in the public psyche as losers and strugglers to be considered real challengers for the premiership. The team's improvement was seen as a minor stirring of a long-sleeping club that would return to peaceful slumber again rather than lead to a full-scale attack on the premiership.

Almost unnoticed, Ryan was putting the pieces together, signing Gould from Penrith as part of the plan. In 1980 Ryan also captured Test warhorse Tom Raudonikis from Wests in a stunning switch of clubs by a player who was regarded as a Wests player forever. Raudonikis made the change at the request of his good friend and advertising whiz John Singleton, who was pumping cash as well as his significant marketing and promotional skills into Newtown.

It would be a lucrative contract that would tempt Raudonikis to leave Wests where he had played since being recruited from Wagga. That switch to the city had been a precursor to a decision that would lead to Raudonikis playing 20 Tests and making two Kangaroo tours in 1973 and 1978.

Raudonikis was a graduate of the old school of Australian half-backs in which toughness, courage and endurance were essential—with a willingness to become an extra forward in defence. Singleton, a long-time Newtown supporter, well supplied with the money to help the club's need for players, earmarked Raudonikis as a vital component in any rebuilding program. 'Tom Terrific' was a crowd-pleaser because of his rugged approach, popular with fans and the media and a proven winner.

'I was 30 years of age at the time and I knew I only had a few years left,' Raudonikis said of the move. 'I loved Wests and I really went to Newtown to make myself more financially secure. The lead-up to the 1981 season with Newtown was a rebuilding time; we bought blokes like Mick Pittman and Peter Kelly. Graeme O'Grady had already been there a year along with Dean Lance.' The decision to sign Raudonikis, the negotiations and the financial agreements were all put in place by Singleton. The final signing pleased almost everyone connected with the club. Newtown now had a born leader and high-profile player in the side. Coach Ryan, however, was not completely won over.

'He didn't want me at Newtown,' Raudonikis said. 'Yet, I taught Newtown how to win, which is why Singo bought me. But Ryan didn't want me there. So Singo said to him (Ryan): "He's coming. You can leave if you like".'

The reasons behind Ryan's lack of enthusiasm for Raudonikis' arrival have never been established but friends of the half-back say it was almost certainly because the coach saw in Tommy an unbeatable rival in the push for media attention.

'That's what it was for sure,' says a player from that time. 'He would have known that Tommy would get more publicity than him and he couldn't handle it. It would be all Raudonikis and not Ryan.'

Raudonikis said: 'But you still have to give Ryan credit—he had some very, very good ideas.' The two men, Ryan and Raudonikis, were worlds apart in application and technique. Gould illustrated the confrontation collision of two different

Good as GOULD

cultures with a story from the dressing room.

Ryan had just delivered a prematch tactical speech, detailing the individual chores of every player as well as the team's playing pattern, and reinforcing the weaknesses of the opposition players that he had drummed into his players at earlier training sessions.

When it was over and Ryan had gone Raudonikis addressed the team and said simply: 'Forget all that. Let's just go out and bash these bastards!'

To Raudonikis, Gould was as good a forward with the ball as he had seen in a long career. 'He reminded me of a Pommy player,' he said. 'He had some of the best skills I've ever seen in a forward. He could get rid of the ball and just read a game of football. He was brilliant. I don't know why his representative career did not kick on.'

Singleton showed he was willing to put his money where his mouth was when it came to supporting Newtown. He attracted startling headlines when it was revealed that he had bet $10,000 on Newtown to win the premiership with bookmaker Terry Page at odds of 50–1. Many would have considered the odds not generous enough. The season's results would prove them wrong. Singleton also had a second bet of $50,000 to $10,000 on Newtown making the semi-finals. If Newtown, who had been renamed the Jets in a 1970s marketing revamp, could just make the final five, Singleton would have the team running for $500,000 to nothing to win the premiership.

Newtown's steady build-up since 1978, when the club had won only two games all season, was startlingly effective by 1981. Ryan had arrived in 1979, Raudonikis in 1980, goal-kicker Ken Wilson was there after three years at Penrith, winger Ray Blacklock, Phil Sigsworth, who would play a Test for Australia, Illawarra's Brian Hetherington, Mick Pitman from Newcastle and John Ferguson from Glen Innes.

FROM PLAYER TO COACH

Ferguson, who was of indeterminate age, proved an elusive and pacy winger for Ryan although eight years later in a famous moment, the coach would query the wisdom of having brought the winger from the bush to the city. It was Ferguson, by then on the wing for Canberra, who set up a try for fullback Gary Belcher and then scored the converted try that levelled the score right on full-time in the 1989 grand final against Ryan's Balmain. Canberra won the title, 19–14, in extra time.

The Jets' build-up went largely unnoticed. Newtown had been tagged as 'losers' and 'also-rans' in the public consciousness for too long to have their status suddenly upgraded by the purchase of a few players. Only Newtown's dwindling ranks of supporters clung to the view that better times were on the way. One of their supporters was future Test centre Terry Hill. 'I was raised in Erskineville and Newtown was my team. One of my happiest sporting memories is watching them play (against Parramatta) in the 1981 grand final. I saw Gus play for Newtown. I was at Leichhardt Oval the night he had a shot at goal that could have won a mid-week cup match. He missed.'

It is a discussion point that has been debated many times over a beer. 'It wasn't me,' Gould insists. 'I didn't take that shot at goal. I don't know who did but it wasn't me. Terry keeps saying it was, but I know it wasn't.'

In 1981 Newtown did not start the season like a side threatening to defy tradition and the pre-premiership predictions. The Jets were beaten 33–9 by Parramatta in the opening round, drew with Wests 12–all and then had their first win of the season 21–13 against Balmain before losing 37–5 to Easts. That was three competition points from a possible eight. Stability soon settled the side, however, and Newtown put together an eye-catching run of seven wins from the next eight matches, beating Manly 20–8, Penrith 24–6, Canterbury 24–14, Souths 30–14, losing 11–9 to Easts before winning against St George

Good as GOULD

20–3, Cronulla 12–6 and Parramatta 14–9. The win against eventual premiers Parramatta in the second round was a gauge of how far the club had come since losing the first-round match 33–9.

Newtown were eventually to finish second to minor premiers Manly on the points table but then lose the minor preliminary final 10–8 to Parramatta who beat Easts 12–8 a week later to be first into the grand final. The results pitted Newtown against Manly in a sudden-death semi-final and the two sides responded with an unforgettable boots-and-all approach.

There was an all-in brawl involving nearly every player on the field and resulted in prop Steve Bowden missing the rest of the season with a fractured cheekbone. Newtown defeated the odds and beat glamour side Manly 20–15. It was a performance built more around bludgeoning than brilliance but it was the win that was sought in a game neither side could afford to lose.

Ryan's tactics as the 1981 season moved into its serious phase was to alternate Raudonikis and Ken Wilson in the halfback role—Wilson for his brilliant kicking in general play and directing the team around the ground, Raudonikis for toughness, will to win and determination. It was a successful formula even though Raudonikis was not happy with having spent 12 weeks in reserve grade. He got back into first grade for the clash with Manly and played for 60 minutes before being replaced by Wilson.

After more than a decade of waiting Raudonikis was determined to be in a grand final side. Newtown had one final obstacle to clear—Easts in the final. Again Newtown were unwanted by punters with as much as 2–1 available about their chances of winning and moving into the club's first grand final since 1955. Bobby Fulton's Easts had been minor premiers but had gradually slipped away in the semi-finals. That slump

FROM PLAYER TO COACH

continued in the final. Newtown dominated proceedings, scoring three tries to one in a 15–5 win. It was a try from Gould that broke a 5–all deadlock at half-time. Nine minutes into the second half Gould raced over after dummying past Easts half Kevin Hastings and forward Ian Barkley. 'It was just one of those things that can happen in a game,' Gould said. 'I had a run, tried a dummy and they fell for it. Sometimes they work, sometimes they don't. They were looking for me to pass the ball.' Again Raudonikis started the game but was replaced with around 15 minutes to go.

The grand final pitted the battlers Newtown against the highly popular Parramatta chasing their first premiership. It was a clash between a Newtown side built around mostly established players against a Parramatta side of lesser-known players but players who were to head on to superstardom for the rest of the decade. Peter Sterling, Steve Ella, Eric Grothe and Brett Kenny were destined to join their Test centre teammate Mick Cronin in Australia's backline.

For a side once again given no chance of winning, Newtown took the fight to the more favoured Parramatta. At half-time Parramatta led 7–6, after Newtown lock Graeme O'Grady scored the first try. Gould had set up the second. Close to Parramatta's line, he had drawn the defence and sent Hetherington over. 'It was looking good at that stage,' Gould remembered. 'We had scored two tries to one by half-time and Parramatta was only ahead because of two goals from Mick Cronin. We were confident of going on with the job in the second half.'

Singleton, with a fortune riding on the result but just as importantly the satisfaction of seeing a side he had helped rebuild bring off an unexpected triumph, was emotionally involved. Working the 9am–noon shift on radio station 2KY at the time, he persuaded the management to let him call the match. Singleton's voice throbbed with emotion in the second

Good as GOULD

half when Raudonikis charged over for a try after running from the base of the scrum and cleverly using referee Greg Hartley as a momentary shield on his way to the line.

It was a pivotal moment in the match. Newtown had clawed its way to an 11–7 lead with around 23 minutes to play. 'We thought we could hold on from there,' Gould said. 'But we knew it would not be easy. Parramatta still had plenty of life left. We knew that.'

The Parramatta backline gradually asserted itself and a try by winger Graham Atkins gave the Eels the lead 12–11 with 15 minutes to go. Then Steve Ella scored and finally Brett Kenny ran 70 metres in the 76th minute to score and put Parramatta's name in the grand final winners' book 20–11.

'It was very disappointing. We all felt sick at the result,' said Gould. 'The team had worked so hard and had done so much to win the premiership and we'd lost. You really do feel devastated losing a grand final. It's a pain that doesn't go away quickly.

'But I suppose we had done well. We had started the season unwanted by anyone and had defied all the critics to make a grand final. I got to play in one and so did Raudonikis. That night we celebrated as if we had won anyway.'

The pain of being beaten in a grand final would soon be replaced by a more tangible hurt. Rumours were already starting to circulate that Newtown's financial status was deteriorating, fast. There were genuine fears that players might not get paid. Eventually, debts of more than $500,000 finished off Newtown and they were cut from the premiership. Arrangements were made to pay the players as much as possible of their contract money with a promissory note for the rest when funds became available. Gould eventually saw a chance to get out—and took it.

The memory of sitting in the run-down Newtown dressing

room all those months before, managing a wry smile at Raudonikis' 'let's bash the bastards' retort to Ryan's more scientific analysis, registered in Phil Gould as two coaching theories colliding. In years to come he would borrow from both Ryan and Raudonikis to shape his own individual structure as a coach.

What was unknown at that stage was the continually intertwining careers he and Ryan would experience in the next decade—when the mantle of top coach would pass from one to the other. But before that happened there was to come verbal brawling in public that would make Raudonikis' remark seem almost gentle by comparison.

PHIL GOULD'S Reflections on
NEWTOWN

Season 1981 was a very special time for me. I came from a club like Penrith that was struggling to make any impression on the premiership at that stage, to be with a club that played and worked hard to make a grand final. It all added up to being an unforgettable experience.

The spirit, friendship and companionship in the Newtown club was as strong as you would ever find in a football team. They were a group of footballers brought together from different backgrounds and from different teams and for various reasons. Some players were considered past their best, some were considered not good enough elsewhere, some were specifically chosen for their potential.

The thing about Newtown was that everyone stuck together so well. Where one player went, everyone followed. It was socially the most enjoyable time you could have. As footballers, they were very tough people, both physically and mentally.

It was during this period that our coach Warren Ryan stamped himself as the best coach rugby league has seen. Much of what he introduced through his Newtown side in 1981 has had dramatic affects on the way the game has been played in the 1980s and 1990s. Ryan's innovations have also significantly influenced the way the rules have been changed to accommodate the style of football he introduced. To my mind he is without peer as a coach.

The 1981 grand final when Ryan's Newtown side took on

FROM PLAYER TO COACH

Parramatta remains one of the supreme highlights of my career. I remember with about 15 minutes to go Brian Hetherington tackled Ray Price under the posts when it looked for certain that Parramatta would score. Hetherington just cut him down.

We had a scrum under our posts and I remember looking at the Parramatta players walking towards the scrum with their heads down. They had thrown a lot at us for little reward. I turned to Newtown's tough forward Mick Pitman and I said, 'We've got these blokes.'

The last 15 minutes are just a blur. They seemed to get a lot of ball and we let in a couple of tries. I guess they gained momentum at the right time and they were able to finish us off.

It took me 10 years to watch the replay. When I finally did, I saw that perhaps it was a game Parramatta was always going to win although it did not feel that way on the field.

A lot of people have made criticism of Ryan's coaching for the changes he made during the grand final like leaving Tom Raudonikis on for the full 80 minutes as well as Kenny Wilson. In lead-up games, Wilson had mostly replaced Raudonikis. I have since been in that position a number of times as a coach. Whether he did the right thing or the wrong thing is simply relative. What is absolutely certain is that any decision Ryan made was designed solely to help us win the match. The same thing we were trying to do ourselves. I don't think anyone can blame Ryan for the changes he made. To my mind, having seen the replay, it does look as if Parramatta was always going to get us as the second half unfolded. Ryan was just trying to stop it happening.

Bulldogs and Bullfrogs

Canterbury in 1983 was a club trying desperately to rehabilitate itself. The euphoria of the 18–4 premiership win in 1980 under Ted Glossop against Bob Fulton's Easts at the SCG had long since evaporated. That was a grand final that was etched into the history books largely through the spectacular try scored by winger Steve Gearin who took a mile-high bomb on the full from fullback Greg Brentnall to dive over in the match and clinch Canterbury's first premiership in first grade since 1942.

The ensuing two years had not been kind. In 1981 Canterbury finished runner-up in defence of its premiership and by 1982, Glossop, the progenitor of the bright attacking football that earned his side the tag 'the entertainers' had become Glossop the contaminated—at least in the minds of some players and one prominent personality at the club.

Signing Phil Gould and other players was seen as a way of strengthening the Bulldogs and perhaps giving new drive and perspective to a club starting to stagger.

For Gould the switch of clubs was motivated by money more than anything else. Newtown after their one glorious season of 1981 had subsequently reverted to form so badly that the money owed to players was severely compromised. Gould found his circumstances so demanding as a newly married man that pursuing his rugby league career with another club became imperative.

FROM PLAYER TO COACH

Gould and Donna were married at a time when it looked as though his rugby league-playing days were over. A second damaging eye injury had seemingly ended his career and he had moved to Coffs Harbour to get away from football and settle down as a married man. But the lure of football was too strong and he decided to play with the local side, figuring the drop in standard would lessen the chances of another eye injury and more damage. He approached Penrith for a clearance and a release from his contract but was refused. If he was going to play football it would be with Penrith, not in the bush. So it was that his career resumed in Sydney rather than being lost to a local side in the far north coast sunshine.

Money remained tight in the Gould household and jobs were hard to get at the time. A well-meaning or malicious acquaintance (the jury is still out on that one) had run into Gould at Penrith Leagues Club one night and, hearing of his employment difficulties, offered to give him a job. The details could be worked out if they met at Parramatta Leagues Club the next day. Gould arrived. The other man did not. Disgruntled, Gould made the long trek back to Penrith by public transport, walking the last few kilometres to his home unit and wife Donna.

Nothing seemed to be going right. With the world seemingly at odds against him, Gould took his last nine dollars and walked across the road to a fast food outlet to buy a chicken and salads for lunch. Instead, feeling things could not get any worse, he took the money into a TAB. He walked out after the last race with around $9000. 'It was a Godsend. I bought Chinese food to take home, we had a night out, paid some bills and used the money to buy a car.'

The move to Canterbury was to consolidate that windfall and hopefully provide the foundation for a solid financial future. It would also be a striking example of division and turmoil

Good as GOULD

behind the public countenance of Canterbury as a happy, family-orientated club.

'Ted Glossop was responsible for getting me to Canterbury on a three-year deal from 1983,' Gould said. 'We'd gone to the grand final with Newtown in 1981 and Canterbury were making overtures to me then. It was obvious Newtown were going broke and I couldn't afford to go broke myself by not getting paid. At that stage we were not going to get paid but as it turned out I finished up with about 85 to 90 per cent of my money which was better than a lot of other people.'

Canterbury's poor seasons in 1981 and 1982 had put enormous pressure on Glossop to get the side performing better. His cause was not helped when Gould fractured a vertebra in his neck and lost the use of his left arm for three months. For Gould it made the season a personal wipeout. Canterbury went on to make the final in 1983 (losing 18–4 to Parramatta), an achievement usually guaranteed to keep a coach in his job for at least another season. Glossop became the exception. During the 1983 season Canterbury's then chief executive Peter Moore held a series of top-secret meetings with Warren Ryan in a car parked not far from where Ryan taught at Belmore High School. The deal for Ryan to take over as first grade coach was set in concrete long before the siren sounded on the 1983 final. Stories, many of them emanating from inside the Canterbury club, started halfway through the season and continued, centred on Glossop's future. It was one of the first examples Gould would see of the skill of prominent Canterbury officials in manipulating the media and introducing destabilising elements into a situation they wanted to change, without seeming to be initiating the idea. Later, when Gould was under siege himself as first grade coach of the club in 1989, it was a system of propaganda Canterbury had perfected.

After five years in the inner sanctum of Canterbury's

administration, Glossop, a school headmaster, was probably astute enough to realise what was happening even before it became public. To Gould, a sideline observer because of his injury, the switch of coaches was not a surprise. From his arrival at Canterbury the prospects of Glossop surviving long-term seemed minimal because of a steady stream of corrosive comments.

'A couple of the senior players like Chris Anderson were unhappy with Glossop and they were looking to unseat him and get someone else to take over as coach,' he said. 'It was obvious halfway through 1983 that Ted wasn't going to be there the next year. Chris used to whinge about everything and say Ted was not doing a good job. To my mind Ted was doing a good job. He'd won a competition for the club so he'd been all right in 1980. Then suddenly he wasn't all right in 1983. I only had one year with Ted and found him a terrific bloke. He was laid-back and preferred to rely on the individual skills of players.'

With the coach's future so unclear, 1983 was a difficult year but Canterbury still managed to finish the preliminary rounds in first place before bowing out in the final to Parramatta who went on to beat Manly in the grand final for their third successive premiership win. They became the first club to win three in a row since St George in their 11-year run between 1956 and 1966.

Ryan's public acceptance of the first grade coaching job at Canterbury was an anticlimax. His arrival at Belmore, greeted with such enthusiasm, would be a detonator to the most explosive four years any club has ever known.

There was no shortage of talent in the club for season 1984. The Mortimer brothers, Steve, Peter and Chris, were there. So was ball-playing five-eighth Garry Hughes. To add to the arsenal Ryan also recruited Peter Kelly, Peter Tunks, Mark Bugden

Good as GOULD

and Terry Lamb. Paul Langmack and David Gillespie were in the forwards as well.

It was a side that suited to perfection Ryan's revolutionary ideas on triumph through intimidation. Quoted warily by bookmakers at 6–1 at the start of the year, Canterbury headed through the season in frightening fashion, establishing themselves as a side capable of physically overpowering other packs, bludgeoning them into submission with tactics both lawful and unlawful.

They paraded a defensive structure that made opposing players wary of venturing into the rucks.

'We had our share of judiciary hearings throughout the year,' Gould said. 'Peter Kelly was down there a couple of times and a few other players were under the microscope.

'The older brigade made it a very, very, brutal side. Opposing sides were beaten before they played us. We only lost five games all year. The scoreboard might have shown we had lost on those few other days but the sides that we'd played were never in doubt about the fact that we had won. We were virtually unbeatable all season.'

Bulldog-style was war with football boots on. No reverse gear, no retreat. In the middle of all the flak, Gould's own career blossomed. He played the first 10 games in first grade, picked up man-of-the-match awards and had caught the eye of the representative selectors.

On the day the City–Country teams were to be announced Peter Moore approached Gould, telling him: 'You're in the side tonight for City Firsts.' It would have been a long-overdue reward and recognition of the player regarded as the most astute and deceptive ball-handler since Arthur Beetson and Bob O'Reilly, but whether it was just a morale-boosting claim by Moore or was based on factual information was not put to the test. Gould broke his ankle that afternoon against North

FROM PLAYER TO COACH

Sydney and he did not recover until three weeks before the end of the season. He played three weeks of third grade and then his ankle collapsed again and he took no part in the semi-finals as Canterbury crunched their way to a 6–4 win against Parramatta in the grand final.

The premiership-decider was a tense and very tight match. Both sides scored a try and Parramatta's Mick Cronin had the chance to level the scores in the final minutes and send the game into extra time. It was one of the few grand finals that has pitted the defending champions against the obvious challenger. 'I'm glad we could play and beat the premiers in the grand final,' Moore would say. 'It is more fitting that way.'

Canterbury's win in the 1984 grand final ended Parramatta's three-year reign as premiers although they would be back in 1986, again under John Monie to regain the first grade premiership—from Canterbury in an emotional match that saw champions Mick Cronin and Ray Price play their last first grade games.

Paul Langmack, then a precociously talented back-rower not long out of school and playing first grade at 17 years of age, remembered the effect Gould had on the side in that premiership-winning season.

'I played 10 games in first grade under Ted Glossop in 1983. The next year Gus was really carving them up in first grade and he was going to play representative football for sure. But he broke his ankle,' Langmack remembered. 'The following week it was between Brian Battese and me to replace him. But they rested Jimmy Leis from the side and picked Battese and me in the same pack. Whoever played best would get the vacancy caused by Gus being injured. Battese and I both played so well they left us both in the side and dropped Leis.

'Gus was Canterbury's best player then. He was like Warren Ryan's quarter-back. He was calling the shots.'

Good as GOULD

Langmack and Gould had first met in 1982 when Gould came down to help the coaches at Langmack's school, Fairfield Patrician Brothers.

'In 1983 I met him again at Canterbury and we played together in 1984–85,' said Langmack. 'He was great to play with. We always seemed to be on the same wavelength. We both liked to be creative. But I trained harder,' he laughed in a pointer towards Gould's less than absolute dedication to training sessions. Langmack reckoned Ryan also appreciated Gould's contribution to the team. 'The times when Gus wasn't in first grade or was in second grade, Warren used to bring him to training and say: "What do you think of these moves?" And Gus would say: "Yeah, that's not bad." Gus is very smart. He had a couple of years at university and he's street smart as well. If you're smart and street-wise and you know a lot about football, you're going to be a good coach because coaching is more the psychology of knowing the pluses and minuses of every player. If you're not street-wise, you'll run into a dead end.

'I know that even Gus would say that Warren Ryan has a great knowledge of football. But Ryan hasn't got people skills. That was his downfall. If he'd had people skills he'd still be coaching now.'

Gould's absence through injury in 1984 caused an upheaval. Eventually half Steve Mortimer was designated to run the side in attack. 'But it wasn't the way Gus used to run the side,' Langmack said. 'I used to see opposition blokes scared to play us. You could tell. They were apprehensive because they knew they were going to get bashed—legally. We had some very big hitters in our team—Tunks, Kelly, Bugden, Johnstone, Folkes, Battese.'

To defeat Parramatta in 1984 Canterbury adhered to a formula that had long been successful for them. For all of their skill and flamboyance in a backline that featured half Peter

Sterling, five-eighth Brett Kenny, centres Steve Ella and Mick Cronin and winger Eric Grothe, who all played Tests and made Kangaroo tours, Ryan had pinpointed what he saw as a fatal but justified flaw—that they all believed in self-preservation.

'Warren had decided that Parramatta had the best backline in the world at that time. But he also thought that they were not very brave. If we could intimidate them and have them worrying about their own welfare rather than trying to use the football, it would suit us,' Gould remembered.

'In those days we used to physically beat sides. But there were also some good sides in the competition who made it tough for us. Balmain were hard to beat. Manly were always around.'

Ryan later stood accused of regimenting football to the same robotic status of the Grenadier Guards outside Buckingham Palace: be tall, be strong, obey orders, do not be distracted and do not speak.

His match plans had the status of the Ten Commandments. They were to be followed without exception and often without room for individual enterprise. Ryan would continually reject accusations that he shackled brilliant attacking players by curtailing their flamboyance, saying it would be idiotic of a coach to stop a player using his gifts to win a game. Nevertheless, the rumours persisted. Steve Mortimer for one never seemed the dominant force under Ryan that he had been with other coaches.

Canterbury made the lap of honour with the J.J. Giltinan Shield and the Winfield Cup after winning the 1984 grand final, looking serene and comfortable and bringing a family touch as the Mortimer brothers Steve, Chris and Peter took their children along as well. It was a scene that bore little comparison to the atmosphere that had often prevailed in the club during the season.

Good as GOULD

Steve Mortimer, a crowd-pleasing favourite, had found himself uncomfortable with Ryan's attitude towards players who liked chancing their arm with flamboyant play. Ryan also dropped long-serving Test winger Chris Anderson, who was club boss Peter Moore's son-in-law, to reserve grade, shaking the foundations of the club severely. Anderson had also been captain. With Anderson gone the captaincy looked certain to go to Steve Mortimer but Ryan had other ideas and broke the news in a brusque and insensitive manner that was often his trademark.

Mortimer was punching the bag in the weights room at Belmore Sports Ground when Ryan approached and said Anderson had been dropped. 'I don't want to see you playing like a traffic cop,' Ryan told Mortimer. 'I don't need a half-back in a dinner suit directing traffic. I want you to be involved.' He then announced that the captaincy was going to Terry Lamb who was in his first year with the club, even though Mortimer was favourite to be appointed NSW captain (and subsequently was). Lamb settled the issue by telling Ryan he did not want to be captain and the job should go to Mortimer (which it did). Mortimer went on to lead Canterbury in three grand finals, winning two of them. Lamb's generosity looked like preventing him achieving his final honour of leading a grand final-winning side, until he made his personal dream come true in 1995 against Manly.

'Ryan had a habit of picking on players,' Gould said. 'In 1984 he talked Garry Hughes into playing again and never used him in first grade the whole year. He gave Steve Mortimer a terrible time as well—an individual player who relied on his instinct and vision. Steve didn't react favourably to the way he was being coached but to his credit he tried to work in as much as possible. Warren used Steve as a scapegoat. He did it at Newtown with Tommy Raudonikis because Tommy was a favourite player there with the media and supporters. After a loss at Canterbury Ryan would often turn to the players and say, "Steve let you down today".'

Gould is convinced that one Ryan decision had more to do with the on-going problems at Canterbury than any other.

'He dropped Chris Anderson three or four weeks before the semi-finals and then refused to go to Anderson's testimonial dinner later in the year,' Gould said. For a club so orientated towards marketing itself as a family-based unit, it was the ultimate treachery. It is likely Ryan's future as a coach at the club was terminated there and then. It was just a matter of writing in the date at the first available opportunity. Remarkably that opportunity would not come for three more years.

'Warren was very anti-establishment,' said Gould. 'He'd constantly turn his players against the NSWRL and he'd always have complaints about the club he was at and how no-one was on the same wavelength as him. But he really did have a way of converting the players into his way of thinking so that anyone out of the circle was an outcast. It was a siege mentality.'

Ryan's strength was his strict and disciplined approach which produced an extremely strict and disciplined football team—a team that would stand up under any sort of pressure that might eventuate in a match. Training sessions would exert pressure on the playing pattern all week. There was nothing that might occur in a match on the weekend that would catch players by surprise. Training sessions were long and would continue until every play and every pattern was so deeply ingrained into the team's psyche that moves became automatic. It is a component of Ryan's coaching that Gould employs himself. 'He taught us to play and he taught us to win—and win often,' Gould said.

For Canterbury supporters though, the culture clash of Ryan's dour strategies compared with the flamboyance of Ted

Good as GOULD

Glossop's 1980 'Entertainers' was sometimes hard to accept, even allowing for grand final success. The media would speculate endlessly about the transformation of a free-running premiership-winning side in 1980 into a methodical, fierce and brutal side in 1984. It was like watching a butterfly become an elephant.

'It would not be so much me getting the ball at training and looking in front of me to see what I would do. My job was to do A, B or C depending on the circumstances that prevailed,' Gould said. 'References to the "Entertainers" of 1980 were of constant concern to Warren. The club supported him for a long while, mainly I think because he was winning. He had promised the club a premiership and it looked as if he would deliver. But things did change remarkably after he dropped Chris Anderson. There are a lot of things that have happened over the past 10 years that I think you can trace back to the fallout in the relationship between Warren Ryan and Peter Moore over the Anderson sacking.'

It was galling for Moore to have to accept that a player he had signed for the club as a teenager, who had boarded at his house, had married one of his daughters and who had played for Australia and 284 games for the club, would be dropped and he was powerless to act.

'Warren was a great coach,' said Gould. 'He was—better than any coach in the game. He had enormous influence on me. But he turned people against the establishment. He gathered people around him and rolled them forward with military-like precision. He had scapegoats and he made scapegoats for the other players. They always had that sort of thing to rely on. Over the years he rebelled against Peter Moore, the club, the NSWRL, referees, the media and anyone else he could think of to attack.'

'I didn't feel sorry for Chris Anderson when he was dropped because he had been part of getting rid of Ted

FROM PLAYER TO COACH

Glossop. His career was pretty much over by then anyway. He was gone as a footballer.'

Anderson subsequently went to England in a deal organised by Peter Moore for the 1984–85 northern hemisphere season. After switching to Halifax he proved an outstanding success as a player–coach, taking the side to a Challenge Cup win at Wembley. Even Anderson's departure incited Ryan—with some justification. Moore also stitched up a deal that allowed Paul Langmack, Michael Hagan and Geoff Robinson from first grade and several young Canterbury players to go across to Halifax as well. They would not be able to return to Sydney until after the start of the 1985 season.

Although Canterbury were premiers in 1984 the cost had been high. On the end-of-season trip there were heated arguments. One topic was a stunning decision by the club management to vote Anderson the clubman-of-the-year award, a decision Ryan opposed.

'Warren was against the family nature of the whole exercise at Canterbury,' Gould said. 'The fact of Steve Folkes being related to the Moores (by marriage) who were in turn related to the Hughes brothers (Moore's nephews). And he hated the idea of the "Entertainers" being rated as Canterbury's best side ahead of his 1984 side. We really had very little to do with it as players. Canterbury was always on the back page but it never really worried the players. We just got on with the job and laughed about it. It was virtually just Warren and Steve Mortimer, or Warren and Chris Anderson or Warren and Peter Moore.'

As distant as the problems seemed to Gould at the time, in an astonishing coincidence he was only a couple of years away from getting a first-hand look at the difficulties of coaching the Canterbury first grade side—especially with the same cast of prominent people—Peter Moore, Steve Mortimer and Chris Anderson—still around.

Good as GOULD

Of all the achievements available in rugby league to a coach, defending the premiership is seen as the most impressive. Winning a grand final is an historic achievement. Climbing the mountain the second year is much tougher. As winners in 1984, Canterbury in 1985 faced that task. Parramatta had won three straight—before that it was back to Easts in 1974–75.

Injuries again took a toll of Gould's efforts in 1985 but he still played 14 first grade games and captained Canterbury's reserve grade side into the semi-finals. By this stage Gould had been joined at Canterbury by Daryl Brohman, his old mate from Penrith. After the disillusionment of Penrith, coming to the professionalism of Canterbury was an eye-opening revelation to front-rower Brohman of how a successful club operated.

'I have nothing but respect for Warren Ryan,' he said. 'He's a great coach and Peter Moore is the best administrator I've known.

'I went to Canterbury when Penrith started to disintegrate. I was going to Parramatta but our secretary, who was Charlie Gibson at the time, spoke to Bullfrog and they gave me a much better deal.

'In my first trial back from my broken jaw (suffered in a State of Origin match), I dislocated my shoulder against St George in 1984 and missed the whole year. I thought this is great. I haven't even played a game for them. But Canterbury were tremendous. They really looked after me. They sent fruit to the hospital. When I was getting my shoulder rehabilitated, I told Moore I didn't have time to get the injury right *and* go to work. I asked for a month's pay and said he could take it out of my contract. He said, "How much do you get?" I think it was $250 a week. He gave me $1000 and told me to have a month off. I wasn't used to that sort of consideration at Penrith.'

Brohman, a big man with a capacity to get the ball away in

tackles, had similar skills to Gould and although they were basically chasing the same first grade position at Canterbury, they were good friends.

'We were both ball-players and we rarely got on the paddock together in first grade at Penrith or Canterbury—it seemed that he was out injured and I was playing first grade or I was injured and he was playing first grade. I think we've always had a deep-seated respect for each other even though there was some rivalry as well,' Brohman said.

In early 1985 injuries had checked the progress of both Brohman and Gould and they were partnered in reserve grade under coach Tony Charlton as the first grade side powered its way towards back-to-back premierships. This year the Bulldogs beat Roy Masters' St George side 7–6 in the tightest of grand finals.

It was a season of fluctuating emotional events. Legendary South Sydney and Test fullback Clive Churchill, the man they called the 'Little Master', lost his fight against cancer not long after friends, family and admirers had gathered at Randwick Racecourse to honour him with a black-tie dinner. It was the year Canterbury half-back Steve Mortimer led NSW to its first State of Origin win. St George failed by just that single point to win all three grand finals.

St George beat Parramatta 24–20 in reserve grade and Canterbury 22–16 in the under-23s but the first grade side lost 7–6 after a field goal in the 72nd minute.

With Gould and Brohman there was no shortage of talent in the reserve grade side. Brohman himself was a State of Origin player, fullback Phil Sigsworth had played for Australia. So had lock Jimmy Leis. Gould and centre Greg Mullane were greatly experienced as were many others in the side.

'I'd been to play in England in the off-season and when I came back to Australia I remember playing against Balmain

Good as GOULD

and this classic "catch the ball, draw the man and pass the ball" manoeuvre we put on,' remembered Paul Langmack, who also had a taste of reserve grade. 'It went from Gus to Brohman to me and I scored against Balmain at Leichhardt Oval. I still remember that try. It was a classic. I was running off two ball-players. Canterbury and Balmain were always big games there.'

Langmack, the teenager on his way to a long and outstanding career that would include grand final wins and a Kangaroo tour before he was 21 years of age, found plenty of common ground with Gould. Langmack's inquisitive mind soaked up Gould's football lore.

'He would tell us about playing at Penrith, and at Newtown with Tommy Raudonikis. He probably learnt a lot from Tommy and from Ryan at Newtown. I didn't play with Tommy but in 1995 he became my coach at Wests. He keeps telling me we young blokes wouldn't have made it in his era because he would have bitten our noses off. That's what the game is lacking a bit now—characters.

'Gus told us the story that when he was playing at Penrith he'd won a few thousand dollars on the punt and wanted to buy a new car. He went to the car yard on a Friday and picked out the one he wanted and took it for a test drive. He asked the salesman to hold it for him until Monday. He said he had the money to do a cash deal. He just didn't have it with him. So he left a deposit. On Monday he was back to tell the salesman that he had lost his money at the races.'

Langmack made no secret of his desire to learn, nominating Gould and Mick Pitman as his tutors when he first came into grade. He would ask one or both of them to watch him play and review his performance. 'That's part of the problem now for young players,' he said. 'They won't go and ask anyone about their game. If you don't ask questions, you don't learn. I tell the young blokes at Wests, if you have questions, come and ask.'

FROM PLAYER TO COACH

It could be said that application and attitude were in shorter supply than ability with Brohman and Gould at times when they were with Canterbury. 'No one was trying all that hard because we all thought we should have been in first grade,' said Brohman. 'But we had a lot of fun. One time we were playing North Sydney and were so far ahead of them—except on the scoreboard—it was embarrassing. I started doing a running commentary on the game from the ruck. I'd be calling players getting the ball and running it up. Gus was laughing and we were having a great time.

'Then Gus took over the commentary. I took the ball up and he called: 'Here comes Brohman, galloping into space.' Poor old Charlo (Tony Charlton), he'd be dragging his hair out because we lost a lot of games we should have won.'

In another match at Belmore in reserve grade, a heckler managed to sting Brohman and Gould in a double-barrelled barrage. 'Even though we were so much better than the opposition, they were beating us easily,' Brohman said. 'They scored a try and as we stood behind the goalposts, waiting for the kick at goal, someone from the crowd called: "Hey, Gould. Why don't you get back to Penrith!" I walked over and put my arm around Gus and said: "Don't worry, mate. They don't know what they're talking about." Then the same voice called out: "And take your fat mate with you." Gus still laughs about it.'

It took a stroke of luck and Ryan's dented ego for Brohman to crack the first grade side even though he was not playing well—and to stay there for the grand final. The Bulldogs were playing Cronulla at Belmore, pitting Ryan against Jack Gibson, who had coached Easts' two premierships in 1974 and 1975 and Parramatta to a treble in 1981–82–83.

'Ryan didn't see it as Canterbury versus Cronulla,' said Brohman. 'He saw it as the Super Coach he believed he was up against the *alleged* Super Coach. By half-time we were down by

Good as GOULD

16 or 17 points. He was pissed off unbelievably and he replaced four players basically, I think, because he was getting beaten by Gibson. I got a start and we finished up getting beaten by six points or so. I stayed in the side after that and I don't think we lost a game on the way to the grand final. Just a stroke of luck. I was in the right place at the right time.'

For Brohman the elevation granted by Ryan paid off and he went on to play the best club football of his career in 1985.

'We didn't start the season all that crash hot and it was a bumpy ride for about seven or eight games,' Gould said. 'Then we lightened up and we lost very few of our remaining games. We just had to get past the drama and concentrate on our football and remember that we were a great club. Canterbury is a great club, and there are fine people at Canterbury. Jarrod McCracken (Kiwi Test centre) asked me once what I thought about Canterbury and I told him it was a terrific place—except for a few people. He said he was surprised that I felt that way after the dramas I'd had there. But he said he felt exactly the same way.'

The pressure started to mount on Canterbury as the season moved into the semi-finals and there was widespread talk that Ryan would be sacked at the end of the year. News too that a couple of prominent officials were licking their lips in anticipation of delivering the notice personally. Ryan and Steve Mortimer were still not seeing eye to eye. The strain became so intense that Mortimer met with Manly coach Bob Fulton the following season (1986) and agreed to switch clubs for 1987. Astonishingly he changed his mind and stayed at Canterbury, swayed by Ryan saying in front of the committee: 'We need you.'

Gould believes Ryan was to be sacked at the end of 1985 even though he had steered the side into the grand final by beating Parramatta. He understands there was an urgent meeting, possibly involving Moore and club president Barry

FROM PLAYER TO COACH

Nelson, when Canterbury beat St George in the grand final to retain the premiership. It would be unthinkable for a club to sack a premiership-winning coach—even though St George had done it in 1956 after Norm Tipping won the premiership. St George went on to win 10 successive premierships which sort of took the sting out of the sacking. Canterbury was not that confident of winning another 10 titles and to sack Ryan would have made the club look ridiculous.

Mortimer has said: 'At the end of 1985 there was no doubt that Moore had it in his mind to give Ryan the shunt. They had a blazing row at the end of 1985 and Moore even indicated to the press as we whooped it up in the dressing room at the grand final that Ryan's position as coach was far from certain. In fact he came to see me to get my opinion about it. I told him that Warren rubbed plenty of people up the wrong way but no-one could argue with the success we were having.'

Ironically Mortimer would fall out with Ryan so badly the next year that he would pursue the Manly deal. Given the fractured circumstances, the bitter in-fighting, the head-on clash of gigantic personalities, the rumours, the headlines and back-stabbing, it stands as a sporting miracle that Canterbury achieved the success it did.

For Gould, it was to be the last year of his association with Canterbury as a player. It had been three years of frustration. He was a lucky charm for everyone when it came to winning grand finals—except himself. He had joined Newtown and played in a losing grand final side. Then he had joined the stronger Canterbury side only to be injured when they won their first grand final and below his best because of injuries the second year. Glory and satisfaction, however, were waiting down the highway at Souths with tough-guy coach George Piggins. Canterbury and grand final wins would loom large and spectacularly in the more distant future.

PHIL GOULD'S Reflections on
THE BULLDOG BREED

Canterbury is a great rugby league club. It is an organisation that really looks after its players. There are many fine people involved with the club and the years I spent there as a player were extremely happy and successful ones. We got to the final in 1983 and won premierships in 1984 and 1985.

Personally it was a difficult time for me because of injury. I fractured my neck in 1983 just before the semi-finals. It was a worrying period because I lost the use of my left arm for about three months and doctors told me again I should retire. It is just very hard to convince people of that age they should give away the sport they love.

I returned in 1984 under my old coach from Newtown Warren Ryan. They were great days. We were a very dominant football team. When you consider the State and international players we had in reserve grade at that stage such as Darryl Brohman, Phil Sigsworth and Jim Leis, it gives you some idea of the strength of the club.

Whatever was going on at a managerial level did not touch the players. It did not matter if it was Peter Moore feuding with Warren Ryan or Warren Ryan feuding with Steve Mortimer, we just went on playing and having a good time.

I felt sorry for Steve Mortimer. He was a great player and I enjoyed playing in the same side as him. He was a very instinctive player and the complete opposite to the type of player Warren wanted.

FROM PLAYER TO COACH

To give Steve credit, he did his best to fit in with the strategies and plays Warren devised, even though it would cause him frustration at times.

Steve was one of the best players I ever played with and he was one of several great players I was alongside at Canterbury. Fullback Greg Brentnall was one of the finest fullbacks I've ever seen. He cut his own career short to go back to live in the country.

My fondest memories are of 1984 when we won the premiership and went away on an end of season holiday to Hawaii, Los Angeles and New Orleans.

There were good young players in the side who were on the verge of turning into great players. David Gillespie was one. So were Paul Langmack and Andrew Farrar. They remain friends of mine to this day. The good thing about Canterbury was that we always knew how to enjoy ourselves. That helps a lot with team spirit. I cherish the days I had playing football with Canterbury. They are great memories for me

The Phantom Coach —Rabbitoh Days

Phil Gould's first training session with South Sydney ended with him staring into space flabbergasted and wondering what on earth he had done in switching from Canterbury.

Someone asked him what he thought and in a moment of rashness and honesty, perhaps accelerated by shortness of breath from running, he spoke frankly: 'What did I think? I thought it was bloody awful. What the hell were we doing?' he gasped.

The players remember being taken aback by the outspokenness of their newest recruit. He was not even a Test player or even a *State* player like their hooker Mario Fenech and, hell, Mario was not complaining about the quality of the session. Only one man was wise enough to hold his tongue, the first grade coach and club president George Piggins. He had personally supervised the recruitment of Gould to Souths so Gould's vast reservoir of stored knowledge from stints at Penrith and more importantly at Newtown and Canterbury under Warren Ryan could be tapped.

Whatever animosity might have been momentarily generated by Gould's outburst was quickly dissipated by a verbal lesson on tactics there and then under the streetlights at a ground at the back of Mascot.

That seminal event involved Gould laying down the basics of his own evolving theories on coaching techniques by drawing diagrams in the sand. The session continued the general air of unreality about Gould leaving a successful club like Canterbury who had been first grade premiers for two of the three years he had been there to join Souths, who were struggling despite a proud record stretching back to the beginnings of the premiership. 1986 was a year that would explore new horizons in rugby league. NSW defeated Queensland 3–nil for the first whitewash in State of Origin history, Monday night football started on Channel 9 in a short-lived experiment to try and duplicate the success of similar programming in America. Channel 9 soon decided that Friday night football was more suitable for Australian audiences. The Kangaroos would remain unbeaten in England and France for the second successive tour and work began on the demolition of the Sydney Sports Ground. In its place sprang the flashy Sydney Football Stadium.

Impending history was of no concern to Gould that night as he again pondered his decision to join Souths. It was not even a club he liked or wanted to be with, but circumstances had conspired to force his hand. Injuries had restricted his appearances in first grade with Canterbury and with the depth of talent in the club committed to fierce defence, he knew he faced a battle to be regarded as anything more than a fringe first grader.

He wanted to play first grade and that meant moving on—but Souths?

Once the pride of the rugby league, the club's red and green colours had been worn with rare spirit and determination for nearly one hundred years, ranging all the way down through the magic years of the 1950s belonging to Clive Churchill, Jack Rayner and co. then the 1960s of Ron Coote, Bob McCarthy, Eric Simms, John Sattler, Michael Cleary and Piggins himself.

By 1985 Souths were close to being broke. The club was becoming more famous for losing to other clubs the local

Good as GOULD

players of great promise who had come through its famous nursery. It was a trend that would continue with Ian Roberts going to Manly, Terry Hill to Easts, Wests and finally Manly, Jim Dymock to Canterbury and then Manly and Les Davidson to Cronulla. The trend would continue.

Souths lacked the financial input from a struggling leagues club to enable it to compete with other clubs for players, and the future looked bleak. Piggins, 40 years of age at that stage and comfortably established after inventing and patenting a device to make unloading trucks easier, stepped into the breach. He became president of the football club and the leagues club and took on the first grade coaching job for nothing—to save money that could be spent on another player or two.

Piggins, whose actions typified the loyalty that is imbued in Souths players, especially locals who have come through the junior ranks, was realistic enough to know he would need a right-hand man familiar with the guile and sophistication of modern coaching techniques. Piggins would bring to the job spirit and fierce commitment. He wanted his offsider to be just as dedicated. The man he chose was Gould.

'I think I started 14 times in 1985 (with Canterbury). Other times I'd play half a game in reserve grade and then stand by for first grade,' Gould remembered. 'I'd broken my jaw in 1982, my neck in 1983 and my leg in 1984. I didn't really want to go to Souths. I didn't like Souths as a club and I'd never been one of those players to go where he would not be happy. I got to Souths Leagues Club with Ross Seymour to talk to their chief executive Terry Parker about a deal. Just before I walked in I said to Ross: "What do you think?"

'He said: "We'll ask for something different. Something he's not expecting. What about $30,000?"

'So we asked for $30,000 and Terry said: "Yes. All right."

'I walked outside and said "Fuck! What do we do now?"'

FROM PLAYER TO COACH

Gould's indecision lingered despite his verbal acceptance of the deal offered by Parker. The situation was complicated by his commitment to playing in Canterbury's reserve grade semi-final side that weekend. Parker rang and asked Gould to come and sign the contract on Thursday night at his home in Coogee. Gould duly attended but suffered a bad attack of cold feet. 'I just couldn't sign the contract. I just didn't think it was me,' he revealed. Parker was shocked and urged him to fulfil his arrangement saying: 'You've got to do it.' Gould replied: 'I can't and that's that.'

By the time Gould arrived home, George Piggins was ringing to arrange a meeting. It was set down for the following Saturday morning—the day of the semi-finals—at Piggins' palatial home in South Coogee. Whatever doubts had existed in Gould's mind about his suitability for Souths were swept away by the overwhelming sincerity of Piggins' efforts to put something back into the club that had given him so much.

'I spent an hour with George and signed on the spot,' Gould said. 'You could see straightaway what a good bloke he was. He said to me: "Look, I'm taking over Souths. We're going through some lean times and I want to get the club back to where it once was. I'm doing it for nothing. I just love the place. I know nothing about coaching but I know I have to get some discipline back if we're going to survive. We have some good young players here and you've been at Canterbury for the past few years when they have won competitions. They're the best side. I need your experience and I want you to come and help us—and help me".'

It was a remarkable and ego-boosting offer. Here was South Sydney wanting to make a Canterbury fringe first grader their major purchase of the off-season ... and the controller of their destiny. As it turned out Souths players were, to put it charitably, not as delighted as Piggins about the quality of the new boy. They thought a player with a higher profile would have been a better proposition.

Souths, with its working-class, inner-city environment, is not known as a club that produces shrinking violets who suffer in silence or keep their opinions to themselves. Locals who have come through the junior ranks know they have to speak out or be drowned in the tumult from their team-mates. The players cold-shouldered Gould but without effect.

'I think that for the first two or three months nobody spoke to me at training and I thought that perhaps I'd done the wrong thing in going there,' Gould said. 'The players thought that if I did anything at all it would be in the lower grades. I'd go home and think bugger it, I'll get out of here and go back to Canterbury.'

Fenech as captain and an influential member of the team was among the players uncertain of Gould's likely contribution. 'When they signed Phil Gould I wasn't overly excited about it.' Fenech said later. 'Gus Gould was a skilful player but he had a reputation for being lazy. I didn't really know him very well but he was nearing the end of his career after stints with Penrith, Newtown and Canterbury so I didn't expect too much.'

Two months later Fenech's opinion changed dramatically when the team for the first trial was announced. 'Gus was picked in the second-row and until then he had not opened his mouth. But when he did decide to talk we just stood around with our mouths open. He was a tremendous communicator and he had an incredible knowledge of the game. When he spoke he made things seem so easy. He made the little things seem interesting and exciting. I knew we had come across a bloke who was virtually going to coach the side. To George's (Piggins) credit he realised it as well and did not let his ego stand in the way. He wanted what was best for South Sydney and if it meant one of the players taking over, so be it. Within five or six sessions I just couldn't believe the amount of confidence Gus had generated. As skipper I was a little apprehensive at first, but like George, I realised it was in the best interests of the team for Gus to run the show. When Gus spoke it was as if he had removed a blindfold we had all been wearing. Everything became so clear.'

Piggins was Gould's support platform despite leaving much of the preseason work to the club conditioners. 'George was always talking to me,' said Gould. 'Always in contact. He'd talk to me at training when the players were ignoring me. I really trained hard in the lead-up. Really hard. I was training with Souths and also at the Police Academy at Redfern where my dad was working with Chicka Moore (the former Kangaroo centre) and some other footballers.'

For the first trial of the season Piggins stuck with the previous year's side, telling them it was their chance to retain their places.

Gould that day played in a winning reserve grade side—a team that had rarely won a game the previous year. The first graders were a side well beaten by Wests. It was an embarrassing performance by the Firsts because there was a scheduled appearance against St George the following week in the Charity Shield and Piggins told Gould to get ready, despite a neck injury. Piggins wanted Gould in first grade to guide the players and especially wanted him at training that week. 'George wanted me to get the players to more fully understand what he was trying to do, especially after they performed so poorly against Wests,' Gould remembered. 'I'll never forget that first training session. One of the big front-rowers played the ball and Mario gave it to half-back Craig Coleman who gave it to Neil Baker who gave it to Bronko Djura who gave it to Neil Baker who gave it to somebody who gave it to the

Good as GOULD

winger who ran 70 metres. The players all screamed out: 'Score it!' and started clapping because the ball had gone along the backline without being dropped. We did that about six or seven times and everyone was feeling very pleased with themselves. I didn't even get to touch the ball.

'George called us in and said: 'That was pretty good, fellas. You didn't drop a ball.'

'Then he turned to me and said: 'Phil, you played with a premiership-winning side. What did you think? Anything we need to know?''

Even now Gould can recall his predicament. Standing there with faces turned his way to hear what the interloper had to say. Should he go along with the popular view and say it was fine or stand his ground and tell the truth? 'Anything you need to know?' he mused to himself. 'You know bugger-all.'

Getting into full stride he addressed the group of upturned faces which had growing shock written all over them. 'That was disgraceful,' he said quietly. 'You have absolutely no idea what you are doing.'

It finished with Gould lecturing on tactics, training and manoeuvres under a streetlight, using a stick to draw in the sand. The enormity of the task ahead was not lost on Piggins who said: 'We'd better come back tomorrow night and get started.'

Gould hammered home the message that nothing was going to change dramatically overnight. It was going to take hard work, discipline and commitment, and lots of it. There would also have to be widespread changes to the way things had been done at Souths. And in the end it might all work or it might not.

As the session broke, amiably, Gould was making his way to his car when Craig Coleman and Mario Fenech called out, asking him to come for a drink. 'I told them to forget it,' said

Gould. 'It was the first time they had spoken to me all summer.'

The point was made. Gould arrived at training the next night and began working with Piggins on a project that would eventually catapult Souths back to the forefront of premiership contention and revive hopes of future glory to match the success of the past. It was also the first practical revelation to Gould and everyone else that he did have something positive to offer as a coach when his playing days were over.

'George Piggins had a terrific understanding of rugby league skills and tactics,' Gould said. 'He knew rugby league very, very well and he had played with some great South Sydney sides and for Australia. He was also intensely committed to Souths. His only problem was a lack of communication with some players who did not understand the game as well as he did. What George saw as a simple move of two to the open and one to the blind needed to be dressed up in a language everyone would understand and respond to. George might think it was a lot about something that was not very important. But if it was what was going to get us rolling as a first grade side, then it had to be done.'

Gould went back to basics, finetuning the playing and training pattern, giving it substance and focus. 'We would work on little moves and little patterns,' he said. 'The first thing I did was to get them to be honest about what they saw as our strengths and weaknesses, the way we should be playing the game and how we could play within our limitations and emphasise our strengths.'

Despite their position on the premiership table the previous year, Souths had a good tough pack of physical forwards, a skilled half-back in Coleman and Neil Baker's excellent kicking game. A young forward named Ian Roberts was in the lower grades and attracting attention although he would not play first grade that year. But the pack included Wayne Chisholm, a recruit from Manly, and Les Davidson, destined for the Kangaroo tour. There was also the renowned South Sydney spirit.

Sceptical at first, Gould came to appreciate the influence of that Souths spirit as much as anyone who had been born within the sound of the clatter of wheels as the trains pulled out of Redfern Station. 'Unless you played there you would just go 'oh yeah' about the Rabbitoh spirit but it really exists,' Gould said. 'Redfern Oval is the genuine thing.'

The Charity Shield appearance by Souths playing to the new pattern was not auspicious. They were belted by St George and it was obvious to Gould, who missed the match with injury, and Piggins that there was a need for on-field direction. Coincidentally Souths were scheduled to play St George in the opening round of the premiership, just three weeks after losing the Charity Shield game, and Gould and Piggins worked overtime to smooth out the rough edges.

'That first premiership game of the year was on a Friday night at Redfern Oval against St George and we were outsiders,' Gould said. 'George picked some of the younger players in the side. We had a bloke called Brad Webb in there and Jason Moon as well. I was looking at the players in the St George team and not really knowing if we could win, but I knew that we had done the work and we would shock them if they were not ready for us and took us lightly. We had a game plan and we won 23–4. We absolutely flogged them.'

It was a telling moment for everyone. Souths suddenly realised they had the players and the ability to make gigantic inroads into the premiership and that they were in the hands of a potent coaching combination in Piggins and a young master in Gould.

Souths went on to win nine of their first 11 games and

FROM PLAYER TO COACH

become the success story of the season. In their achievement they earned Piggins a Dally M award as coach of the year.

Souths beat Illawarra 13–10 in the second round and lost to Jack Gibson's Cronulla side 14–nil at Ronson Field in the third game before stringing together four wins in a row against Wests 29–4 at Redfern Oval, Penrith 15–8 at Penrith, Easts 8–6 at Redfern and Norths 31–13 at North Sydney before a 26–2 loss to Canterbury at the SCG ended the run.

The loss to Canterbury was embarrassing. The Bulldogs played with just 12 men for 79 minutes after prop Peter Kelly was sent off for the first tackle in the game after about 30 seconds. It remains the record for a first grade send-off.

That afternoon was the first time Gould had lined up against his former Canterbury side and former team-mates and friends such as Paul Langmack and David 'Cement' Gillespie. Langmack, something of a prodigy who was in first grade, with Canterbury, as a lock forward at 17 years of age, could trace his links with Gould back five years. Gould arrived one day with Penrith lower grade coach Mick Hartas, who was also Langmack's coach at Fairfield Patrician Brothers, to offer advice. 'Mick had greyhounds and Gus loves a punt,' Langmack recalled.

In the second-round clash between Souths and Canterbury and again when the two teams met in the mid-week premiership, there was no place to hide. The second-round game, a Monday-night battle at Belmore Sports Ground, produced fireworks from the start. 'It was one of the toughest games I ever played in,' Langmack recalled. 'There were all-in brawls, the lot. The next day I thought I had been in a war.'

There was an explosive moment when Souths forward Les Davidson took the ball up hard and was smashed by the defence. Fenech went to dummy half and the referee whistled a penalty for Canterbury being off-side. Fenech disregarded the ball to charge into the Canterbury line, sparking a fight on-field.

Good as GOULD

'Gus just grabbed me when the fighting started and said "lay down. We're too smart for these blokes,"' said Langmack. 'So we just kind of wrestled around.'

Anticipating that Canterbury might try and take him out of play, Gould changed his own playing style that night. 'He was like a half-back in the match. He would just stand and pivot,' Langmack remembered. 'I'd be shouting: "Gould, Gould" to the forwards.

'And he'd be singing out: "Come and get me."

'He wanted Cement (Gillespie) and me to come and get him. But he was just off-loading the ball all the time and had blokes running off him. We couldn't get to him.

'I sang out once: "Why don't you have a run."

'He called out: "You wouldn't be fast enough to catch me."

'So we're having this big argument all through the game. Then the one time we didn't move up on him, he slipped through and scored the winning try. He knew just when to run.

'His classic ploy was running acrossfield and dummying to a bloke—and then accelerating through the gap. He was very quick over 20 metres and very strong around the hips.'

It was that strength that would deflate hard-man Gillespie's ego when Souths and Canterbury played in the mid-week pre-season match on March 19 at Lismore. The match was enmeshed in controversy even before kick-off when Canterbury coach Warren Ryan declared publicly that Gould (not Piggins) was coaching Souths and Gould was using techniques he had learnt from Ryan to do the job.

'We were young Turks and we thought we were indestructible,' said Langmack. 'Cement was a big hitter even then. I could read the play and I would call out who was going to get the ball when the opposition was in possession. I'd say to Cement: 'Here comes Gus, give it to him!' Cement raced in hard and Gus gave him the hip and Cement just bounced off him. And Gus is running off laughing and singing out: "You don't know how to tackle!" Cement had steam coming out of his ears. He was screaming: "I'm going to kill him!" Two minutes later Gus got the ball and I called out to Cement to make the tackle. And Gus did it again! Cement landed on his back twice.'

Canterbury won that match 6–5 but Souths had every reason to be pleased with the way the season was progressing.

Although Souths beat Canterbury in the fiery premiership match via Gould's late try, it was a game that attracted attention for reasons other than the score. Fenech and Canterbury's Paul Dunn were swinging punches at each other in the opening minutes. Within seconds it seemed that Fenech had taken leave of his senses. He chased players around the ground, trying to get them to stand and fight. While chasing Canterbury's Billy Johnstone, Fenech collided with another Canterbury player and started fighting him instead. In the process Fenech tore his already ripped jumper from his shoulders to make throwing punches easier. When order was restored referee Bill Harrigan sent Fenech and Dunn to the sin bin. It was also the game in which thousands of television viewers saw Fenech abusing Piggins for calling him from the field because of an ankle injury that was curtailing his mobility. Through the turmoil of that night, Gould kept his head and engineered a win. His coolness under fire kept Souths in a winning position.

There was no burning bush of revelation, but it was another indication of Gould's graduation to the ranks of potentially great coaches. He had learnt that he could influence players, design effective game plans and handle himself and a team under pressure. Having young alert players in his side who were willing to learn made it easier for Gould. 'Just that one game when we beat Canterbury was enough for young

Good as GOULD

blokes at Souths to catch on and say: "Hey, this is the way to go and this is what we have to do to achieve it." We ended up having an excellent year and we went within a point of the minor premiership. We beat some really good sides along the way even though we were beaten in the semi-finals by Balmain (36–11) and Canterbury (16–2).'

The significance of Souths' improvement hit home on May 18 when the Rabbitohs beat eventual premiers Parramatta 13–6 at Redfern Oval. With a win against grand final runners-up Canterbury under their belt as well, Souths were well-credentialled premiership contenders.

That season Parramatta were minor premiers on 37 points from Souths (36), Canterbury (35), Manly (33) with Balmain beating Norths in a play-off for fifth after both sides finished on 30 points.

Piggins' generosity in ensuring Gould's contribution to Souths was widely recognised and helped establish him as a potential coach of the future. 'Phil Gould was a major buy for the club,' Piggins said. 'He was a tremendous help to the club and I am not ashamed to say I learned a lot from him.'

Gould remembers the season with considerable affection. Souths' first grade side was a success. The under-23s won the premiership. Les Davidson made the Kangaroo tour and Craig Coleman, Mario Fenech and Ian Roberts all showed signs of the players they would develop into in the years to come. 'George was the coach. Basically my job was to get his ideas across to the players and advise him on the way we should play certain teams,' Gould said. 'George was always very kind publicly about my contribution.'

Fenech was captain that year but when he was absent for one game with injury, Gould led the side. 'Supporters wrote in complaining because I walked the team onto the SCG for the game and didn't run them on,' said Gould. 'I said, well make

FROM PLAYER TO COACH

Craig Coleman the captain and he can run them on and I'll just walk out at the back of the team.'

It was Coleman, one of the great characters of Souths and of rugby league, who gave Gould one of his funniest moments in a match. In a game entering its final minutes, Souths were given a penalty kick 20 metres from the opposition's line in easy goal-kicking range. With Souths ahead, Gould elected to kick for the line so the team could retain possession and play down the clock rather than go for goal and surrender possession if the kick missed. Coleman rushed up and begged Gould to go for the goal: 'But if it misses, we'll lose the ball,' Gould explained patiently. 'That doesn't matter. I need this kick. We're only ahead by six points and I've taken us with six and a half,' replied Coleman. Neil Baker kicked the goal.

What was shaping as the revival of Gould's playing career at Souths represented instead a final flamboyant flourish. Injuries which had troubled him for years kept recurring with greater intensity, making playing difficult and reopening the option of retirement, and coaching. 'I had always thought that coaching would be an option later down the track,' he said. 'I had signed with Souths for two years but during that first season I struggled to train and play. I had a bad groin and lower back problems that virtually stopped me from training.' Barely able to take part in training, Gould's approach was a forerunner of that of Canterbury veteran Terry Lamb a decade later. Piggins was happy enough with Gould's limited training appearances, especially as the side kept winning with Gould as the on-field general to ensure that everything that had been practised at training was put into effect.

Given a double chance in the semi-finals because of their second place on the table, Souths faltered disappointingly, missing key players. Gould and Neil Baker missed the semi-final loss to Canterbury with injury. The following week against Balmain, Mario Fenech was sent off early in the second half and Baker (groin) and Gould (ribs) only came on at half-time.

It was a quick and disappointing exit after such a year. Gould's future was decided just before Christmas 1986. He announced his retirement—then toyed with the idea of a comeback in 1987. 'I had a rest at the end of 1986 and the doctors wanted to operate on my back. I wanted to give it time to recover before deciding what I would do. I had two private training sessions before Christmas 1986 and the pain was still there and the enthusiasm to play was mostly gone. I just wasn't hungry to play any more and injuries over the years had caught up with me.'

At his former club Canterbury, Gould was gone but not forgotten. Canterbury president Barry Nelson had always made it clear that he eventually wanted Gould back at the club as a coach. The club had identified his potential in that area as early as 1984.

Warren Ryan was also a factor in wanting Gould back at Canterbury—although his reasons might not have been more pragmatic than those of Nelson. 'Warren was going on about me being at Souths and giving them his coaching ideas and coaching the club the Warren Ryan way and all that sort of thing,' Gould said. 'He saw it as weakening the opposition as well if I left Souths and came back to Canterbury.'

Uncertain, Gould took time out to spend a week or so building a verandah with his father at his parents' home. Tested by the heavy labouring, the groin and back problems returned just as Souths were due to start preseason training which would involve extensive road runs.

'My girl friend at the time was on holidays at the Gold Coast and I kept thinking that I would rather be up there with her than training,' Gould said. 'I'd really just had it. I was worn

FROM PLAYER TO COACH

out from a hard physical season. And after all the years, and all the injuries, I just thought: 'That'll do me.' So I gave playing away and accepted the reserve grade coaching job with Canterbury.'

For Gould it was a decision that was to bring considerable glory, enormous controversy, fame, infamy and, a few years down the track, a leading role in the greatest crisis ever to hit the game—Super League.

PHIL GOULD'S Reflections on
SOUTHS

Playing with South Sydney was an extremely enjoyable time for me even though it was for only one season.

I can look back now and see 1986 with Souths as being the springboard to a coaching career for me.

I will forever be indebted to coach George Piggins for the kind recognition he gave me for most of that season for my contribution to the club and to those players who ultimately accepted me as a team-mate and friend.

We were extremely unlucky that year not to win the premiership.

Possibly a lot of our players were too inexperienced to realise how close they went. Parramatta went on to win the 1986 premiership and we had beaten them twice during the season. That is how close we were to winning the premiership.

Perhaps if we had managed to get through and play Parramatta in the grand final, we could have made it three wins. It just was not meant to be. We got injuries at the wrong part of the year and after finishing second on 36 points to Parramatta's 37, we were beaten by Canterbury 16–2 and then Balmain 36–11.

My friendship with George Piggins, Craig Coleman and Mario Fenech will last as long as I do and so will my memories of the club.

In the following three years, Souths remained competitive, winning 43 out of 66 matches. That is the best percentage

FROM PLAYER TO COACH

behind Cronulla, who won 45.

George Piggins and the players proved themselves people of immense talent. South Sydney is a tremendous football club.

People talk a lot about the spirit at South Sydney but it is a very real thing. The supporters are knowledgeable and committed. They cheer when you win and they stick when you lose in a way that few other clubs can boast.

Unless you have played there you cannot fully understand South's spirit. It is unique in Australian rugby league.

Souths have been under a lot of pressure in recent times to hold their spot in the competition. Financial problems have meant the club has struggled in the 1990s. Only the hard work of a lot of important and kind people has helped the club survive. I for one hope there will always be a South Sydney. Tradition and heritage mean a lot to me and to South Sydney.

The Smooth-As-Silk Premiership

After six rounds as a coach in the 1987 premiership Phil Gould's shoulders were slumped as low as his Canterbury reserve grade side was in the competition. For a man with many natural attributes to bring to coaching and whose entry into coaching ranks had been keenly awaited by people who had recognised his analytical mind, it was disappointing. Here was his reserve grade side struggling to make any impression—and the coach struggling to change the situation.

Gould had tried almost everything he knew to turn things around but nothing had worked. There had been tactical changes, positional changes and training changes. The players had been spoken to, chastised and criticised without any noticeable affect. Gould's dilemma can be a common one for coaches.

Looking after a first grade side is easier because the potential and quality of the players is well known. If the line-up is not strong, a coach is unlikely to be publicly criticised. Reserve grade line-ups are less obvious. Coaches there are more anonymous. Winning a premiership gives them individuality. So does overcoming difficulties.

Gould's performance with the reserve grade side eventually turned out to be praiseworthy. The crumbling artifice of Warren Ryan's coaching structure at Canterbury contributed to the early problems. The final result was the quickest elevation to first grade success by the youngest coach in the history of the game.

FROM PLAYER TO COACH

Gould steered his reserve grade side back on track by sitting them down and talking about what they were trying to achieve, what the players saw as priorities and re-defining their challenge. It was a forerunner to the approach he would employ at all levels he was to coach: to get the players on side, mesh everyone's ambitions towards a common goal and devise appropriate tactical plans.

The reserve grade side of '87 staged a dramatic turnaround and with a late surge, made the semi-finals. The achievement left Gould in an obviously favourable position to be considered for the first grade position if Ryan ever did leave.

Ryan's coaching style had given Canterbury first grade premierships in his first two years 1984 and 1985 plus a grand final place against Parramatta who won the 1986 grand final 4–2— a record low score and the only tryless grand final ever played. It was impossible to consider sacking a coach with such a near impeccable record of success but by 1987 Ryan was far from being the most popular man at Canterbury. The players seemed loyal enough but there was growing animosity between Ryan and club officials, particularly then secretary Peter Moore. Ryan was convinced Moore had access to at least one section of the media that he could manipulate to slant the news to suit Canterbury's image as a family club and discredit perceived troublemakers who would not follow the party line.

Whether it was the years of drama under Ryan stretching back to 1983, inter-club wrangling or simply time catching up with players and coach is still open to debate, but 1987 was the poorest year Canterbury had known in nearly a decade.

The first grade side struggled, eventually failing to make the semi-finals. That came down to the last preliminary match of the season against St George, who were still coached by Roy Masters. If Canterbury could beat St George, they would finish third. It was a lacklustre Canterbury side that lost 16–14.

Good as GOULD

Ironically the match was at the SCG where Canterbury had enjoyed so much success in the past. That year, the famous old ground was the graveyard of their semi-final hopes.

Ryan had already announced that 1987 was to be his last year at Canterbury even though he still had a year to run on his contract. Masters, for so long his adversary, had also announced that he was stepping down at St George to pursue a career in the media.

It had been a turbulent year at Canterbury. The first grade side beat eventual premiers Manly 18–6 in one game but generally the side's performances were patchy. Along the way the relationship between Gould and Ryan became fractured and finally fragmented in a fierce argument in the dressing room in front of the players. It stemmed from remarks Ryan had made to his players in the lead-up to the second round match against Souths at Belmore Sports Ground. Under pressure to keep Canterbury's semi-final drive going, Ryan told his players not to reveal to anyone the tactics that were to be used in the game against Souths. Ryan made it clear he thought someone in the club was leaking his tactics to Souths. It was not hard to reason that the person Ryan was talking about was Gould, who had spent the previous year at Souths and was a personal friend of many of the Souths players.

There is no security system in a football club. Ryan's words were being repeated to Gould by friendly first-graders almost as soon as they were spoken.

The blow-up came the next week-end at Belmore. Gould was giving his reserve grade players their half-time talk when Ryan attempted to enter the dressing room with his players to begin their preparations. 'Get out of here you prick,' Gould yelled, bringing immediate silence to the dressing room. It was a tirade that captured the attention of everyone who heard it—and there was no shortage of witnesses. 'He bored it right up

Wazza. He couldn't say a word back,' said one player.

Paul Langmack, was in Canterbury's first grade side and making his way through the dressing room when the explosion happened. 'Ryan was convinced Gus was feeding tips to "Tugger" (Souths halfback Craig Coleman),' Langmack said. 'He called Ryan a dickhead and cut loose. You know how it is when you're somewhere when something happens that doesn't involve you but you're in the middle of it—I just kept walking thinking: "Hey. Isn't this good!"'

Veteran five-eighth Terry Lamb was another first grader close by and recalled the incident this way: 'We walked into the dressing room to prepare for the match and Phil was addressing the reserve grade players. Warren walked over to make his contribution when Phil erupted over what had been said about him and said: "Get out of my life!" Lamb says there was never any spying episode at all.

Naturally the episode made the newspapers, adding to the drama and pressure on Canterbury. Gould says he had never leaked any of Ryan's plans to anyone. 'I was coaching the reserve grade side. I didn't know what he was doing in first grade,' he said.

Quoted later in another newspaper interview, he claimed that it was simply another example of Ryan not being able to handle pressure. 'Ryan has a weakness which we have seen twice in the past two years,' said Gould. 'He cannot handle pressure. When he senses the tide of events turning against him he has all the excuses ready. In the lead-up to the Souths game he knew a loss would put him in a very precarious position for the five. That's what caused him to make the remark behind closed doors to the first grade side about their match plan because Phil Gould was a mate of Souths halfback Craig Coleman. It couldn't be his fault if they lost.'

Gould said there had been another example in the game

Canterbury had lost that year 32–2 to Manly at Brookvale. 'When Manly won, he blew up in the dressing room, blaming the referee, touch judges, the League, "company" journalists and so on.'

Ryan retaliated by saying he was amused by any allegation that he could not handle pressure. 'Look at my record. Five grand finals in the 1980s. In the nine years I've coached, teams I've coached have made it into six grand finals.'

Ryan was coaching Balmain at that stage and cryptically summed up coaching at Canterbury. 'At Canterbury the biggest enemy was in your own camp—a publicity machine in the front-office undermining you. The pressure there (Canterbury) is from within, not without.'

The outburst from Ryan did not surprise his players. They had become used to his passion for secrecy, and they used it as a base for practical jokes. 'We'd be training and Terry Lamb would say: "Wazza, there's a man inside the big dog" (Canterbury's gigantic mascot that sits on the hill.) 'He'd look up and stare before realising what was happening and he'd say "Just keep training". Or there would be some bloke walking down the lane alongside the ground who had stopped to look through a hole in the fence. Peter Tunks or me would gee Ryan up by saying: "It's a spy, it's a spy. It's Roy Masters spying." He'd race over and tell the bloke to rack off. We'd just be standing there laughing.'

Spying in rugby league, while not common any more in these times of extensive video access to opposing teams in action, was once a regular occurrence. So was duplicity as teams took any advantage they could. Gould was standing in a pub one night after training, drinking with team-mates when Roy Masters walked in and joined them. Over the course of a few drinks he told how he was having trouble with his Test second-rower Les Boyd. According to Masters, Boyd was having personal problems and as soon as someone mentioned his wife's name, he would lose his temper and his game would be shot to pieces.

Knowing they would be playing Masters' Wests team in a couple of weeks and figuring that Masters had inadvertently dropped the information while partially under the influence, the players filed the tip away in their minds under 'useful information'.

'When we played Roy's side, one of our players mentioned the forbidden words in Boyd's ear during a tackle. It was like setting a match to gunpowder. He just exploded and tore us apart. We still had bruises days later. It's a funny thing but I'd never seen Roy in that pub before that night and we never saw him there again.'

Even allowing for Ryan's passion for secrecy, which some players thought he took to obsessive lengths, he seemed to have a fair point about Canterbury's ready access to the media, particularly newspapers, to get the club's point of view across. Gould's turn on that score was coming.

As first grade coach the success that came was mixed with tension and interclub fighting that made him wonder if it was all worth it.

With the 1987 season over and Canterbury needing a first grade coach the decision to appoint Gould was made hastily. Although the club's former Test winger and Peter Moore's son-in-law Chris Anderson had been tipped to return from coaching in England to take the job, it did not happen.

Gould was appointed and starting picking up the pieces of Ryan's erratic relationship with champion half-back Steve Mortimer, realising the need for harmony and the binding of wounds. 'Our troubles were publicised in the papers far too much in 1987,' Terry Lamb said. 'It got to the stage where you couldn't open up a newspaper without finding Canterbury up in headlines.'

Good as GOULD

Although conceding there were problems at times with Ryan's autocratic approach, Lamb also says other clubs were getting used to Canterbury's playing style and were better equipped to handle it. Another factor was that while the famed and brutal Canterbury defence continued to be an asset, the side's attack fell away sharply to be the fourth worst in the premiership.

Gould had deduced that Ryan would be leaving at the end of 1987 even though he still had a year to run on his contract but was uncertain whether he would be appointed. 'Warren was worried about the lack of recruitment by Canterbury and the number of players who were leaving the club and not being replaced,' Gould said. It had also been a tough year for headlines and Ryan's running battle with Mortimer had provided a continuing edge. An extraordinarily gifted player, Mortimer could pivot, sprint, chip and chase, zig zag and sidestep. He relished being given a free rein to run through his repertoire of tricks. But Mortimer's way was not the way of Ryan, who wanted strictly regulated and controlled football. It was a contrast in styles that was always going to lead to conflict and could never be satisfactorily resolved. As it turned out Mortimer also continued to be in the headlines in 1988, starting with Gould's decision to overlook both him and Terry Lamb for the first grade captaincy and give it to Peter Tunks.

Mortimer saw Ryan's departure as the chance for his own career to be revived but the years were beginning to catch up with his phenomenal pace and intuitive play. With 'Turvey' Mortimer out injured, Gould settled on Michael Hagan and Terry Lamb as his half and five-eighth combination and won three games which took the club to the top of the premiership. It was impossible to make changes when Mortimer came back. He was listed as a fresh reserve for the next game against North Sydney. 'It was all very difficult because Steve had always been such a great player and an idol at Canterbury,' said Gould. 'He felt a need to prove himself again after three years of living under the pressure of Ryan as coach. But he was not playing as well as he could and that was a problem for me. He was one of the greats but I honestly think that he was letting his previous dramas with Ryan interfere with the way he was thinking about his football in 1988. I thought he had three or four big games left in him and I wanted to use them so that both he and the club benefited. He became a strike weapon. Steve put pressure on himself because he demanded that he go straight back into first grade. Eventually he did go into first grade and broke his wrist. That's always a possibility with players who are as old as Steve.'

Mortimer suffered the injury in Canterbury's 26–nil win over St George and it basically solved the problem. He was not expected to play again that season, relieving Gould of the continuing pressure on who to choose on selection nights.

'The stress was significant. I was coaching first grade for the first time and I did not want these sort of problems about a player I respected enormously,' said Gould. 'But I had the other 50 players in the club to worry about as well and the responsibility of picking the team that would do best for the club.'

The 1988 season under Gould started on the right track with a 21–10 win against the Gold Coast, followed by 22–18 against Cronulla. 14–10 against Easts and 22–17 against Canberra. It was not until the fifth round that Canterbury suffered its first loss of the season, going down 8–2 to Illawarra at Wollongong. Three more wins in a row against St George 22–8, Souths 16–12 and Penrith 18–12 followed by an 18–nil loss to Manly were enough to lift Canterbury into the top three—and they were not displaced all year.

Theirs was a remarkable exhibition of professional, and

Good as GOULD

disciplined rugby league, a contrast to the unevenness of the previous year. The stability and camaraderie reflected the commitment Gould had made to the players at the start of the season: to make the first grade side competitive again.

'It helped that we all knew Gus. He was well respected by the team,' says Langmack. 'He said from the start of the season that everything was on an even-footing. He said we were all mates but there might be times during the year when he might have to drop one or more of us. We all just said: 'Yeah, that's sweet.'

An enthusiastic Gould and a first grade side looking for a new direction were made for each other. Years of playing under Warren Ryan had brought success but not total enjoyment and satisfaction. Gould was a chance to have both.

'He was helped by having players in the team who were winners and who were sick of playing football the way we had,' Langmack said. 'Gus told us to go out there and play to our ability and for each other. There was a touch of the old Newtown and South Sydney style.'

Canterbury were to play their future grand final opponents Balmain only once in the preliminary rounds, losing 19–8 on the Tigers home ground Leichhardt Oval. Despite that win and then defeating Newcastle, Parramatta and Wests in a month of success, Balmain looked only the remotest of chances to make the grand final after a shaky start and the ongoing struggle of that season.

The Tigers lost two of their first three (Norths 24–4, Parramatta 10–30, Newcastle 16–20) and ended the first preliminary round with the unimpressive figures of six wins and five losses for 12 competition points. It was a masterstroke produced by Tigers chief executive Keith Barnes mid-way through the season that rescued the club's plight.

The Great Britain side was touring Australia that season

FROM PLAYER TO COACH

and in strict secrecy Barnes negotiated to have the team's captain and centre Ellery Hanley—then regarded as one of the top three players in the world—join Balmain. Barnes got to the NSWRL to register Hanley at 4.55 on June 30, just five minutes inside the deadline for signing players for that year.

Hanley, then a brighter more personable player than the sullen grump he would later turn into, metamorphosed Balmain. From strugglers they became sensational and staged a gripping charge for the final five. With Hanley an inspiration, Balmain won nine of their last 11 games including five in a row against Illawarra 24–12, North Sydney 30–20, Parramatta 22–6, Newcastle 18–16 and Wests 22–16. The Tigers wrapped up the year by beating Penrith 16–14 and Brisbane 20–10.

They were vital successes because at the end of 22 rounds Balmain had achieved what looked to be impossible at one stage and had sneaked into equal fifth place on 30 points, with Manly and Penrith, behind Cronulla's 34 points and Canterbury's 32 on an incredibly congested points ladder.

Manly took fourth place on better for and against points leaving Balmain to play (and beat) Penrith 28–8 to claim fifth place outright.

At that stage it looked as if Balmain had done enough in making the five to keep sponsors, supporters and officials happy. The club had played 22 preliminary rounds and, including the match against Penrith, had to get past every other semifinal side in four successive weeks to make the grand final and become the first side since the introduction of five team semifinals, to get that far from a play-off.

Somehow the players and coach Ryan, recalling his experience with Wests under–23 side those years earlier in making the grand final from fifth, achieved the remarkable. They beat Manly 19–6 in what was the Tiger's third tough match in eight days. Balmain then showed the resolution of heroes to continue their dogged campaign, beating Canberra 14–6 and then Cronulla 9–2. The last win carried them into the grand final against Gould's Canterbury side that had travelled a much smoother route.

Although an 18–14 loss to Souths in the final round at Belmore had cost Canterbury the minor premiership, the side still finished second and moved into the grand final the easy way by beating Canberra 19–18 and then Cronulla 26–8.

The win against Canberra had its desperate moments after Canterbury had led 16–6 at half-time. Two quick tries, from winger John Ferguson, an old team mate of Gould's from Newtown, and Peter Jackson, levelled the score at 18–all. It took a field goal from Terry Lamb with seven minutes left to play to get Canterbury out of trouble.

So the stage was set for a grand final of infinite appeal and speculation on numerous levels. There was the master coach Warren Ryan of Balmain up against the club he had coached for four years to three grand finals and two premierships and matched against the man who had replaced him at Canterbury, Phil Gould. It was master against pupil.

There was great appeal and emotion in Balmain's headline-making and much admired drive to even get to the semi-finals after a play-off and then keep the momentum going to make the grand finals. Then there was Hanley, nicknamed the 'Black Pearl', whose form had been so outstanding. Could he do it again in the grand final? Could Balmain, in their first grand final since 1969 when they achieved legendary status by beating 5–2 on favourites Souths win this one? Balmain's coach that day was Leo Nosworthy, the last coach to win a first grade grand final at his first attempt. Could Gould duplicate that feat and also become the youngest coach in history, at 30, to win a grand final?

The duel between Ryan and Gould through that season was

intense. Canterbury five-eighth Terry Lamb told how he had been speaking to Balmain prop Steve Roach during State of Origin training that year after the first Canterbury and Balmain game. 'Blocker told me that Warren said before the game in May: "I don't care if you never win another game this season. This is the one I want!"'

After the win Ryan declared publicly: 'Today, Canterbury looked as if they had been coached by Bullfrog (Peter Moore).'

Gould had had his moments as he wrestled with the various pressures of being the youngest coach in the premiership and in his first year in the job. Gradually earlier goals that had risen from perhaps just having a successful season, to making the semi-finals, to making the grand final and finally winning the premiership, started to become reality.

'That year we were scheduled to play Brisbane at Lang Park and we'd lost a little bit of form, (Canterbury had lost 30–18 to Norths the previous week),' says Langmack. 'We all went to have a team dinner at La Rusta, an Italian restaurant in Leichhardt we used to go to with Ryan. It was about a week before the Brisbane game. Everyone had to drink—red wine—sambucas—anything. It was the Thursday night before we were to play. I remember (Peter) Tunks got up all emotional and said: "We've got to win this one."

'Then Gus got up and started getting teary-eyed when he was talking about the team. That's how it was in 1988. We were all for each other.' Canterbury went to Lang Park and beat Brisbane 25–10.

The game against Canberra at Seiffert Oval was preceded by more bonding. It was in the third last round and Canterbury needed to win to ensure a place in the top three and continue the push for the minor premiership. The loser would be fourth and deprived of the double chance in the semi-finals.

Good as GOULD

'It was probably the most memorable game I ever played in because of the preparation,' says Langmack. 'We went up the day before in a mini-bus. We met at Belmore, trained and then set off with Gus doing the driving. Joey Thomas was the bookmaker. Everyone was betting with him. Ken Stuart (former Souths hooker) had a pub and we stopped in to see him. You could see all the locals looking at us and thinking: "What are these blokes doing? They've got to play football tomorrow." We were all on the punt and in the pub.'

Any advantages the bonding session had generated were slow to emerge. After 10 minutes Canterbury were down 12–nil. They recovered to win 23–16. 'It was hard but we got away with it,' Langmack says. 'Gus was at the dressing room door when we came off, hugging us as we came in. He's a very emotional sort of bloke. We hit all the pubs on the way back.'

For Langmack, success in 1988 made amends for what he saw as the disaster of 1987, even allowing for the effort the players had contributed.

'When we were beaten by St George in that last game of the season at the SCG we knew we were not going to make the semi-finals and it was a disappointment,' he says. 'We knew we had not played well all season, what with the dramas between the administration and coach. I always remember our centre Tony Currie saying at the end of the season, "We can win this competition if we train hard and stick together." But no-one really gave us much of a chance of winning.'

The length of time a coach is of value to a club is in direct proportion to the fresh ideas and motivation he provides. Wayne Bennett is the only coach Brisbane has ever known and he will be in his ninth season in 1996. Other coaches seem to reach their use-by date quicker.

'Warren Ryan's not really the sort of coach to stay too long at a club,' Langmack said. 'He stayed four years at Canterbury because of the success we were having. It was probably a year too long. There was too much drama. But every time there was drama with Ryan and the committee, the side would play well. We seemed to thrive on the drama ourselves but in the end I think we all just needed a change.'

Gould brought a less tense atmosphere—while still maintaining discipline and control. He was also more prepared for his team to attack but he admitted he had inherited a well-established defensive pattern which made it easier to concentrate on working the team with the ball.

The emphasis on attack and the extra time available because the team already knew how to defend, allowed Gould the chance to broaden the rugby league horizons of his players in remarkable ways. 'At training one night he was trying to teach me something about playing lock,' Langmack says. 'He told me to go and stand by the goal posts and watch what he did. He ran in my position all night. I just stood and watched what he did and where he was putting people and where he was putting them through gaps. It was probably the most I ever learnt that night. He was so young he could run around with the team. Other coaches couldn't.'

Grand final day 1988 dawned brightly, with the expectation of an exciting day at the Sydney Football Stadium.

The match that eventuated was absorbing, but the pivotal moment came and went in a flash in the first half and the entire crowd of 40,000 and millions more watching on television knew it. Ellery Hanley, Balmain's trump in the battle, was flattened in a high tackle from Lamb. Hanley was heavily concussed, disoriented and as he groggily left the field propped up by two Balmain trainers, his prospects of returning looked minimal. Under the rules of the time, Hanley was allowed 10 minutes to recover in the head bin. If he could not return in 10 minutes he had to be replaced. He returned just before half

Good as GOULD

time and stood on the wing, seemingly not knowing if he was in Sydney or Leeds.

Hanley did not come back for the second half and Balmain slid steadily to a 24–12 loss to a Canterbury side that always had the look of winners about them. This was the first grand final ever played at the Sydney Football Stadium after decades of matches at the adjacent SCG.

On grand final day Balmain grabbed an early 6–4 lead when Ben Elias was first to the ball after putting up a kick. But by halftime Canterbury led 10–6 after running in a 70 metre try from broken play.

In the Balmain dressing room at half time trainers and medical staff worked desperately to get Hanley alert enough to return to the game but it was useless. Speculation remains intense even now about the way Hanley was injured and put out of the game.

Gould is adamant that the injury was just one of those things that can happen in a match and not a deliberate ploy to spot Hanley. 'Hanley was a good player but he was not a major concern for us in that grand final,' Gould says. 'We always thought we had him covered. I don't think he was mentioned all that much at training. We were more concerned about Benny Elias' work at dummy half.' Elias is certain however, the felling of Hanley was the turning point.

'Without a doubt,' he says. 'There is absolutely no question about it. We were in a very dominant position at the time. Ellery had such a great psychological effect on our players, he was sorely missed in the second half. Everyone looked up to him. At half-time I begged him to go back on the field but he couldn't.'

While stopping short of saying Gould had pinpointed Ellery for special treatment, Elias says that obviously the Englishman was going to be closely marked. 'He was the best player in the competition three months out from the semi-finals. If you don't target the best player in the opposition side, there must be something wrong with you. I've never heard Gould tell a player to knock someone's head off in a match but I think Terry Lamb knew the importance of Hanley to Balmain. If you had to go and ask Lamb to go out and do it again, he wouldn't be able to knock Ellery out in 20 attempts. It was just one of those things.'

New Zealand's former Test captain Gary Freeman still cannot bring himself to watch videos of the 1988 and 1989 grand finals, both of which Balmain lost. 'It's too painful,' he says. 'Everywhere you go someone says: "Gee you blokes should have won those games." What we should have done and what we did do don't matter. We lost. I can't remember that tackle on Hanley. When things are happening on the field at 100 miles an hour you don't see everything. But I do remember that he played sensationally for us that year.'

Langmack insists Hanley was not a target for his Canterbury side that year. 'He wasn't a problem. He was never mentioned in the tactical talks about the match. Gus regarded Ellery as a weakness. All he ever did was run from dummy half and always to one side of the field—I can't remember if it was to the left or to the right but it was always to the same side,' Langmack says.

Lamb insists the tackle was not illegal. He meant it as a ball-and-all tackle. Whatever problems Hanley suffered came from him hitting his head on the ground, he says.

Gould prepared his side quietly and with little fanfare, switching training sessions to Newtown Police Boys Club where the players would be supervised by Johnny Lewis, the trainer behind the world boxing championships won by Jeff Fenech. 'We were really very confident going into the match. I doubted if Balmain had the point-scoring ability to test us out,' Gould said. 'The way things turned out they came up with a try from a bomb and another in the final minutes when the game had been decided. It looked that way on paper and that is the way it turned out. We had a lot more attacking power in our Canterbury side. The start was going to be the biggest hurdle for us. Balmain were going to come out full of hype and emotion. It was essential we settle into our regular pattern as quickly as possible.'

The match ended on a sentimental note. With the premiership under lock and key, Gould called Mortimer to the sideline. Mortimer was a long way from fully fit and was still troubled by the broken wrist suffered earlier in the year but he had been named as a fresh reserve for the grand final as a tribute to his previous contributions. With his arm heavily padded to protect his wrist, Mortimer ran onto a football field for the last time. Gould kept his promise that Mortimer would get to play. The match ended with Mortimer moving to dummy half and taking the ball up for the last time.

The celebrations were long and noisy as the players, coach, officials and supporters celebrated deep into the night. Dawn found the die-hards still revelling in the delight of a premiership win.

That first dawn also officially ended the 1988 season and heralded the start of planning for 1989. Gould was appointed coach on a new two year deal. It should have been the springboard to a wave of success for the club. Instead the unknown future was grim and unfulfilling. Frustration and bitterness were to accompany Canterbury's attempt to defend the premiership. Acrimony between the coach, the players and the committee were destined to spill over into the public arena. Not only would Canterbury fail to defend the premiership, the club would fail to make the semi-finals.

Before long Gould would discover first hand the truth in

FROM PLAYER TO COACH

the haunting words of Warren Ryan that at Canterbury the enemy was often within rather than without. Short of players and sceptical of Canterbury's efforts to rebuild with quality signings, Gould was himself forced to seek out and sign players to try and fill in the gaps.

More and more he would come to believe that he had been set up for failure in 1988 by a committee more interested in letting the playing strength dwindle so a new coach in Chris Anderson could return in triumph and take over knowing the coffers were full and recruiting players would not be a problem. More and more Gould came to believe that his win in the 1988 grand final had stunned a committee who expected him to fail and then depart. Instead he had won the premiership. Canterbury had no choice but to sign him again. In time Gould would come to see his reappointment as a poisoned chalice.

PHIL GOULD'S Reflections on
BRILLIANT BULLDOG DAYS

It was a real shock to me to go into the coaching ranks in 1987 and become totally responsible for the welfare and performance of a group of players.

George Piggins had been extremely complimentary about my contributions at Souths, but he had still been the man who was handling the media and who lived and died by the team's results every week. Now I was all alone as a coach.

I remember when we won our first game of the season then for the next six weeks we lost without ever looking like winning. It all culminated in a massive loss by something like 40–4 to Parramatta at Parramatta Stadium. I started to doubt if I was the man for the job and if I had any real future in coaching.

After the Parramatta debacle we all went back to the Leagues Club at Belmore for a drink. I made the players stay until closing time. I said anyone can celebrate when they win. I'm going to show you how to celebrate when you lose.

We went for pizza around the corner when the club shut. There I ran into a bookmaker friend of mine who started making fun of the way the team was playing and the way I was coaching. I took the bait and said: 'what price are we to make the semi-finals?' He said: 'You're a 100–1.'

I pulled out the little bit of money I had in my pocket—about $60 or $80—and said it was a bet. We won 13 of our next 14 games and squeezed into the final five by beating Balmain in the last premiership round.

FROM PLAYER TO COACH

After that miserable day at Parramatta I sat down with the players and we started to talk about what we were doing. It was not so much why we were losing. It was more about what we were *not* doing in trying to win.

We talked about what our careers really meant to us and what football really meant to us. We talked about how they would turn up and play each Sunday—but how they would go home shaking their heads because they had not contributed what they wanted to contribute. They were only really sending half of themselves out to play. They were fearful of going flat-out in case they made mistakes. We decided that whatever talent everyone had we needed in the team and it was no good leaving initiative in the dressing room. I have retained that philosophy ever since.

The turnaround at Canterbury was almost immediate, even allowing for a few close calls along the way. With the new found confidence the players felt in turn giving me greater confidence in my ability to coach a football team.

To make the semi-finals from where we had been after seven rounds was an outstanding achievement by the players. I think when I look back that if I had not enjoyed that success in the second half of the 1987 season I would not have even been considered to take on board the first grade job in 1988.

Warren Ryan stood down because he felt that he was not getting enough support from the management and that there was a weakening of the club's strength in anticipation of Chris Anderson's return from England.

When I took the first grade job in 1988 I was told by Peter Moore that it was a one-year deal because Chris Anderson was coming home to coach the side in 1989. Moore said that he would speak to Souths chief executive Terry Parker and arrange for me to take over as first grade coach at the club in 1989 when Chris took over at Canterbury. I was astonished to hear about the South Sydney component. At that stage George

Good as GOULD

Piggins was doing a fabulous job as coach and seemed unlikely to step down—especially as it would mean bringing a paid coach into a club under financial pressure.

There was no pressure in 1988 because no-one expected us to win anything following Warren's departure. We'd lost a few senior players and were being tipped to run about 10th. We'd only recruited four players—a couple of reserve graders from Penrith named Brandon Lee and Glen Nissan as well as Souths lower grade player Joe Thomas (now my reserve grade coach at Easts) and an unknown player from Brisbane, Robin Thorn.

It was just a dream season. We started strongly. Young players developed quickly under the guidance of the senior players. I was greatly assisted by experienced players such as Terry Lamb, Steve Folkes and Peter Tunks. Looking back I honestly wonder if I was a good coach then by today's standards. But we were all mates and had played together and there was a real feeling of camaraderie and a sense that everyone was contributing to a common cause. It was not until half-way through the season that we started to believe in ourselves that we could win the premiership. We set ourselves a test against Canberra at Canberra. When we won that game I was convinced the premiership was as good as ours.

When I think of winning a first grade premiership at my first attempt I still shake my head. Knowing what I now know about coaching, I shake my head even more about the win in 1988. I owe so much to the players in that team.

Our end of season trip was a tremendous affair. All 30 players went away. We beat Auckland for $20,000—winner take all—and our $10,000 share went into the holiday fund along with $10,000 we won for backing ourselves to win the premiership and $10,000 from our Punters Club. We converted it into about $US24,000 in Hawaii and Peter Moore took half and I took half. I had 30 blokes to look after and Bullfrog had four blokes. Yet we managed to spend the money at the same pace. Amazing.

The Feudin' Fightin' Family

In 1989 Canterbury were the defending premiers. They were confident, they were filled with ambition, they had the J J Giltinan Shield and they had the Winfield Cup sitting in the Leagues Club. They seemed a happy family ... in fact they were an accident waiting to happen.

From the short period between the whistle to start the first game of the season and the full time siren at the last match, Canterbury, champions of the League would be in shreds. Players would be bitter toward each other. First grade coach Phil Gould and the committee, especially chief executive Peter Moore would be estranged.

Gould would quit after being told by Peter Moore that there was no guarantee that the destabilising tactics of 1989 that had caused such unrest, would not be repeated in 1990.

Accusations of treachery would abound. Canterbury would once again show its skills in manipulating sections of the sporting media to do its bidding. Moore would again be accused of being a giant spider at the centre of a web, the man pulling the strings.

Former champion half Steve Mortimer and former Test five-eighth Tim Pickup would go public with their criticisms of coach Gould and he would return the complaints in an equally public way.

It was a blood-letting that horrified supporters, players, sponsors and officials.

Good as GOULD

The lacerations to Canterbury's public image of a family club were deep and painful.

First blood was drawn early in the year. Gould was having a drink in the bar of Canterbury Leagues Club when word came via a steward that Peter Moore and football club president Barry Nelson wished to talk to him in the dining room. Nothing really unusual about that. Nelson and Moore were there most nights after matches. Certainly nothing for Gould to worry about, even though the side had been beaten 16–8 by St George that afternoon at Belmore Sports Ground.

The ground had been heavy and Canterbury was backing up after losing a mid-week Cup match to Souths on the penalty count after the scores and the tries scored had been equal.

The first grade side was still in good shape. Three successive premiership wins against Gold Coast 8–2, Cronulla 22–2 and Illawarra 16–4 had Canterbury up with the leaders after four rounds.

Moore was drinking with Nelson at a table when Gould walked in and sat down around 10pm. They quickly brought up the subject of team selections in first grade. 'Why are you embarrassing us with the players you're picking in first grade?' Moore demanded. 'We've bought a lot of new players this year and you're not using them.

'What are you talking about?' retorted Gould.

In a remarkable outburst Moore went on to relate his dissatisfaction with the selection of a first grade line-up that had won three out of four premiership matches—a record any other chief executive in the premiership would have warmly appreciated.

The truth was that Canterbury's administration had dug a hole for itself with its wildcat recruiting without consultation with its first grade coach. Players had been signed without any thought about how they would fit into the first grade pattern.

FROM PLAYER TO COACH

A prime recruit—at least from the administration's point of view—was New Zealand centre or winger Mark Elia. When Gould asked Moore which players he thought should be in first grade, Elia was the first name mentioned. Not so much on ability, but because he had cost $95,000—it was embarrassing to have Moore's judgement held up to costly ridicule by playing him in reserve grade. Gould said he did not consider Elia as good as players who were already at the club but, in the interests of compromise, he would include the Kiwi in the first grade squad for the next week-end. That would entitle Elia to at least ride on the team bus.

Moore then started to talk about players who had been brought to the club and were not getting much time in first grade—players such as Bal Numapo, a Papua New Guinea Test player and Darren Curry.

'Darren Curry—you've had him on the bench for first grade. He might be better off playing a full game in reserve grade for fitness.'

Gould: 'Fine. I'll drop him back to reserve grade five-eighth.'

Moore: 'And Bal Numapo. He's a centre mate. Not a winger where you've been playing him.'

Gould: 'I've already told you he can't play the game. But if you want I'll play him in the centres in reserve grade.'

It was then that Moore started to look a little concerned as he ran the reserve grade line-up through his mind. Numapo would be in the centres, Curry would be five-eighth. Greg Mackey had been bought as a first grade half but had been playing five-eighth in reserve grade so Moore's son Kevin could play half-back.

'If Curry is five-eighth where does Mackey play?' Moore asked. Gould: 'He'll have to play half-back.'

Moore: 'What about Kevin.' Gould: 'He'll have to miss out.'

Good as GOULD

With that Moore stood up, slammed his napkin onto the table and said: 'You're the one who wants him out of this club. You're the one who's got it in for Kevin. I'm not going to let you ruin my marriage and my family.' Moore then turned to Barry Nelson and said: 'I quit' and stormed from the room leaving Nelson and Gould stunned. Nelson moved to go after Moore saying to Gould: 'Don't worry, he's just a little touchy about his family.'

With Nelson gone Gould's mind flashed back to an earlier discussion that season with Moore about the quality of the players for 1989. After watching the reserve grade side concede 66 points in a trial, Gould had turned to Moore and said that there was not a potential first grader in the line-up.

Moore asked quietly: 'Does that include Kevin.' Gould responded: 'Yes. I've played with Kevin and I've coached him. He's not a first grade half-back.'

Moore eventually returned to the dining room and the atmosphere calmed a little over a couple of drinks. The conversation again turned to Kevin Moore. 'I've told you before that I don't think Kevin is a first grader,' Gould said. 'I've told you that he could be a first grade hooker if he's prepared to work on his game—but that doesn't suit you. Anyway what's this all about? You're the one who came up with this idea of wanting the teams changed. You're the one who wants to give Bal Numapo a run in the centres and play Darren Curry at five-eighth in reserve grade, not me.'

Moore then said: 'Does that mean if Numapo doesn't play in the centres, Kevin stays in the side?' Gould: 'Yes'. Moore: 'I'll have him on the first plane home.' And he did.

It was the first time Gould had really come face to face with the intensity of Moore's paternal feelings.

At times Canterbury's staff would read like a Moore family reunion. His son was in reserve grade, his son-in-law Chris

Anderson was coaching, another son-in-law Steve Folkes was a trainer and eventually a reserve grade coach on a reported contract of $100,000. Later Moore's daughter Lyn (Anderson), Chris's wife, would take over as marketing manager of the club as well.

Folkes and Anderson were former internationals with extensive experience. Lyn Anderson was well qualified in marketing but their filial association with Moore still raised eyebrows.

When Super League was stopped by court action in 1996 and the Adelaide Rams franchise declared null and void, many of the players signed by the club would be funnelled towards the Moorebank Rams in the Metropolitan Cup competition. At that stage Peter Moore was the recruitment officer for Super League. His son Kevin was coach of the Moorebank Rams.

Seasons later when Chris Anderson took over as first grade coach at Canterbury, he used Kevin Moore as first grade halfback for a time but Moore would switch to dummy half in general play because it suited the team better.

For a season that would end with star five-eighth Terry Lamb in tears after the final match over the frustration of not having been able to do better, 1989 started with some brightness. As defending champions Canterbury knew they would be under additional pressure in every match. Every move would be scrutinised by a media and public anxious to know whether the previous year's premiership won by a 30-year-old coach was a sign of things to come or just a fluke.

Outside pressure did not worry the players or Gould. It was again the enemy within, that former coach Warren Ryan had warned about, that would destroy Canterbury's chances.

There is no doubt that Moore had considerable influence on some rugby league writers in newspapers and magazines.

The ones who support his theories, publish his propositions

Good as GOULD

in a favourable light find him constantly accessible. Others, preferring to tread a more independent path, can find access to Moore considerably restricted.

It is reasonable to say that a lot of people were not particularly surprised at the savage criticism and character evaluation Justice Burchett afforded Moore when he classified him as 'totally corrupt' for the way he conducted himself in the Super League battle with the ARL.

For Phil Gould in 1989, the euphoria from the previous year's grand final win, did not last.

The alarm bells were clanging loudly enough to drown out Big Ben before the season had even started. There had been a constant and serious drain on Canterbury's playing staff for several seasons. It had been a major worry in 1988. By 1989 the situation had not improved. In fact it had worsened to—to critical.

At the end of the 1988 Canterbury had lost players of the calibre of Test centre Tony Currie to Brisbane, clever five-eighth Michael Hagan to Newcastle, fullback and dual Dally M winner Mick Potter to St George. Steve Mortimer had retired, prop Mark Bugden was gone. So was winger-centre Sandy Campbell—to Easts. Tough utility back Chris Mortimer had already departed the club at the end of the 1987 season for Penrith at the urging of his close friend and Penrith captain Royce Simmons. Mortimer revealed he was motivated to leave by Peter Moore's indifference to plans to stage a testimonial year benefit for Mortimer's tenth year with the club. Rugged prop Peter Kelly had also switched to Penrith at the end of 1987.

Satisfactory replacements were never found for either Mortimer or Kelly even though Gould took Canterbury to the 1988 title. Gould says the total number of players who had left the club in the previous three or four years was around 30.

'Part of it was that they had played in winning Canterbury

sides and had aroused the interest of other clubs,' Gould says. 'I accept that. It's football. What I could not accept and still cannot accept is that Canterbury made such a minimal effort to replace the players who had left. We played a trial match at Parramatta before the season started and Canterbury's reserve grade side was beaten by 66 points. It was an obvious signal to any responsible management that something was wrong and needed fixing in a hurry. After the loss I told Peter Moore that there was not one player in that Canterbury side that I could ever use in first grade. Unless we got replacements in a hurry we were going to have to play the season and try and defend the first grade premiership with a pool of around 20 players. It was ludicrous.'

To Gould the final piece of the puzzle fell into place when Canterbury appointed Chris Anderson as under-23s coach. It was not an appointment Gould endorsed. To antagonise a first grade coach, even more importantly a premiership-winning first grade coach, by appointing someone not to his liking to the coaching staff would be unthinkable at any other club. At Canterbury, if people could see what was happening, they were not prepared to raise any objections.

'I was not a bit happy about Chris' appointment,' said Gould. It was Bullfrog's way of arrogantly saying that it did not matter how many premierships I won or how successful the club became, I was going to be replaced by his son-in-law. It was him publicly revealing that he had total control of the club. Not the board of directors, not the members, not the players and not the supporters. Just him. It was basically Moore throwing petrol on the embers of the fire that had raged when Ryan was coach. A lot of people had worked hard to bring stability to the club and it worked. We had won the premiership. Now Peter Moore was making it obvious the whole thing was going to start all over again.'

Good as GOULD

Gould's theory has always been that he was intended to be a sacrificial lamb as Canterbury's coach. Moore wanted Ryan out and, at the end of 1987, he got his way. The club had to find someone in a hurry to take over and steady the ship for a season until Anderson was ready to take over. Canterbury would then throw its financial resources into building a team Anderson could take to a premiership win.

Half-back Steve Mortimer confirmed that theory during 1989 but admitted he had initially been the first person approached to coach Canterbury in 1988 when Ryan left. Mortimer said the agreement was that he would coach for one year and then let Chris Anderson take over. In an interview in the *Sunday Telegraph* headlined: 'Steve Mortimer says Gus Must Quit', he declared:

Phil Gould must go—and take his mates with him. I have known Phil Gould for many years as a player and as a coach. As a player he was what we call a humble footballer, a good grade player who never really hit the heights before finishing his career at Souths—a club he is obviously fond of.

After Phil stopped playing, he coached the Canterbury reserve grade side. When I was asked if I would coach Canterbury last year as a caretaker coach before Chris Anderson took over I said no. I said I wasn't the right person for the job and I said I didn't think that Chris should come into the job straight after coaching in England. I suggested Phil was the man for the job and my judgement was proved correct when Canterbury won the premiership last season—a mighty achievement for a coach in his first year. Unfortunately with the success I saw a change overcome Phil Gould. As Canterbury was winning, his profile grew as quickly as the headlines, and then, as the club approached the 1989 season, even faster. I feel in any sport that a true champion will be secure in his own ability. Unfortunately there are some people who achieve champion status but cannot handle it. Although Phil never achieved the great heights as a player, as a coach, he did. He enjoyed the sensation and I am afraid he lost perspective of what he stood for. The current situation at Canterbury where coach and a committeeman are engaging in a public slanging match should never have taken place. Phil is looking for reasons for his lack of success this year. He is critical of the committee, but let me say that last year Phil Gould never had a more staunch supporter than Peter Moore. Moore supported Gould all the way last season. The situation this season where people have tried to antagonise Moore into a confrontation should never have taken place. Peter has never made a secret of the fact that he would love to see Chris Anderson coach at Canterbury. He is open about it, but he had enough admiration for Phil Gould's ability to try and sign him to a long term contract. If there is a cancer in a body, doctors try and cut it out. There are cancers at Canterbury and they too must be cut out. Sadly last year's success didn't kill the cancers, they grew off it. There are influences at Canterbury not in the best interest of the club. One such influence is Phil's manager Ross Seymour. There are a couple in the playing ranks too. One is asking other players to join him at another club. Now Phil says he has a contract from Canterbury in his possession which he hasn't signed. Obviously there must be some doubt in his mind. So don't sign it Phil. Leave. Go and let Canterbury fight its way back. Adversity always brings out the best in good players. There are other clubs who want Phil Gould. Let them take him. The Bulldogs are better off without him.

Phil Gould says having compromised Canterbury's theory of him only being a one-year coach by winning the 1988 premiership, the club did the next best thing. He could not be sacked so Canterbury tried making his stay at the club intolerable and weakened the playing strength by not signing experienced first grade players.

Committeeman and former Kangaroo and Test five-eighth

Good as GOULD

Tim Pickup, who clashed heatedly and publicly with Gould during the season, says he had absolutely no knowledge of such a plan. 'I can't say it didn't happen. I can only say that I knew nothing about it. Nor did the rest of the committee,' he said.

Pickup eventually wrote an open letter to *Rugby League Week*, taking exception to Gould's constant fault-finding with the strength of the Canterbury side. In the letter Pickup referred to Gould as a whinger and a media superstar. 'I only did it because of what Phil was saying in the papers every five minutes. He kept criticising the make up of the team and the players we had,' Pickup said. 'I respected Gus for what he had achieved at Canterbury in winning the premiership. The bone was quite rightly pointed at our committee by Phil and the media that we needed some good players and that we had wrongly let some good ones go. But can you think of any club that would have let its coach go so far and still keep his job.'

In reply Gould referred to Pickup as an errand boy for Peter Moore and insignificant in the overall pictures. Peter Moore bought into the argument from New Zealand, where he was manager of the Australian team. In Rotorua, Moore told two journalists that it was very likely Gould would be leaving the club at the end of 1989. He said Gould's public utterances had been caused by the frustration of financial problems caused by gambling. It was mentioned that Gould had become a bookmaker at the greyhounds at one stage of the season.

The crux of the matter was whether Gould would reply to an offer from Canterbury to stay on as first grade coach. Moore finally put into words on July 13 the rumours that were floating around. He said Gould had accepted an offer to coach another club in 1990 and would be quitting the Bulldogs. He said Gould should have kept his mouth shut. Moore said he was outlining the situation to set the record straight.

FROM PLAYER TO COACH

In yet another open letter in the saga, Moore declared:

Phil's recently published statement that Tim Pickup is very insignificant, merits comment from me. Tim Pickup is certainly one of the power men behind Canterbury's great success in the past 10 years, and as most players at Canterbury will agree, is a genius. Tim's comments about Phil were factual and undeniable. It is particularly true that Phil's business partner and football adviser Ross Seymour approached me, despite his denials, on three occasions as early as March and April. Seymour told me that he and Phil had accepted a better offer for 1990. When I asked Phil on May 5 what was going on, all he said was: 'Ross shouldn't have said that!' There were no denials. In May, Phil told Leagues Club president Gary McIntyre that he had a really big offer and would not be here in 1990. In June the management committee called Phil in and asked him to sign for 1989-90. He picked up the contract, said he would consider it, and walked out of the room. On five occasions over the next four weeks I asked Phil to bring the contract back but he refused. Finally Barry Nelson asked Phil Gould to sign the contract but he still refused. When I came to New Zealand, Phil had many times in the media failed to respect a verbal coaching agreement and on six occasions failed to sign a contract. Obviously Phil of his own choice, has no contract or agreement with Canterbury in 1990.

Pickup was of the opinion that Moore should have intervened much earlier in the dispute. Pickup says he was only prompted to speak out because of the lack of response from the club to Gould's criticisms.

During the season Gould's frustration would over flow and he would say: 'We've patched up our first grade with players that other clubs don't want.' He also said: 'There should be a broom through the place.'

Canterbury's opening sequence in the defence of its premiership crown in 1989 was three successive wins. Gold Coast,

Good as GOULD

Cronulla and Illawarra all fell. Not great scalps perhaps and there had been problems, but optimistically Gould started thinking that things might not be as bad as he had feared. He was prepared to overlook the fact that Canterbury could only beat lowly-rated Gold Coast 8–2 after the score was 2–all at half-time on a wet field. 'Gold Coast were the real winners of that game,' he remembers. 'Make no mistake, we didn't deserve to win.'

Canterbury was more impressive in beating Cronulla 22–2, and then Illawarra 16–4 at Wollongong Stadium in some of the worst conditions ever seen in a premiership match. Torrential rain for days leading up to the game turned the showground into a mini-lake and water flowed across the field throughout the match.

At that stage Canterbury were equal competition leaders. Lamb was playing well, so was the forward pack—with David Gillespie maturing more and more into a tough and feared prop.

The problems started with a 16–8 loss to St George in the fourth game, worsened with a 34–4 hiding from Canberra on a heavy track that lessened the effectiveness of Canterbury's big pack. Things eased fractionally with a 30–6 win against Easts at the Sydney Football Stadium—but it would be the club's last away win of the season.

The next 16 weeks brought seven away losses and two away draws (6–all with North Sydney and 18–all with Souths).

After the win against Easts, it was Souths who sent pessimism levels rising again with a 10–2 win at Belmore Sports Ground, ironically making sure of the win with a safety first approach they had learned from Gould of cutting down mistakes and waiting for chances. A 16–8 loss to Newcastle in Newcastle meant Canterbury had lost four out of their last five games and there was obviously a need to regather enthusiasm and re-build morale.

FROM PLAYER TO COACH

A 10–4 win against Balmain in a clash of the previous season's two grand finalists helped a little, but the following week's 38–4 hiding from Penrith meant that nothing much had changed. This was Canterbury's fifth loss in seven games and established a pattern of performance that lasted all season of winning a game or two to raise hopes of a revival and then losing a couple of matches to concede more ground.

There was obviously something lacking. And Gould knew it. 'We just could not seem to get things together. We were trying. The side was trying hard and playing with enthusiasm. But we were not winning close matches and we were not winning regularly enough to consolidate a place in the five,' Gould said. 'We also did not have enough experienced or talented players. The lack of recruitment was becoming more obvious. Generally we were not playing with any less intensity than the previous year. Teams were just playing better against us.'

The internal structure of support was also starting to crumble. Gould and Moore were not getting on.

The run of uncertain form continued, with a 25–10 loss to Cronulla also bringing the suspension of Joe Thomas and David Gillespie for a total of 12 weeks for a spear tackle.

Performances in home matches at Belmore Sports Ground maintained Canterbury's faltering drive for the semi-finals, including a run of three successive wins against Brisbane (22–8), Wests (26–8) and Gold Coast (14–8) six weeks before the semi-finals started.

For Canterbury the semi-final chance came down to an historic match against Canberra in Perth in the third last game of the season. It would be the first time a first grade NSW rugby league premiership had ever been played on the West Coast. It was scheduled for a Friday night and beamed live back to Sydney by Channel 9.

Good as GOULD

The history-making aspects of the match were lost on Gould and the Canterbury players.

The match was effectively an 80 minute sudden death semi-final that had arrived four weeks early. If Canterbury won, they would still be in line for a semi-final place. If they lost, they were out. They lost.

Ahead 14-6 at one stage, the Bulldogs were run down by a late scoring surge from Canberra, highlighted by tries from Laurie Daley and Ivan Henjack in an 18-14 win.

Referee Bill Harrigan did not impress Gould with his performance that night. Giving full reign to his fury at Harrigan's performance, Gould went to the referee's room and invited him to come into the Canterbury room and see the pain that was being suffered. 'I wanted him to see what his decisions had done to this team. I wanted him to see for himself how upset the players were at his decisions, especially the ones that were wrong and the pounding we had taken. It was the end of a season of hard work and he had been responsible.' Harrigan declined the invitation to the Canterbury room and took the matter no further, even though he could have reported the incident to the NSWRL and asked for an inquiry. It was not to be the end Gould's heated clashes with Harrigan.

As the status of each man grew in their respective categories of rugby league, their paths continued to cross and their confrontations became more heated and more public. Eventually the ARL was forced to call both of them to Phillip Street to manufacture a truce, which will be discussed in a later chapter. At that stage of his career in 1989 Harrigan was simply an irritant to Gould.

The real antagonism Gould felt was towards Moore, Pickup and the rest of the Canterbury committee he felt had let him and the club down with their reluctance to provide him with enough quality players to keep the first grade side competitive.

Darryl Brohman was back at Canterbury at that stage as reserve grade coach, continuing the relationship he and Gould had enjoyed at Penrith as players and at Canterbury before Gould left to join Souths. 'I was back in Brisbane in 1988 when Phil won the first grade premiership,' said Brohman. 'I was coaching the Brisbane Broncos reserve grade side the first year they were in the premiership. I wasn't much of a coach and we didn't make the semi-finals. My marriage had just broken up and at the end of the season, Brisbane gave me the flick. The Frog (Peter Moore) rang me and asked if I wanted to coach the Canterbury seconds because Gus would love to have me do it,' he said. 'I took the job and came to Sydney. The first night I arrived something went wrong with the arrangements about where I had to stay—I've forgotten what it was—but they said you can stay at Gus' place tonight. It turned into ten months.'

For Brohman it was a first hand look at the eccentric and often erratic life style that Gould embraced then—and still does to a large extent. He is not an insomniac but conventional sleeping hours are not on his schedule. Sleep is something that is taken when it comes, usually when it is impossible to stay awake any longer.

A live telecast of Wimbledon or the US golf open will keep him up all night watching. So will watching and re-watching videos of opposing teams. He will study opposition sides, not only for their overall strengths and weaknesses but the individual skills players in the sides have. 'He might still be up at 4am looking at videos. There would be a pile of pieces of paper where he had picked 20 teams and then discarded them,' Brohman said. 'He's a nightmare for a reserve grade coach because he keeps changing sides. He takes losses to heart very deeply. It might not always show on the outside but getting beaten hurts him badly.'

Gould and Brohman were an unusual coupling as flatmates, linked by their jobs as coaches and a background at Penrith.

'I didn't pay any board,' said Brohman. 'I didn't have any money. Gus ended up supporting me for about ten months. I was depending on him more than he was depending on me. He was tremendously generous. It was nothing for him to come home and give me a couple of hundred dollars and say "Let's go out" or "have a bet". Sometimes I would go off to work in the morning and return home at night and he wouldn't have moved. I'd think, what is this bloke on about?'

Eventually Gould's behaviour would get the better of Brohman. 'We would get out for a few drinks on a Friday or a Saturday night or after games on Sundays,' said Brohman. 'I had a job that involved 7am meetings on Mondays. I missed six or seven in a row. I just couldn't get there because of the way I felt after the drink. In the end I had to give up that job because it was too hard to get there.'

Brohman was an eye-witness to Canterbury's demise in 1989 and still remembers Gould's courage in holding on against the odds of a committee against him and a chief executive with a son-in-law with ambitions to coach first grade. 'I remember 1989 being such a bad year,' Brohman said. 'Canterbury was disintegrating. The underlying thing was that Gus was really dirty on the Bullfrog for letting so many good players leave and not replacing them or replacing them with players of considerably less talent.'

Brohman says one example was the club's recruitment of Elia. The club had let Tony Currie go and at that stage he was probably the best centre in the world. 'Elia was nowhere near as good,' he said. Halfback was also a major problem following the retirement of Steve Mortimer. Canterbury had not made any plans to cover Mortimer's departure. The job was covered by Peter Moore's son Kevin and paternal pride and expectations ran high. Kevin was a competent half-back who had proved adequate when called in to first grade but was not seen as the permanent answer to replacing Mortimer. However Canterbury's reluctance to shop for a half-back left Gould with few real choices to fill the position. Terry Lamb played there some of the time, so did Jason Alchin.

Peter Moore explored the possibility of Kevin being transferred to another club to avoid accusations of favouritism but no offers of any significance were received. In fairness to Kevin, he was in a no-win situation. Had he not been the son of the club chief executive, his career might have settled into a reserve grade niche and his performances would have missed the spotlight.

Former Kangaroo Paul Langmack, who later switched from Canterbury to Wests, remembers a match which emphasised Gould's talent for motivation when the coach selected a bunch of players who had not been going well. 'It was done to show some of the first graders that they were not guaranteed first grade positions if they were playing badly. Gus did it to show that there were players pushing for first grade places and they could play well. I was about the only recognised first grader and I was captain. Greg Mackey was in the centres. Joe Thomas was lock,' he said. Against the odds Canterbury won—beating Parramatta.

Daryl Brohman's demise came soon after Gould's departure. 'We both got the arse together. Bullfrog rang me and said: "Daryl matey . . . Gus is going and I think you might have to go too." And that was that.'

Gould's own departure was not so clean and decisive. After a season of wrangling and almost murderous exchanges of verbal firepower between Gould, Moore, the committee and Mortimer, it was a seemingly impossible repair job to put all the pieces back together again—but they tried. Gould and Moore had extensive talks in an effort to work out what had gone wrong and whether relationships could be repaired. Initially talks were promising. They met at Belmore Sports Ground and sat in the grandstand to talk things over. The thaw led to a second meeting at Bankstown Trots where more progress was made.

'I wanted an assurance that if I stayed as coach I would not be subjected to the dramas and innuendo of the 1989. I wanted to know that anything that happened in the club would stay in the club and out of the papers,' said Gould. 'I was sick of all the drama and I knew our supporters and players were sick of it too. We spoke to the senior players about making a new start and at first everything seemed all right. I was happy with the changed conditions, the players were happy and Peter Moore said he was happy. Then he changed his mind.'

Moore contacted Gould and said he was having second thoughts about the first grade coaching job and was suddenly not so certain that all of the problems of 1989 would not be repeated in 1990. 'I said: "I thought everything was sweet,"' Gould said. 'Moore said: "I've changed my mind matey." I said: "Does that mean you can't guarantee that all of the problems of this year, the newspaper headlines, the disputes, the committee . . . everything won't happen again." He said: "That's right." So I called it off. If I couldn't be comfortable at the club I didn't want to be there at all. I didn't want to put myself, the club or the players through another year like 1989.' The final parting came at a Chinese restaurant in Campsie, where Gould's contract was paid out.

FROM PLAYER TO COACH

Sometimes tyrannical former Kangaroo Ron Willey, ironically a former Canterbury junior, had been coaching at Penrith with outstanding if controversial success. Willey, who coached Manly to the 1972–3 first grade premierships and NSW to the State of Origin success in 1986, was enormously experienced. Tim Sheens had lifted Penrith into the semi-finals for the first time in 1985 but their inexperience led to a 38–6 hiding from Parramatta in the first sudden death game.

Willey took the 1988 Penrith side to equal fifth where they lost a play-off to Balmain 28–8. The next season he steered Penrith into second place but they then lost back-to-back games, to Balmain 24–8 and Canberra 27–18.

Willey raised Penrith's ire for playing then up-and-comer Brad Fittler in the semi-final against Balmain instead of the seasoned veteran Chris Mortimer. Willey also delayed the decision on Fittler until minutes before the match, further antagonising Penrith players and supporters who said the manoeuvre was both wrong and disruptive. Willey was not the most popular coach in town at Penrith despite having a final year of his contract to run. After that the story becomes one of two versions.

The first is that Penrith sacked Willey and opened negotiations with Gould simultaneously, with the approval of Peter Moore.

The second is that Willey and Penrith parted company amicably and that Gould co-incidentally happened to be on the market at the same time after quitting Canterbury.

The first theory has plenty of support and logic. Especially as Willey said he was stepping down from coaching but almost immediately accepted an offer to coach English club Bradford Northern. Gould prefers to support the coincidence theory. 'I did not know anything about the Penrith deal until after I had stepped down at Canterbury. I was on the market and then approaches were made.'

Penrith boss Roger Cowan insists Willey was not sacked, saying it was a mutual decision to part company. There is no doubt however that the sudden availability of the Penrith coaching job at a time when Gould was uncertain about staying at Canterbury, added another dimension to the equation.

By an odd coincidence Gould was opposed by his former half-back at Canterbury Steve Mortimer for the Penrith coaching job but won on the first ballot.

Paul Langmack was also a peripheral player as the coaching game of musical chairs continued. Once Gould's destination was either confirmed or hinted at, depending on which story you accept, he spoke to Langmack about changing clubs. 'In 1989 I had a year to go on my contract but Canterbury gave me a release—but not in writing,' said Langmack.

'Gus was going to Penrith and he wanted me there as well. The day I went to get the release was the day it was in the paper that Willey was gone from Penrith.

'Bullfrog smelled a rat. He said: "I'm busy at the moment, can you come back this afternoon." By the afternoon, he'd spoken to Gus—I think he'd spoken to Gus the night before and he'd quit—and they cancelled my release. I'd shaken hands with Frog earlier and everything about the release. He just said to me: "I can't." I said: "All right." I think we always knew he (Gould) was going to Penrith.'

Langmack, still one of the most polished performers in the premiership, has no real regrets about the way things worked out and boasts an enviable record of personal achievement. 'I was lucky it all happened early for me,' he said. 'I started thinking it was just a normal career. The Frog used to tell me I was the luckiest bloke ever, to have had it all happen so early. The first year we played in the final I was straight out of school and I'd scored a try in a semi-final. We won the competition in 1984 and 1985. We made the grand final in 1986 and I went on a Kangaroo tour. By 1988 I told myself that I wanted to win four more grand finals, but your goals change.

'The funny thing is that I enjoyed 1995 (at Wests) under our new coach Tommy Raudonikis more than any other year and we didn't even make the semi-finals,' Langmack said. 'I learned a lot of useful things playing under Gus, Warren Ryan and Chris Anderson. I have a lot of time for Anderson. We won eight of the first nine when he took over in 1990 then we lost six in a row and just missed the semi-finals.'

Langmack remains a close friend of Gould's to this day and supports the theory of 1989 being a one-year deal by Canterbury before they put Anderson into the job. 'Gus is an emotional guy and he felt there was a set against him by management because they hadn't bought anyone,' Langmack said. 'Because we were close to the coach we stuck with him. But I think he was only meant to be a fall guy for a year. The script didn't go according to plan. He beat them all."

The bitterness and wounds of 1989 have been slow to heal. In 1995 Tim Pickup was at Randwick races with some Canterbury players when Gould walked past. Not a word was spoken.

PHIL GOULD'S Reflections on Leaving
CANTERBURY, 1989

It was always going to be difficult defending the premiership because of the loss of a lot of good players at the end of 1988 and poor recruiting. The Canterbury side that won the grand final in 1988 never took the field together again. Senior players noticed a change in the club.

In 1988 my reserve grade coach was Ken Wilson and my conditioner was Jim Tuite. I guess Peter Moore suspected me of trying to start my own network at the club because he made life difficult for both men. They resigned despite saying they wanted to stay and help me. Peter Mortimer became conditioner. We did not find a reserve grade coach until February when Daryl Brohman took the job.

Season 1989 was a very difficult year. On top of a lot of problems simmering beneath the surface, we also had many injuries and the problems of an extremely wet season.

We trained at four or five different venues. Our gear was never ready on time. That was one of the things we spoke to Peter Moore about at the end of the year when he agreed the club could have done more to help our cause.

Despite some poor games we were still in contention with about five games to go even though I always knew we would struggle to make the semi-finals. Season 1988 had been a carefree period without bitterness or wrangling. For coach and management problems to return again in 1989 was just too much for players who had been with the club for any length of time.

FROM PLAYER TO COACH

Steve Mortimer in his first year of retirement took advantage of the situation between Peter Moore and myself to write his scathing article in a Sunday newspaper. It all went back to 1988. Steve started the year in first grade but to be brutally honest his priorities seemed to me to be more in promoting a tourist centre at Coffs Harbour where he was seen to be a figurehead for new resorts. He was also replaced as captain in 1988 for disobeying instructions.

It started around game five against Illawarra when I kept sending out instructions he ignored. I sacked him as captain, saying if he wouldn't follow instructions then I would get someone who would.

Later in 1988 we were playing Warren Ryan's Balmain side at Leichhardt Oval and Steve Mortimer made it a personal vendetta. He wanted to beat Warren Ryan playing the type of flamboyant football that Ryan had refused to let him play at Canterbury. It was a disaster and brought about our downfall.

The next day at training Steve Mortimer was sitting on the grandstand steps waiting for me, to apologise for his performance the previous day. He said he had been very sick all week and it had affected his judgement. He was distressed at his own performance and distressed at having cost Canterbury a win. He was also upset that Warren Ryan had used the win against Canterbury to get square with Steve with some comments in the media about the way he played.

I told Steve I was disappointed in his performance and if he was sick he should see the doctor. It turned out he did not have a virus but was below peak fitness. Steve was not playing well.

I felt a lot of it had to do with his attitude to playing because of what had happened during his years under Warren Ryan and I considered it something I could not repair. I told Steve I was going to use Jason Alchin at half and that his first grade position was in jeopardy.

Good as GOULD

I remember Steve asking me to come to his house at Illawong, where he virtually attacked me for my decision. He wanted to know who I thought I was to drop Steve Mortimer and how did I ever think the side would function without him at half. He was the reason Canterbury was having any success and I was obviously getting carried away with my job. He virtually dared me to drop him from the side and got very emotional about it all.

I listened as politely as I could because in reality my mind was already made up.

He came to me a couple of days later and decided to take the option of a mystery virus—which is how it was presented to the media. It was suggested Steve would need six weeks to recover. The truth was the doctor had estimated Steve needed six weeks of training to get his fitness up to first grade level.

In my mind I think Steve was saying he was pulling out for six weeks and telling me I would be the one to suffer most because the team would fail.

We won our next five games without Steve Mortimer. When he was ready to play, I named him as a fresh reserve to use when sides were tired. And it worked well. Bob Fulton used the same ploy in 1987 with Paul Shaw and won a grand final. Everyone praised Fulton's ploy but because I was doing it with Steve Mortimer, it was a different story.

I still had plans for Steve around grand final time—to use his experience in the starting side but management intervention and a loss combined to give him a chance in first grade again.

I put him back in and two weeks later he broke his arm against St George and missed the semi-finals, returning for only a token visit on grand final day. Had Steve been more patient he would have enjoyed the same glorious exit from rugby league on grand final day as had Ray Price, Mick Cronin and Royce Simmons.

FROM PLAYER TO COACH

The Steve Mortimer saga was a valuable learning experience for me. In 1991 I would not surrender to pressure to reinstate Royce Simmons in first grade. But I made sure he was there for us at semi-final time.

Steve's attack on me in the newspaper came from his own bitterness at being dropped in the middle of the season, his bitterness at weeks on the interchange bench and his frustration at having to sit there on grand final day and watch Michael Hagan help bring off victory as the number one half-back in the club.

I have always admired Steve Mortimer as a player, but I have never forgotten what he tried to do to me in 1988 and 1989. I still believe Peter Moore was the motivating force behind the attacks by Steve Mortimer and also Tim Pickup. It was another example of the Canterbury propaganda machine in top gear trying to paint a different picture of the club to the public than the one that really existed.

What Steve wrote did not affect me too much but it certainly widened the gap between the senior players at the club and him.

They complained to management and asked them what they intended to do about the column.

Peter Moore promised he would act. To this day, I believe he was one of the prime movers in Steve Mortimer and Tim Pickup going public with their attacks.

The Canterbury propaganda machine in those days had become adept at damage control and getting chosen journalists to paint a favourable picture of the club.

Steve Mortimer to me is one of those footballers who did not know when to let go, and who remained somewhat bitter since retirement.

Having said that, I will add that Steve is also a hard worker for charities. It is pleasing to see him putting his name and profile to good use.

Good as GOULD

When all the dust finally settled at Canterbury at the end of the 1989 season, everything I had suspected would happen, had happened. And that was despite all the pretence and all the promises from Peter Moore that everything that had been wrong with Canterbury had been corrected and we could look forward to a productive 1990.

My feeling all along had been that Peter Moore would not let his son-in-law Chris Anderson come back to a club that had put together three or four premierships.

That scenario would put too much public pressure on Chris to continue the winning sequence. Chris' job would be so much easier if, for whatever reason, Canterbury's prestige and potential had been on a downhill spiral. Whoever came along and coached the side in those circumstances could re-build slowly and with purpose. There would be no demand for immediate success.

Whether or not the theory was right was open to varying personal interpretations. But it had certainly been ingrained in me and in all of the Bulldog players. And there was also plenty of evidence to support the idea.

Canterbury Leagues Club president Garry McIntyre and secretary-manager John Ballesty confided in me several times that they thought the concept had credibility.

By late 1988 and early 1989 Canterbury had resumed its policy of signing a lot of young players, as part of the future picture. This happened to coincide with the appointment of Chris Anderson as under-23 coach. In a few years time the crop of young players would develop into first graders and provide the then coach with the foundation of a good team.

I freely admit that I did not handle things in 1989 as well as I might have. I am not making excuses but I was 30-years-old and defending a premiership we had won against all odds. It was also the first time in my life that I found myself in a situation where I felt I was not wanted.

FROM PLAYER TO COACH

I fell back on my natural instincts when the fireworks started and started giving as good as I was getting. With hindsight it might have been better for me to have bitten my tongue and gone along quietly. But I was not like that then and I am not like that now. I reacted pretty badly to a lot of the things that were being said by Peter Moore, Tim Pickup and the Canterbury club because lies were being made up to justify the stories that were being told and the circumstances they were trying to create.

For example I had absolutely nothing to do with signing players for 1989 although the club maintained a pretence to the media that I did. For years Canterbury had boasted of its great recruitment record. The only year they recruited poorly was the year they decided that it was convenient to say the coach had been solely responsible for signing new players. The only players who came to the club after the start of the season were bought simply because we needed to strengthen the reserve grade side.

I did not regard the Canterbury committee as an independent body. My view was that the club was run exclusively by Peter Moore. But to this day if anyone ever asks me, I say that Canterbury is a super club and the people in it are super people.

When it came about, our parting was long and protracted with at least one false dawn. Peter Moore called me to Belmore Sports Ground one day for a talk and said basically that we as a club and as individuals had experienced a very difficult year. We sat and talked for around three hours about everything that had gone wrong. The orchestrated attacks in the media, the club's buying policy, the rumours. I told him I had not handled it well but said in my defence that I was 30, in my second year of first grade coaching and defending a premiership. I had been looking for more support from him and it had not been forthcoming. I told him that rightly or wrongly there was a feeling that he had been death-riding us all season and did not care if

Good as GOULD

we won or lost. In the end he conceded he had not given me the support a first grade coach should get and proposed a truce.

I can still picture the scene. We were sitting in the grandstand at Belmore, the semi-finals were on and Canterbury were not there, and Peter Moore said we would give it another go and try and work together. I went home and got a phone call from him about two hours later. He had been sitting in his office having a drink. He said: 'Phil I apologise for the whole season. I am sorry for what we did. I know we can make a go of it and we will.'

We called the senior players together and they aired their grievances. Moore and Barry Nelson were there to hear the players say that Mortimer and Pickup should keep out of things they knew nothing about. The players talked about the feud in the media and asked Moore if he had been happy to see us get beaten. Moore said no to the question and said everything was now in the past, that the club was starting afresh. The next week the whole club had a meeting about starting anew.

Two weeks later there was a report in a Sydney newspaper revealing that Ron Willey was quitting Penrith. That day I got a phone call from Peter Moore, saying, 'If you get an offer you can accept it.'

I said to him, 'What do you mean? I have a contract to coach Canterbury.' He said again that if an offer came I should take it.

I said, 'I don't want the job at Penrith. I have a job coaching Canterbury. We were all going to start anew.' He said, 'Sorry matey, can't do it.'

We agreed to meet at the Bankstown Trotting Club the next day for talks. When I arrived Moore was drinking at the bar with Chris Anderson and Garry Hughes, his nephew.

He came over to me and I said, 'You said you were giving

me your guarantee that things would get better. Are you saying things will be as bad in 1990 as they were in 1989?'

He replied, 'Yes. You won't feel comfortable here.'

I said, 'Well, I quit.'

He said, 'Meet me tomorrow and I'll pay you your money.'

We met at a Chinese restaurant in Burwood. He paid me and I was no longer the coach of Canterbury. Not long afterwards Chris Anderson was appointed first grade coach.

Putting Pride into the Panthers

Walking into Penrith Park for the first time in eleven years was like entering a time tunnel. Gould had played with three city-based clubs, had worked his way to the fringe of representative teams before having his momentum stopped by injuries, had played in a first grade grand final and coached Canterbury to win a first grade grand final. Looking around Penrith Park it seemed that it might still be a few more years before news of what was happening further east of the Blue Mountains reached the club.

In his mind Penrith in 1990 could be cut out like a template and fitted neatly onto a similar scene from his last year at the club in 1979—except for one thing: There was now a first grade side full of exceptional promise.

In the years Gould had been away Penrith had stumbled a little but generally the momentum had been significantly on the rise. Former first grade prop and captain Tim Sheens had taken over in 1984 and had streamlined the club's professionalism and approach. That year the club missed the first grade semi-finals by just a point, bouncing back from equal 10th in 1983.

In 1985 Sheens took Penrith to the semi-finals for the first time after they beat Manly 10–7 in a play-off. There they lost the first sudden death game to Parramatta 38–6.

From that point Penrith were always competitive, finishing eighth in 1986 after losing a succession of close matches, before falling apart in Sheens' last season, 1987, and dropping to 12th. Former Kangaroo fullback Ron Willey, who played with Manly, Canterbury and Parramatta during a long career, took over in 1988 and got the club again headed in the right direction.

Willey was probably the most experienced coach Penrith had signed. He had taken Manly to the first grade premiership in 1972–73 and then coached Balmain and Souths. A firm believer in an eye for an eye philosophy, Willey generated plenty of headlines as he took Penrith to a play-off for fifth in 1988 (they lost 28–8 to Balmain) and second, before the semi-finals, in 1989. Penrith's challenge was brief in 1989. The side lost 24–12 to Balmain in the first semi-final and then 27–18 to Canberra the next week.

The second match was marked by Willey's shock decision to use up-and-coming Brad Fittler, a future Australian Test and World Cup captain, as first grade five-eighth ahead of the vastly more experienced Chris Mortimer. Willey was astute enough to recognise Fittler's enormous potential but rash enough to use him prematurely and paid with his job for the dissension and uproar it caused in the area. However Willey's no-nonsense approach gave Penrith much to be proud of in 1988–89 and, more importantly, gave Gould a solid, experienced side for 1990.

Chris Mortimer was still there. Brad Fittler was continuing to improve, Colin Van Voort was emerging as a forward of the future. Prop Paul Clarke, a reserve grader with promise from Balmain, had joined Penrith. Another prop and second-rower Barry Walker had fought his way into first grade calculations. Versatile Steve Carter, who would play State of Origin football, winger Paul Smith and forward Joe Vitanza were also prominent among the players pushing up from lower grades.

The future looked good. It always had at Penrith. Supporters though were growing increasingly restless with the long term vision. They wanted to see something tangible happening in the present. Gould was the man who would deliver for them.

In 1990 Gould would take Penrith to the grand final, sparking unprecedented scenes of celebration in the area. In 1991 the premiership would finally come to the foot of the Blue Mountains ending 25 years of waiting and coinciding with the club's silver anniversary.

Such grandiose ideas were not in Gould's calculations as he walked back into the Penrith camp in October 1989. Emotionally drained from the Canterbury experience, the familiar surroundings of Penrith, where he had served his own rugby league apprenticeship, were a balm to his own bruised psyche. His return had been orchestrated but it was unclear who was waving the baton.

Had Peter Moore reneged on his initial offer for Gould to stay on as Canterbury coach once he saw a chance to encourage him to move to Penrith and leave the way clear for Chris Anderson to coach Canterbury? Had Gould been involved in his own agenda? A retrenchment at Canterbury where he realised his use-by day might either have expired or would expire sometime during the 1990 season, would mean his contract being paid out. He could then sign a new deal with Penrith. Was Penrith's former coach Ron Willey the man caught up in the turmoil? There are pointers indicating Willey might have been sacked by Penrith and the circumstances dressed up in the best possible attire to save any embarrassment.

Officially all parties involved are giving accounts of the incidents that synchronise. Gould says he left Canterbury when Peter Moore made it obvious that their relationship would continue to be rocky in 1990. He did not enter into any negotiations with Penrith until he was approached by the club's chief executive Roger Cowan to coach the first grade side.

FROM PLAYER TO COACH

Roger Cowan says the job at Penrith was not even vacant until Willey decided to step down because of other interests he wanted to pursue. With Willey gone and Gould available, nominations were called for the first grade coaching job. Gould was preferred to his old Canterbury antagonist Steve Mortimer. The Penrith account includes a declaration that Willey also was not happy with the club's new direction that would include a full time coach, because he lived too far away at Manly to make the drive five days a week, 12 months a year.

Yet Willey would uproot himself just weeks after saying he could not accommodate a fulltime coaching position, and move to Bradford Northern in the English premiership as a fulltime coach. Willey did not see out the English season after falling out with players at Bradford Northern over training methods they considered old fashioned. He returned to Sydney after about 10 weeks.

For Gould, Penrith's potential was obvious and his appreciation of the talent available grew with each passing week. 'The promise was certainly there, but there was still work to be done,' Gould remembers. 'By mid-season we were looking better and players like David Green, Joe Vitanza, Steve Carter, Barry Walker and David Smith had become regular first graders. We also had Greg Alexander, John Cartwright, Mark Geyer and Brad Fittler. The club also had a component of older players as well like Peter Kelly and Royce Simmons.'

Peter Tunks, who had followed Gould to Penrith from Canterbury, was another player approaching classification as a veteran. The front-row of Kelly, Simmons and Tunks proved a problem for Gould as the 1990 season progressed. The trio boasted vast experience of first grade football in the Sydney premiership but were coming to the end of great careers and were lacking both the consistency and approach that Gould was demanding. When Penrith's premiership challenge went off the rails for a couple of weeks during the year with back-to-back losses to Cronulla and Canterbury, Gould fearlessly dropped Simmons, despite his legendary status in the district, and Tunks. He called Simmons, Kelly and Tunks to one side after the loss to Cronulla and told them he was not satisfied with their combined contribution. He said all three lacked the mobility he wanted in first grade and unless there was a decided improvement the following week against Canterbury, changes would be made.

Gould's tone made it clear that status, captaincy and friendship would not be influences in his decision. When the team to play Easts was read out after Penrith's 24–2 loss to Canterbury, Simmons and Tunks were in reserve grade and Chris Mortimer was the new first grade captain. Lock Colin Van Der Voort the new hooker. They were selection decisions that underlined Gould's determination to be his own man as a coach, and to make the hard calls when he had to. He had done it at Canterbury by dropping at various times Steve Mortimer, Paul Langmack and David Gillespie. Now the trend was continuing at Penrith.

But dropping Simmons was a bombshell and the shrapnel slashed through the air around Penrith, inflicting deep wounds. Simmons remembers the situation with mixed feelings. His initial anger has been tempered by time and the responsibilities he has faced as a coach, first with English club Hull and then with Penrith. 'I was upset at the time,' he says. 'Really upset. I didn't think I had played too badly against Canterbury, even though we lost, and I was not expecting to be dropped even though Phil had spoken to us the week before.'

Simmons admits that being dropped just sharpened his determination to get back into first grade and taught him a lesson he put away to use when he became a coach. 'When Phil originally dropped me, I was dirty but I still trained hard and did everything that was required. I look back now and see things a bit differently than I did then. I probably deserved to be dropped. Now I'm a coach, I look back and see that a coach has to make hard decisions, and if he doesn't he is not doing his own job properly. I'm in that position myself now and I've got to make some myself. I just thought at the time that Phil could have given me more of a hand to get my spot back. He could have gone more into what I was doing wrong and how to fix it.'

With time to re-evaluate a difficult decision, Simmons even admits that Gould was probably right in his assessment of the Penrith front-row. 'There was not room for all three of us (Simmons, Kelly and Tunks) in the side,' he says. 'We were getting on a bit and getting a little slower underfoot. I just thought I could have been given a couple of programs to go and do to overcome whatever problems were in my game. That didn't happen. He just called me over and said I was in the seconds.'

Simmons says that as a coach, he now goes out of his way to break the news gently to any player he drops. 'I take them aside and tell them the reasons and I show them videos to explain why they are being left out of the side.'

'After 12 years in first grade it is always going to be hard for anyone to accept being dropped and I was no different when Gus told me,' Simmons says. 'We had been mates since he had been playing at Penrith. There were no hard feelings in the end and Gus helped me win a premiership and that is something I will never forget. The second year (1991) we got on well. To tell you the truth I could have handled the situation a bit better as well. Things were strained for a while but I came back from coaching in England to be his assistant coach at Penrith and when he left to join Easts he helped steer me into the first grade job.'

To Gould, dropping Royce was hard. But no harder than dropping Tunks, who had changed clubs to help Gould strengthen Penrith. 'All of the concentration was on Royce being dropped. That was because he was a Penrith player of long standing, a former Test hooker and the team captain. But I felt sorry for Tunks as well. No-one at Penrith cared as much though. Royce was dropped because he wasn't playing well at the time. He had become set in his ways and the approach he had to the game and was not changing. He was in a rut. I don't think his game had matured the way it should have over the years. Previous coaches like Tim Sheens and Ron Willey were mates of his. Perhaps something should have been said to him earlier.'

The furore over Simmons being in reserve grade gathered sympathetic support from a group of peripheral minor sponsors, whose efforts had the effect of inconveniencing Gould as much as possible in the years to come. At one stage in 1993 the sponsors campaigned to have Gould sacked and Simmons take over. The attempt was quickly put down by Penrith's management but it at least indicates the seriousness with which Simmons' demotion was seen.

The immediate upheaval in 1990 of Simmons being dropped was quickly lost in the revitalising of the club's premiership challenge. Penrith won six of the next seven games to move permanently into the top three. A season that had started indifferently was back on target.

The opening two rounds of the premiership saw the Panthers lose 19–10 to Parramatta followed by a 24–10 win against Balmain. The Balmain game saw Alexander move to fullback in an effort to take greater advantage of his attacking skill and give him more room to move. The disadvantage of the Balmain game was that Alexander was sent off for a high tackle after he collided with Tigers centre James Grant who chipped and chased, a minute before half-time.

As worrying as it was for all concerned in the Penrith camp

at the time, the incident turned out to be a bonus. Alexander was quickly cleared of the head-high tackle charge by the judiciary. Convincing video evidence and the presence of Gus Gould Q.C. (temporary) quickly convinced the tribunal that Alexander's clash with Grant had been accidental. For Gould it was the chance to put into practice the legal skills he had picked up during his two years of doing law at the University of NSW. 'I couldn't believe how good he was,' Alexander said later. 'He was better than any solicitor could have been and I was exonerated.'

In different circumstances, with different priorities Gould has frequently displayed the verbal finesse, mental agility and motivating speeches to influence and sway opinions. His carefully constructed speeches to the State of Origin teams were highlights of the preparation before matches against Queensland. Before one game he took the players to the Sydney Football Stadium the night before a State of Origin match and had them stand in the positions they would occupy at kick-off in the game. Before another State of Origin match he sent the players home to be with their families so they could fully understand how important the series was to them and the rest of the rugby league supporters in New South Wales.

There was another example in club football. In 1990 Penrith was scheduled to play at Newcastle's International Sports Centre against a Newcastle side that was chasing a semi-final place after winning nine matches in a row. A full house—and it was—meant 30,000 Newcastle supporters urging their side on and making life as miserable as possible for an opposing side.

When Penrith arrived in Newcastle by bus, Gould abandoned the normal routine by taking the players to the beach instead. They walked along the sand, had their team talk and took the time to absorb every word their coach was saying away from the intimidating atmosphere of the claustrophobic Newcastle Stadium dressing rooms.

To increase the pressure on the opposition, Newcastle had also declared the day as a salute to the men and women who had worked so tirelessly to reclaim the city after the devastating earthquake that had caused millions of dollars in damage. Before the match started there was to be a ceremony for the earthquake workers, which would further inspire the crowd.

At the beach, Gould was dealing out his own motivational tactics as he talked to the Penrith players.

'Fuck the crowd, fuck the earthquake, fuck Newcastle and fuck the Knights. Fuck them all. We're here to win a football match. They want to see us beaten. Go out there and spoil their day for them,' he barked. Penrith players listened, followed his tactics to perfection and won 20–6.

Gould's verbal tirade against Newcastle and its players and population was not personal. Like all of Australia he was saddened by the plight of Newcastle's population and the damage they suffered. But he knew that Newcastle's rebuilding would not be influenced one way or the other by the result of a football match. The result of that football match however was vital to him and his players.

It was not all flamboyance and the unexpected that set Gould's coaching apart. He was also methodical enough to call the weather bureau before a match against Brisbane in the third last round in 1990 at Penrith Park. Told that a wind change was expected late in the afternoon, Gould told his players to defy convention and run against the breeze in the first half if they won the toss. The players hung on in the first half and came at a tiring Brisbane strongly in the second with the wind at their backs for an 18–2 win.

After 22 rounds Penrith had won 15 games, lost six and

drawn one to be sitting on 31 points in a tight scramble at the top of the competition table. Canberra were minor premiers on 33 points on for and against from Brisbane, also on 33 points, with Manly 30 points and Balmain 28 making up the five. Balmain sneaked in with a 12–4 win against Newcastle in a play-off for fifth.

Gould's Penrith's side by semi-final time barely resembled the team that had started the season. Props Peter Kelly and Peter Tunks had departed for most of the season with serious injuries. Fittler, after being held back for the opening few games, had been chosen in first grade for the fifth round clash with Brisbane at Lang Park. He scored a smart try from dummy half and was in first grade to stay. Just as importantly, the team had been re-aligned to suit the circumstances. Greg Alexander's stint at fullback was over. He returned to half-back in the match against Manly at Brookvale in round 20. Royce Simmons was back as hooker after continued substantial form in reserve grade, taking over from former Parramatta player Paul Taylor. David Greene had emerged as a safe fullback, Fittler was in the centres, Steve Carter at five-eighth.

Alexander had recovered spectacularly from a disaster in the round 19 clash with Balmain at Leichhardt Oval under lights. In the first half his poor pass to winger Alan McIndoe had gone loose and been kicked ahead by Balmain centre Tim Brasher. The ball rebounded from a goal post to James Grant who scored a try that meant a 9–4 win to the Tigers and in time meant the difference between fifth place and missing the semi-finals.

Gould's tirade against Alexander in the dressing room at half-time, possibly influenced by the fact that his old antagonist Warren Ryan was coaching Balmain, lifted the paint from the walls.

He accused Alexander of unprofessionalism and lacking the discipline to be a real leader and contributor to the team when the going got tough. Team-mates watched open-mouthed as Gould berated Alexander in a voice that could be heard a mile away, telling him that he was in debt to every player in the side for his mistake in the first half and he expected it to be repaid.

'We're going to ride home on your shoulders for the rest of this competition and you bloody well better be up to it,' Gould said. 'From now on you'll be calling all the plays in matches and whether we win or lose will be up to you. If you don't get it together, we lose.'

Alexander later credited the blast as being the cross roads of his career, making him determined to become a more consistent player and the reason he was appointed first grade captain in 1991.

'We were never one of the popular picks to win the premiership from the moment the ball was kicked in the first game,' Gould remembers. 'We were always in touch with the top three but we were still always somewhere between 16–1 and 20–1 with bookmakers. Probably our best performance of the season was against Canberra in the 17th round. We went into the match as 5–1 outsiders and missing Mark Geyer, Peter Kelly, Brad Fittler and Greg Alexander we won 23–2.'

Into the semi-finals Penrith supporters held their breath. The club had lost its only three semi-final appearances—one with Tim Sheens in 1985 and two with Ron Willey in 1989. Would 1990 bring a different result or would it be more losses and further promises of potential for the future?

Penrith allayed any fears about their fragility under Gould by winning the first semi-final 26–16 over Brisbane in easy fashion after leading 18–2 at half-time and 24–2 early in the second half. 'I was not surprised that we won so easily. We had beaten Brisbane in the Channel 10 Cup and in both premiership rounds. They just had no answers to us that year,' Gould said.

FROM PLAYER TO COACH

The next game was against Canberra, coached by former Penrith stalwart Tim Sheens and looking for back-to-back premierships after beating Balmain in 1989 in extra time. The winner would go into the grand final and wait to play the winner of the loser v Brisbane clash in the final.

Before the match Penrith players hardened their resolve in a team get-together in the dressing room with the players linking arms and shedding tears at the emotion of the moment. 'I had tears in my eyes as well from the spirit they were all showing. As they walked out the door I said to myself: "This one is as good as over. They won't lose",' the coach recalls.

Penrith did not lose—but it was tense. The final score was Penrith 30 Canberra 12 but only after Canberra had led 12–10 with five minutes of normal time to play. Alexander kicked a goal to level the score and in extra time, the Panthers scored another three tries.

Gould could only mumble replies to questions from the media in the dressing room after the match as his own composure showed signs of cracking. After 24 years of trying, Penrith was in its first grand final in first grade.

A week later Canberra clinically disposed of Brisbane 34–2, establishing themselves as Penrith's final hurdle to the 1990 premiership.

The two weeks leading up to the grand final were an explosion of celebration. Whether that spirit of celebration was premature and eroded the will-to-win in the side or was an incidental part of a grand final build-up remains open to argument. Penrith celebrated hard and long. The district came to vibrant life as it delighted in the pride of the achievement of the first grade side had generated.

The main street became a brown and white strip as shopkeepers decorated their premises in the club's colours. For the gastronomically inclined there were brown and white doughnuts

Good as GOULD

and brown and white bread. Everywhere there was unending debate about the Big One. The grand final. How it would be played? Who would win? Players when they appeared in public were feted as heroes.

Gould could have curtailed the availability of the side to its supporters and kept them in cotton wool for the two weeks, away from distractions. Instead he chose to let them be involved in a motorcade, public appearances and the media's demands. As a former Penrith player and resident he realised more than most exactly how important the success of the team could be to the area and its supporters.

Penrith's chief executive Roger Cowan said: 'The two weeks before the grand final was an extraordinary period. Penrith just lit up. The place really came alive.'

Gould made a point, however, of playing down the constant demands for player access and remains convinced to this day that the instant celebrity status of the players was not a problem in the grand final lead up. 'The place did go berserk,' he said. 'There is no doubt about that. But I think we handled it very well. I don't consider the excitement of the occasion to have been a problem.' Mark Geyer does. Of the scene in the dressing room after the win in the major semi-final he says: 'I was screaming myself hoarse, shouting over and over: "This is the greatest day of my life!" In hindsight, I think it was there and then that we lost the edge which had made us such a competitive force in a demanding season. We'd made the grand final, yet by the way we were carrying on after the final, you'd have sworn that we had won the premiership. All of it was premature.'

The big day was not structured to suit the already jaded nerves of a predominantly young team making its first grand final appearance. Extra time in the reserve grade grand final followed by the planned pre-match entertainment running behind time as well combined to put the schedule around 30 minutes behind the clock.

It was a malfunction that should never have occurred. But it did. The influence of the delays on a Penrith side running high on emotion and finely tuned to start the game on time can only be imagined but the players believed it had had a bearing on what happened.

'The delay was the same for both sides but at least Canberra had been in a grand final before. Officials kept coming in and saying: "Another five minutes",' Gould recalled. 'After the third or fourth time your minds starts to wander, people start to get cranky. When you weigh it all up you probably lose nothing on the field but you're feeling nervous enough as it is without that sort of problem.'

Canberra jumped to a 12–nil lead in the opening minutes of the grand final, after half Ricky Stuart laid on tries for winger John Ferguson and Laurie Daley and the match seemed as good as over despite a strengthening of Penrith's defence as the players recovered from the onslaught.

The Panthers got back to trail 12–10 after Alexander put Brad Fittler in for a try just before half-time and Paul Smith for another one seven minutes into the second half.

But Canberra moved to 18–10 in the second half when replacement winger Matthew Wood scored and a late try from Alexander still left Penrith trailing, 18–14, when the full-time siren sounded.

To win the grand final, Penrith would have had to defy the tradition that teams have to serve their apprenticeships by losing one first. Against their will, Penrith had added their own name to the list of teams whose experiences proved the adage.

The loss did not stop celebrations by the players and supporters. They were disappointed but they partied like winners. 'My wife found me sitting in front of the garden outside the leagues club in the middle of the night, dirty on the world,' Simmons would recall.

Coach Gould accepted that losing the grand final was part of a learning curve. 'We came back into the match when we had to after trailing 12–nil early,' he said. 'We had all pulled together through the season and we stuck together when we lost. We knew we could come back and win one.'

PHIL GOULD'S Reflections on
PENRITH'S NEAR MISS

When I arrived at Penrith in 1990 I was in a state of confusion. I had been planning to be coaching Canterbury in 1990 and all of my strategies and programs were in place for a club I was no longer with. Instead I was at Penrith, and to say the least, fairly emotionally strained. It had been a difficult period in 1989 dealing with Peter Moore. In hindsight I did not handle the situation very well at all. I never stood a chance against the relationships he had built up with the media. I would have been better off at the time just letting things roll and leaving under my own steam. But all that was in the past.

My job was now with my old club Penrith. The Panthers had shown potential and it was always my thought that they could be competitive in 1990. We had a very enjoyable year with very few hiccups. The most disappointing part of the season was having to drop Royce Simmons and Peter Tunks but we all got over that. I think it might have made Royce a better player and a stronger person. He tells me nowadays that it has made him a better coach for having gone through it all as a player. I was in the early stages of my coaching career and I guess it was really at Penrith that I started to develop the training techniques that I use today. I had good senior players like Simmons, Peter Kelly and Chris Mortimer, who was in the final year of his career after joining Penrith from Canterbury. He was a great inspiration to the club and of great assistance to me. We made the semi-finals in all three grades and the future looked very bright.

Good as GOULD

After only four or five rounds in 1990 I said to Roger Cowan, the Leagues Club boss, that whatever we achieved in that year we would improve on in 1991. I put the cross bar up a lot for myself because we finished second in 1990 so anything less than a premiership in 1991 would not have been acceptable. The day of the 1990 grand final we played and lost very gallantly to Canberra. Things just did not go our way. Canberra's Ricky Stuart had the ball on a string. His kicks would go over the sideline where Greg Alexander's would bounce in the field of play. We were in with a great chance of winning with only ten minutes to play when we trailed by only two points 12–10. But we dropped a ball on the second tackle of a set play and the wrong man picked it up from Penrith's point of view because Laurie Daley set up a try. We stood in the middle of the football field after full time and the players looked devastated, especially Royce. At that stage I'm sure he thought he had lost his chance to go out as a winner. There were a lot of tears but I pulled them all together and we went up on the dais to get our silver medals. I said to them all as we gathered on the field: 'Next year we'll come back and replace these silver ones with gold.' It was at that moment, standing distressed at the Sydney Football Stadium as a beaten grand final side, that we made a commitment and began our preparation for the grand final of 1991.

Penrith's Greatest Day

With 40 minutes to play in the 1991 grand final, Penrith's recurring dream of a first grade premiership was again on the verge of turning into a nightmare.

After a consistent and dedicated season of endeavour, Penrith were again playing Canberra in a grand final and were again in trouble.

Ahead 6–nil early after a try from Royce Simmons, Penrith had slipped to trail 12–6 by half-time following two tries by Matthew Wood—the first from a chip by half Ricky Stuart, the second after Bradley Clyde, Mal Meninga and Laurie Daley had combined.

Half-time could not come quickly enough for a Penrith side feeling the pressure and in need of revival. By the time Phil Gould had finished with the players during the half-time break the players were desperate to get back on the field. It was safer.

Playing against Canberra was formidable but not as frightening as staying in the dressing room with Gould, who had forcefully put his message across that the team was not playing well. 'I did rip into them. We had gone off our game plan and lost our way,' Gould says. 'We were going well until Royce scored an early try and we led 6–nil. We got caught up in razzle dazzle after that and tried to match Canberra at running the ball adventurously. We went from ahead 6–nil to trailing 12–6 and going backwards.'

Those in the dressing room accustomed to hearing Gould's

precise analytical speeches at half-time, were stunned at the anger in his voice. 'I hope you're all having a good time out there,' he said. 'I know the television people are happy with the way you're playing because it looks good. And the crowd thinks it looks spectacular. But if you keep playing the way you are, you'll be sitting out there in the middle of the ground again at fulltime crying your eyes out because you will be losers again.

'What about doing it my fucking way? The way we've been doing it all year. The way that got us into this grand final in the first place. Take the ball up for the full six tackles, kick for the corners and let's get back into this match.'

Gould reckoned that the performance of the 1991 side in the opening 40 minutes of the grand final threatened to duplicate the effort of every other team Penrith had produced that had manoeuvred itself into a position to win something.

'I told them that they were going to be losers as well unless they started playing and performing the way we had trained, the way we had planned and the way we had played all year in getting ourselves into the grand final.'

For the next forty minutes the Panthers went out and played the way they had been coached to perform. Carefully, deliberately and with neat precision Penrith clawed back into the match, opening up the chance of celebrating its silver anniversary 25 years in the premiership by carrying off the silver J J Giltinan Shield and silver Winfield Cup.

Season 1991 is one that Gould remembers for its consistency and real purpose. The heart break of the previous year when so much hard work had ended so disappointingly in a grand final loss had healed.

As often happens, the mending of Penrith's broken confidence was the strongest part of the club's reformed character.

In 22 preliminary rounds, Penrith won 17 games, drew one

(against Newcastle 18–all in the second round) and lost only four, Wests 12–8, Canberra 20–nil, Brisbane 20–12 and Cronulla 12–12.

The club finished on 35 premiership points and took its first minor premiership ahead of Manly and Norths (both 29 points), Canberra on 28 and Wests sneaking in on 27 points after beating Canterbury 19–14 in a play-off.

The season did not start without a considerable jolt of controversy from both Gould and the NSWRL. For the first time the controversial draft system was in operation. It lasted just the one season before being defeated in the courts by players and coaches opposed to its limitations, but while it was in operation, Penrith picked up former Test prop Paul Dunn from Canterbury as the club's 15th selection and Western Suburbs winger Graham Mackay as their 31st choice.

The draft allowed teams to recruit players on a roster system based on where the club finished the previous year. It was in reverse order with the wooden spooners getting first choice and the premiers last.

Penrith's choices were sound despite their belated chance. Dunn's experience was vital after Penrith had lost Peter Kelly and Peter Tunks from the previous season with injuries and both players retired. Mackay was not well known but under Gould quickly developed into a tough and resourceful winger who could kick goals, who went on to play for Australia in a Test against Papua New Guinea and win selection in the 1992 world cup team.

There were some faces missing from the side that had gone to the grand final the previous year. The wonderfully durable Chris Mortimer, Peter Kelly, Peter Tunks, Paul Taylor and Alan McIndoe had all departed. Mortimer and Tunks would continue their careers with English clubs. Kelly was retiring because of consistent back trouble, Taylor was going back to continue his career in country football and McIndoe was rejoining his old club Illawarra.

Gould handed Penrith a jolt as well by selecting Greg Alexander as the first grade captain in place of Royce Simmons. Gould made a tough decision based on the needs of the club both present and future, irrespective of what his personal thoughts might have been on an issue.

To Gould, Royce was an affable and durable soldier who had toiled hard and willingly for the club for 14 years. His loyalty was unquestioned but the very attributes he brought to the club were a double edged sword. After so long with Penrith there was no guarantee that Simmons could automatically command a first grade position, week in and week out. It was better to give the captaincy to someone whose inclusion in first grade was automatic. Someone like Alexander.

'It had taken some time but I really thought that Alexander was ready for the captaincy of the side,' Gould remembers. 'He had been on a Kangaroo tour and come back a more experienced and more mature player. Royce was in the last year of his contract and I was not convinced that he would play a lot of first grade football. He was at an age when players tend to get injured more and take longer to recover. They find it harder to hold their form.'

As things turned out in 1991 Gould's expectations were fulfilled. Simmons did not play much first grade in the preliminary rounds—only six matches as a selected player and five from the interchange bench—and Alexander proved an able captain. 'Losing the captaincy did not come as such a big shock to me but it was still disappointing,' Simmons says. 'I could see it coming. I knew it was my last year and I was prepared for whatever happened.'

The decision had more affect on Alexander. He was too embarrassed to confront Simmons about the switch.

FROM PLAYER TO COACH

Eventually Simmons approached Alexander, saying: ' "There is no problem. I'll give you 100 per cent support. If you want any help just call." Greg had given me great support when I was captain and I was determined to give him the same.'

Penrith's year opened worryingly when they led Brisbane 16–2 in the second quarter of the Lotto Challenge before losing 20–16. The result meant that Penrith had lost the finals of pre-season competitions in 1990 and 1991 as well as the 1991 grand final—three key-match defeats in 12 months. It was a worry but Gould cooled the apprehension by saying the record would be improved by the end of the season. With almost detached professionalism, Penrith opened the season in convincing fashion with a 32–10 win against Illawarra before drawing 18–all with Newcastle. Five weeks of wins against Souths (36–22), Canterbury (26–6), Cronulla (17–10), Balmain (14–nil) and Easts (32–6) followed, meaning the Panthers were undefeated for the opening seven rounds. A tough and bruising 12–8 loss to Wests, now coached by Gould's coaching nemesis Warren Ryan interrupted the sequence but a 32–8 win against Manly and 14–12 against St George refloated Penrith's campaign.

The 20–nil loss to Canberra was due to both sides missing key players to State of Origin commitments and Penrith having young hooker Darren Tuite sent off. In the reserve grade match of the same round Simmons, who had a shocking year with injuries, had to be helped from the field after suffering ankle ligament damage.

The performance record of the Penrith side did not come easily. Gould had long ago summed up the potential in his team and knew they could win the premiership if they remained totally focused. 'The only problems we had in getting to the grand final were the problems we created for ourselves,' he says. 'I always felt we would be there based on the way the side was playing and the talent we had available but we had to keep the pressure on ourselves and not slacken off.'

Two weeks before the end of the preliminary rounds Gould spoke to Simmons secretly, saying he was assured of selection in every first grade side for the rest of the year, starting with Balmain at Penrith Park. Penrith won the match 41–12 and thousands of supporters from both sides stayed behind after the fulltime siren to see Simmons do a lap of honour to commemorate his last game at the ground. Even when things had looked to be at their blackest for Simmons because of injuries and form, Gould had never really lost faith in the tough little hooker. He had always intended bringing him back into first grade for the big matches. He just wanted to be perfectly sure that Simmons was ready to handle the challenge before he went public with his decision.

'What I did was all for the good and I know Royce will appreciate it in years to come. It was all about getting him ready for that one big game, the grand final,' said Gould. 'There were times when he probably got angry and frustrated about what was going on. But I just had to be sure in my own mind that when we got down to the semi-finals, that he would be 100 per cent fit to play and last as long as he was needed.'

In the semi-finals, Penrith took the express lane to the grand final, beating North Sydney 16–14 in the major semi-final. Penrith led 12–nil at half time and were comfortably placed. Replacement Penrith fullback Tony Xuereb became the 'X Factor' when he threw an intercept pass near his own line and then miscalculated the velocity of a Norths kick into the Panthers' in goal. On both occasions Norths scored tries to open up the game again. Finally a penalty goal from Alexander gave Penrith their winning margin and a place in the grand final for the second successive year.

Canberra qualified for its third successive grand final by

beating Norths 30–14, setting the scene for the second meeting in two years of the same sides to decide the grand final.

This time the fanfare at Penrith was more subdued. The best wishes and hopes of the local businessmen and club supporters was still directed towards the Panthers but the public outpouring of joy was put on hold until after the grand final.

For the big game Gould decided on a different approach. Maintaining his reputation for meticulous research, Gould pondered the fact through numerous sessions with a video player, that Manly, Wests, and Norths had all led Canberra in their matches during the finals series before being beaten. He decided that the opposing clubs had all taken the field pumped to the eyeballs with emotion and had used up their full supply quickly, giving Canberra the chance to come storming back into the game. Gould told his players to simply go the same pace as Canberra in the match from the opening whistle. If Canberra went slowly, so would Penrith. If Canberra stepped up the pace of the match, so would Penrith.

To sidestep the pressure building up at Penrith, Gould and his players spent the night before the grand final at a motel in Sydney. The grand final was a short drive away from the motel but it represented a bridge the club had been trying to cross for 25 years . . .

And now here it was half time and the dream was threatening to go up in smoke again. How many chances does a team get to win a premiership? If this one got away pride and prestige in the Penrith area would be irrefutably damaged. Supporters could forgive one lost grand final. To lose a second one after dominating the premiership all season and winning the minor premiership by six points would be classified as a massive choke under the ultimate sporting pressure.

'At least they realised at half-time they had buggered up a

Good as GOULD

good thing,' Gould recalls. 'So they set about fixing it up.'

Down 12–6 at half-time, coincidentally the same score Penrith trailed Canberra at half-time in the previous year's grand final, the Panthers prepared themselves for the fightback. Kicking with accuracy and tackling with venom, Penrith gradually swung the ascendancy back towards themselves. A feud that would continue to ignite for years to come would be born in the second half of that 1991 grand final.

Referee Bill Harrigan sin-binned Mark Geyer for 10 minutes over his outburst when a try by Penrith winger Paul Smith was disallowed. Smith crossed in the south western corner of the Sydney Football Stadium after Penrith had secured a loose ball. As Harrigan was about to award the try, which video replays showed was scored without a hint of impropriety, touch judge Martin Weekes ran onto the field to report Penrith prop Paul Clarke for using a swinging arm to the face and head of Canberra's Mark Bell.

It was a humiliating mistake by Weekes' who had named the wrong man. The player involved was Brad Fittler not Paul Clarke, at the time though the exact identity of the culprit was immaterial. Harrigan, listening to Weekes, astonishingly disallowed Smith's try that would have levelled the score at 12–all. Even more stunningly Harrigan waved Geyer to the sin bin for 10 minutes.

In two almost simultaneous decisions Harrigan could have ripped the heart out of Penrith's challenge by denying them a try and cutting the troops to 12 men. Geyer said later that he felt desperately alone sitting in the sin bin knowing that his recklessness might have cost Penrith the grand final. He was so nauseous, he wanted to be physically sick. He also fumed at the decision by Harrigan to send him to the sin bin. The more he fumed the angrier and less approachable he became.

After the match Gould was asked by a journalist if he had

considered replacing Geyer because he had gone to the sin bin. 'Sure I thought about it,' Gould said. 'But who was going to get close enough to tell him.'

Geyer made amends when he finally returned to the playing field to a score that had not changed in his absence. Penrith still trailed 12–6.

He linked up in a move with Alexander, Barwick and Fittler for Brad Izzard to score. Alexander's conversion made it 12–all.

Then with six minutes to play Alexander broke the deadlock with a wobbly field goal that struggled desperately before falling over the cross bar.

It was around that time that the grand final went into some romantic time warp designed by a god who believed that champion footballers should be sent out as champions. The gods decreed that Royce Simmons, Mr Penrith Rugby League, the man who had been the backbone of the side for more than a decade of mostly pitiful returns, the man who had been dropped the previous year and played in a losing grand final side, who had been stripped of the captaincy at the start of the season, was about to be rewarded for all those setbacks. Having scored the first try, Simmons found chance giving him the honour of scoring the last one as well, the try that would carry the Panthers into history.

Canberra's Scot Gale, who had replaced half Ricky Stuart in the side, took a line drop out and kicked short. The ball bounced freakishly to chest height and seemed to hang in the air until the giant Geyer came thundering towards it at full pace out wide. He looked and saw Simmons in support and got the ball to him quickly for Simmons to score. Alexander's conversion established a seven point buffer of 19–12 and Canberra were out of time and finished.

'I don't think I have ever enjoyed a moment as much as I did when Royce scored that try,' Gould says. 'It was really special. It meant so much to everyone.' The players rushed to embrace Simmons and tears stared to flow. Later other fluids would flow copiously from the leagues' club taps and wine bottles as celebrations raged for days. But the initial single moment when Penrith realised victory was finally in their grasp was celebrated with Royce.

Accepting the Winfield Cup and JJ Giltinan Shield Alexander declared: 'This has got to be the best feeling of my life. I know how much the other blokes (Canberra) feel. Gus said to us before the game, there's not a group of blokes that deserve to win this more than we do. We've all grown up together, we've lived in each other's pockets since we were kids. That's the best feeling of all. To be a team member. This is not only for us, it's for the Penrith district. They stuck behind us for all those years and now we've finally won it. The bloke that lifted us was Gus. He is a genius. I don't know how to explain Gus. When we were down 12–6 at half-time he somehow lifted us again and made us believe we could do it.'

Simmons took his turn to speak and rocked the crowd with his honesty. 'This is the greatest day of my sporting life. I want to have a schooner with everyone of you,' he said.

Penrith quickly began their redefinition of the words 'party' and 'celebration' as drinks flowed for days after the grand final win. The morning after the grand final, players, spectators and partygoers were asleep on the lawn and in the gardens near the leagues club.

Realising the vast amount of money on hand from the happy supporters, armed bandits raided Penrith Leagues Club, escaping with an estimated $400,000 the day after the grand final. Despite that drama, pubs in Penrith were full to overflowing; the match was replayed over and over again.

To Penrith the job was done. The grand final had been won. Mission accomplished. But there was one little detail they had overlooked. In 1987 the International Rugby League board had agreed to stage a world club championship between the northern and southern premiership winners. It was scheduled for a week after the Sydney grand final in England. The concept of a world club championship had struggled for acceptance in Australia and grand final winners had not fared as well as their reputations had suggested they would. The primary reason was that teams that won the Sydney premiership regarded it as the ultimate achievement for the season and would be off celebrating immediately without giving a second thought to playing another game.

Penrith were no different. For a week Gould wondered if he could even get a team together to make the trip to England to play Wigan in Liverpool. Players were nowhere to be found. The pubs, the clubs, were the domain of the players. He would round up a couple and they would disappear as soon as he turned his back to look for more.

Gould's detection processes were not helped by the fact that he was very competitive himself when it came to celebrating the grand final win. At one stage Penrith inquired about whether they could pull out of the match but were told they had to make the trip.

Finally a deal was made between the players and Gould, after enough of the team was rounded up to make a quorum.

The deal was if they made the trip they could continue celebrating until they arrived in England. Once in England they would have to do some moderate training and stay sober until after the match. The deal was struck. Some players though would try and slip through the net . . .

Mark Geyer was ruled out injured. 'MG waited until the last minute and then rang and said he could not find his passport. He knew there was not enough time to get a new one before we were supposed to leave. There was no option but to leave him at home,' Gould says. 'About an hour later Greg Alexander rang to say he had lost his passport and could not make the trip. 'I said: "You're an hour too late Brandy! MG's already used that excuse. See you at the airport." In the end we were pulling players out of pubs to make up the numbers.'

Gould remembers the challenge for the world club championship as the most frivolous and wasted journey of his life. 'None of us wanted to be there. We got off the plane somewhere in England and then we got on a bus for hours until we arrived in Liverpool,' he recalls. 'Then we were taken to a dark and unpleasant hotel. It was depressing to be there in the cold weather and in an area where no-one knew anything or cared anything about rugby league. We were virtually ignored by the people who were staging the match.'

Staging the game at Anfield Stadium in Liverpool, a city fanatical about its soccer team, was another of the English Rugby League's periodic flights of fantasy about trying to spread the code further afield than its roots in Yorkshire and Lancashire.

The Penrith players stuck by their word and stayed off the drink until the match was played. Despite the limited preparation and reluctance to play at all, Penrith fared better than the 21–7 loss to Wigan suggests. Wigan were keen to win and had trained and prepared accordingly. French referee Alain Sablayrolles penalised Penrith 14–7 in the first half and the result looked predictable.

'We were down 10–nil after about 12 minutes,' Gould says. 'I looked at the Penrith officials and said "We've come a long way to get handled like this. We could have stayed at home and this referee would still have penalised us!"'

Despite the absence of five players from the winning grand final side—Simmons, Fittler, who was with the Australian team in New Guinea, Geyer, Paul Smith and Col Bentley, who had other commitments—the Panthers did as well as they could. Wigan's winning margin was inflated by a late intercept try, and six goals from Frano Botica.

The loss was just about the final straw for Gould. His temper and good intentions exhausted by the fact that he was thousands of kilometres away from where he wanted to be in Australia's warm sunshine, he took drastic action. Marching into the nearest travel agency he requested a seat on the first plane back to Sydney. He got one.

It cost him $3000. At the time it seemed like a cheap price to pay to get away from England's gloom.

Had Gould known he was heading back to a season that would scar his soul forever, he might not have been in such a rush. Ahead lay the death of a player and then a dreadful disintegration of a football club, the story already told in these pages of the Ben Alexander tragedy and its aftermath. For Gould the only ray of sunshine lay east and further down the track in a fortuitous 1995 move to Eastern Suburbs (Sydney City Roosters).

PHIL GOULD'S Reflections on
A YEAR TO REMEMBER

From the first day we returned to training in preparation for season 1991, there was a feeling we could win the premiership. It was a year the side played with great determination and enthusiasm every week.

I have always said that to win a premiership you have to do things right over a long period of time. It's not just a matter of turning up on grand final day and playing.

It was a tribute to the team that it never relented at any stage from what was necessary to prepare each week to get the job done.

1991 was the year Penrith came of age as a football club. Supporters had waited a long time for success and that we got it is a highlight of my life—to know I was not only an integral part of it, but I was also on hand to enjoy it.

There were many people at the club who worked very hard for a long time and endured major disappointments and criticisms over the years. All of it was forgotten on a day that will long live in my memory as we carried the J J Giltinan Shield around the stadium.

I drove back to my Penrith house with my mate Ross Seymour after the grand final to get ready to join the players at the Leagues Club. What we didn't know was that there were road blocks set half a kilometre in all directions from the club. The sea of people made it impossible for anyone, including the team bus, to get access to the club.

FROM PLAYER TO COACH

The same thing happened to Ross and me. We had no way of getting near the place. It was pandemonium.

Eventually getting there, Ross and I were able to disguise ourselves while we walked through the foyer and up the stairs to the main entertainment area where the celebrations were being held. All we did to hide was pull our jumpers over our heads but it was enough.

It was a funny experience walking through a crowd of highly excited supporters unrecognised. I think if we'd been recognised in the hysteria we would never have made it to the club. We would have been killed in the crush.

What followed was a night of great celebration. I was especially pleased for players in that Penrith side who had grabbed the chance to show what they could achieve. Players who might have had little recognition at other clubs and had now won the game's ultimate prize—players such as Paul Clarke and Greg Barwick, as well as long service players like John Cartwright, Col van der Voort, Greg Alexander, Royce Simmons, and the up and comers such as Steve Carter and Brad Fittler.

I recall being at the team hotel the morning of the grand final and watching the under-23's match on TV. They were talking history and mentioned Mark Bugden (Canterbury) being one of the few, if not the only, hooker to score a try in a grand final. Royce Simmons turned to me: 'Is there any chance I might score a try?' I replied: 'You're a million to one!'

As it turned out Royce scored *two*—two tries and won the game for us.

The achievement that day was the culmination of two years of very hard work. The club developed a powerful pattern of play, matched with great skills. Greg Alexander confirmed to me that he was one of the best half-backs of all time. His performance on grand final day probably went unheralded by most

Good as GOULD

media people, some of whom over the years had been critical that he had not reached the heights they expected.

On grand final day 1991, there was no better half-back in the rugby league world.

BOMBING AWAY: Phil Gould pressures the opposition with a towering kick in his playing days with Penrith. *Photo Rugby League Week*

SKILFUL: Gould, who possessed exceptional ball-distributing skills as a player, off-loads in a game for Canterbury-Bankstown. *Photo Fairfax Photo Library*

SANDWICHED: Gould draws in three defenders while playing for Newtown against Eastern Suburbs. *Photo Fairfax Photo Library*

CRUNCH: Gould on the receiving end of a hard but fair tackle while playing for South Sydney against Balmain. *Photo News Limited*

ON THE BOIL: A confident Gould weighs it up and steps off his left foot as he prepares to take on the opposition's defence in his last season as a player, with the South Sydney club. *Photo Fairfax Photo Library*

PRECISE EXECUTION: Gould drops the ball in readiness to stab-kick it with his right boot when playing with South Sydney. *Photo Fairfax Photo Library*

EMOTION: Gould in a rare expression of jubilation during Canterbury-Bankstown's 16-12 win over South Sydney in 1988 at the Sydney Football Stadium. *Photo News Limited*

MASTER GREETS PUPIL: Warren Ryan congratulating Gould, whom he coached as a player with Newtown and Canterbury-Bankstown and later recruited as his reserve grade coach at Canterbury-Bankstown, after Balmain lost the 1988 grand final to the Bulldogs. *Photo Fairfax Photo Library*

SWEET VICTORY: Canterbury-Bankstown boss Peter 'Bullfrog' Moore (right) and Brandon Lee, who played with the premiership-winning team, sharing a moment of the celebrations with Gould after the 1988 grand final. *Photo Rugby League Week*

WINNERS ARE GRINNERS: Jason Alchin (left) and Paul Langmack chair Gould from the Sydney Football Stadium after Canterbury-Bankstown's victory over Balmain in the 1988 grand final. *Photo News Limited*

THAT WINNING FEELING: Penrith players Graham Mackay (left) and Paul 'Nobby' Clarke hoist high Gould at the Sydney Football Stadium after the Panthers' first premiership win in 1991. *Photo Fairfax Photo Library*

TALKING TACTICS: New South Wales players (from left) Brad Fittler, Laurie Daley, Ben Elias and Ricky Stuart discussing the game plan with Gould before a State of Origin clash with Queensland. *Photo Fairfax Photo Library*

INSTRUCTIONAL: Gould, flanked by two of his trump players Brad Fittler (left) and Laurie Daley in the background, calling for the rehearsal of a set move from the remainder of his troops during NSW State of Origin team training. *Photo Fairfax Photo Library*

DELEGATING AUTHORITY: Gould signalling his requirements from the NSW players in the build-up to a State of Origin clash with Queensland. *Photo News Limited*

DO AS I SAY: Gould laying down the law as the NSW State of Origin team assembles for training. *Photo Fairfax Photo Library*

SOAKING IT UP: Chief playmaker Ricky Stuart absorbing Gould's instructions as NSW prepare for a State of Origin game against Queensland. *Photo Fairfax Library*

THE ENFORCERS: Tough-tackling front-rowers Glenn Lazarus (left) and David Gillespie, in preparation for State of Origin combat with Queensland, flank Gould at the NSW team's training. *Photo Fairfax Photo Library*

TENSION: The intensity at which State of Origin games with Queensland are played shows on the faces of Gould and NSW team manager Geoff Carr (right). *Photo Fairfax Photo Library*

WHAT'S THAT?: Gould gestures his disapproval of an on-field incident during a 1994 State of Origin game. *Photo Fairfax Photo Library*

TROUBLE AT CRONULLA: Referee Bill Harrigan ordering Gould to vacate his sideline position during the 1994 Cronulla-Sutherland v Penrith game at Caltex Field. *Photo News Limited*

MOTIVATIONAL: The note on dressing room blackboard, which helped stir Penrith to its 10-8 win over Canberra in a crucial 1992 game at Penrith Stadium, acts as a backdrop while Gould conducts his post-match media conference. *Photo News Limited*

HARD ACT TO FOLLOW:
Jack Gibson (left) and Arthur Beetson, who plotted the Roosters' last taste of premiership success as coach and captain respectively more than two decades ago, meet up with Gould at Sydney City's function to launch the 1995 season. *Photo Rugby League Week*

CONGRATULATIONS AND COMMISERATIONS: Gould and his Queensland counterpart Paul 'Fatty' Vautin exchange greetings after the Maroons ended New South Wales' three-year reign as State of Origin champions with a clean-sweep win of the 1995 series. *Photo Fairfax Photo Library.*

AIR STUART: Gould and Ricky Stuart's manager, John Fordham, on their arrival back in Sydney by private plane after meeting in Canberra with the champion halfback at the height of the scramble to sign players in the early days of the ARL v Super League war. *Photo Fairfax Photo Library*

From the Mountains to the Sea

All Illawarra winger Nigel Roy wanted to do was cut a new deal with a new club which would reward him financially while providing him the chance to play with a strong line-up.

Roy certainly did not intend to cause a dramatic upheaval and re-evaluation of the coaching, training and recruitment policies of Eastern Suburbs club.

But that is how it turned out.

Roy had talks with Easts in 1995 but rejected their offer and eventually signed with North Sydney for less money.

It was a decision that sent shock waves through an Easts board trying to cope with the embarrassment of losing a player to a club offering poorer terms. It was also not the first time a player had spoken to Easts, and then signed elsewhere.

'That's not going to happen again,' thundered president Nick Politis. The consequences of Roy's decision would ripple through the rugby league premiership, eventually drawing Phil Gould from Penrith to Eastern Suburbs.

After losing Roy, Easts at least had the foresight to try and work out the reasons. Coach Mark Murray, in charge of the first grade side and with the imprimatur of former first grade coach Jack Gibson on his forehead, was well liked. Gibson had been deeply involved in Murray's recruitment from Queensland after a run of disappointing seasons under a variety of coaches had lowered the status of Easts to that of an also ran.

By 1994 Easts were getting restive. A new board that

Good as GOULD

included James Packer, son of Kerry, was anxious to make an impact but was having trouble recruiting players of sufficient qualifications to make their ambitions a reality. To define the problems and find an answer, Easts called in players' manager Wayne Beavis and asked why so few, if any, of his clients were coming to the club.

Beavis said his involvement with Easts had been limited by an apparent lack of interest in his services from the management. It was his understanding that Murray and Gibson much preferred to deal directly with players rather than managers. Beavis said the perception held by many of his players was that Easts was not a club that immediately grabbed attention when it came to discussing premiership contenders. None of his clients were particularly interested in going there. The club was not especially competitive. The coach was not well known, had not made much of an impression and the overall prospects did not look good.

Beavis, Politis and Packer talked about all the reasons why Easts were having difficulties. How players liked to go to a strong, winning club and how players were inclined to follow a coach to a new club. Warren Ryan had proved that when he moved from Newtown to Canterbury and again when he joined Wests. On both occasions, many of his former players had also signed with the new clubs. Easts realised that as painful as it might be, changes had to be made to the recruiting, training and coaching staff. The alterations were vital if the club was ever to be a success at building a team capable of challenging for the premiership.

'It was no slight on the people who were at the club. And Beavis made that clear,' Gould said. 'Easts were just keen to make a move to strengthen the side and wanted to look at their options. It was the perception players with other clubs had of Easts that was the problem.'

Beavis was asked by Easts who the top young player in the

game was at the time and he unhesitatingly replied: 'Brad Fittler'. Fittler was a Beavis client but he was under contract to Penrith for another two years. James Packer asked if he could meet and talk with Fittler. Beavis asked Gould if he had any objections.

'The first thing I did was go to Penrith and check Brad's contract. I wanted to make sure he was well and truly tied up with us before I let him sit down with officials from other clubs,' Gould said. 'Then I agreed. I thought it was good experience for Brad. He had been at Penrith for all of his career. Meeting other officials and talking to other clubs would not do any harm. It would widen his experience.'

Fittler would verify to Packer and Easts that all that Beavis had told them was the truth. Players were not keen to come to Easts for any number of reasons.

Beavis was then asked which coaches would be able to influence the movement of players. He mentioned leading representative and premiership coaches like Wayne Bennett, Gould and Tim Sheens.

In the meantime life went on at Easts, with the club signing Terry Hermansson from Souths but missing another couple of players they were chasing.

Then Easts settled on Gould as the man they wanted. He was invited to Bondi Junction for talks. At that stage the scenario was that Murray would serve out the final year of his contract in 1995 and Gould would take over in 1996. Gould had intended taking a 12 months break in 1995 to recharge his batteries after a non-stop career as a player and coach for 20 years. He would then be available to coach again. If Easts had a vacancy he would be a candidate.

Persistent rumours accelerated the situation. A story in the *Daily Telegraph* pinpointed the likelihood of Gould joining Easts and forecast Royce Simmons taking over at Penrith.

Good as GOULD

'I really was going to have 12 months off and just relax. Penrith had got me down. The drama of the previous few years had taken their toll. I wanted a break from football. I just wanted to take stock for a year, watch a lot of football and see who was on the market for 1996 if I joined a new club,' he said.

'That would have coincided with Mark Murray's departure at the end of 1996,' Gould remembered. 'But talk about the move changed the schedule. I got the offer from Easts the day before I resigned.'

It was a painful parting for Easts and Murray but both parties coped with a difficult situation with professionalism. Easts held Murray in the highest regard and appreciated his hard work as a coach but were confronted with a situation that was not improving. Murray was paid out in full for the remaining year of his contract and left with warm words for Easts and the time he had spent there.

To some commentators, Murray's departure and the signing of Gould was not necessarily a beneficial move for Easts.

'If Gould is so good, why is Penrith letting him go?' queried Jack Gibson.

Speculation was rife that Easts had signed Gould weeks before the official announcement was made and that he had been involved in lengthy talks for some time.

In fact Gould had several times decided to call off any idea of joining Easts. It seemed negotiations were going on endlessly and were not reaching any real conclusion. The prospect of leaving Penrith after so long and immediately joining another club was also starting to weigh more heavily. Talks with his father, a couple of close friends and Beavis finally convinced him to be patient. Finally the deal was struck.

'A lot of reports were saying that I had been having talks with Easts but I hadn't,' Gould said. 'Whatever was happening at Easts was happening without them speaking to me. They were a club looking to improve and player recruitment was high on their list. They were having trouble attracting key players. In their own minds they felt that perhaps a change of coach could rectify that.'

Easts concern about player recruitment mirrored the problems faced by many clubs in the premiership. The increased status of coaches, based on their success rate, had conferred upon them Super Star status comparable with the elite players in the game. From near anonymity 20 years before, coaches had become almost the focal point of the game. They were a self-supporting industry, generating additional headlines and viewpoints.

Coaches' opinions would be sought consistently by the media, often in preference to those of a player. Some had their own newspaper columns. Gould and Fulton were in the *Daily Telegraph*. Warren Ryan was in the *Sydney Morning Herald*. Other coaches wrote for regional and suburban newspapers. There was an almost frenzied drive from the media for coaches and their opinions. Fulton and Gould were also panellists on radio station 2UE—Gould after being released from a contract with 2GB at his own request. He had verbally agreed to new terms with 2GB but the station chose not to stand in his way when the 2UE offer eventuated. St George's Brian Smith and Ryan were at the ABC along with former Newcastle coach Alan McMahon, who was appointed Illawarra coach for 1996.

Gould joined Easts as an interested observer for the remaining few games of 1994 after Murray stepped down. Loyal club man Arthur Beetson was appointed caretaker until the end of the year. Easts finished 1994 in 13th place in a 16 team competition. With four more clubs joining the competition in 1995, there was no way Easts could have withstood the extra competition for players and rebuilt its line-up under its previous structure.

Good as GOULD

Gould showed the extra effort needed to acquire an elite coach was worth the trouble. For 1996 rugby union surrendered Wallabies Darren Junee and Peter Jorgensen, St George released five-eighth Andrew Walker and the club also signed Great Britain Test vice-captain Phil Clarke. Australian Test winger Graham Mackay also switched to Easts from Penrith.

Halfback Adrian Lam and prop Jason Lowrie quickly developed into top class performers under Gould. Lowrie played Tests for New Zealand and Lam was declared an honorary Queenslander and played State of Origin against New South Wales as well as retaining his status as a Test halfback for Papua New Guinea, the country of his birth. Lam's conversion from Papua New Guinean to Queenslander and back again is still the subject of some curiosity.

Under Gould in 1995 Easts were resurrected as premiership candidates, underlining again his ability as a coach and his astuteness in building a competitive team with skilled recruitment of playing staff.

There are only a certain number of class players to go around and even fewer champions in modern day rugby league. No more are being manufactured en masse. For clubs hungry for success, it is a matter of recycling the champions and bidding extraordinary amounts of money for their signatures, rather then waiting for new stars to emerge or develop their own. If the coaching name is big enough and the attendant charisma is there, players will come. Never in the history of the game in Australia has it been so hard for a middle-of-the-road club to improve dramatically unless cash, high profile coaching, club stability and success abound.

With Gould in charge and fielding a stronger team, Easts made a sustained charge at a place in the new-look 1995 eight team semi-final series, failing by the narrowest possible margin. For an exhilarating ten minutes in the final match of the season, Easts were in the final eight. The situation developed as Easts crushed Balmain 44–10 at the Sydney Football Stadium and other unlikely results in other matches fell into place.

The final 11 weeks of the premiership were always going to develop into a tense struggle for Easts (who had been uncomfortably re-named 'Sydney City Roosters') as far as semi-finals were concerned. The structure of the draw meant that every club had to endure a difficult five weeks of successive matches against leading sides Canterbury (the eventual premiers), followed by semi-finalists Canberra, Brisbane, North Sydney and grand finalists Manly. With 14 competition points from 11 games Gould knew the team needed to win at least one game in the horror run as well as five out of six of the matches after that. It looked difficult but it almost came off. Gould set his side to peak motivation and capacity for each of the games in the horror run but he always had a particular focus on Manly as being the most vulnerable.

The first week came and went with a 22–14 loss to a Canterbury side missing five regular first graders. Canberra scraped home 17–16 on the strength of a Ricky Stuart field goal in the final minutes. It was a tense and fierce struggle in which the Easts did well—but it was still a loss. There were still three matches in the horror run to go. Gould has always believed Brisbane can be one of the most fragile sides in the premiership because of their limitations in the forwards, whose prowess does not match that of the stunning backline. His expectations looked like being fulfilled when Easts played Brisbane at ANZ Stadium in the 14th round on Sunday July 2. Easts led 20–12 with 30 minutes to play and looked likely to hold on but were finally swamped 36–20 in a result that looked decidedly more convincing that it was in reality. Brisbane coach Wayne Bennett turned things around when his side

Good as GOULD

trailed 20–12. He replaced his entire front-row of Glenn Lazarus, John Driscoll and Andrew Gee and switched Wendall Sailor from the wing to the second-row. He also put highly promising John Plath into the fray at five-eighth. The switches revitalised a Brisbane side that was floundering.

Three successive losses lessened interest in Easts as a semi-final candidate. A 28–34 defeat by North Sydney did nothing to stop the losing momentum despite an enthusiastic effort from all of the Easts players that saw them score five tries to four. It was six goals from North's champion halfback Jason Taylor to Andrew Walker's two goals that made the difference. The loss pushed Easts down to 10th place on 14 points—16 points behind their next opponents, unbeaten competition leaders Manly.

Coach Bob Fulton had done an excellent job with Manly. The side had trampled its way through the premiership, running up some stunning scores on its way to 15 successive wins. Souths had been beaten 42–18 in the first round, Norths fell 30–nil, Auckland 26–14, the Crushers 38–10, St George 24–6, Canterbury 26–nil, Brisbane 23–4, Norths (a second time) 36–6.

There was already talk of Manly becoming the first side since St George in 1959 to go through a season unbeaten.

On the afternoon of Sunday July 16 at Brookvale Oval Manly was the side setting a red hot pace in the premiership and Easts were a side coming off four successive losses, staring a fifth in the face and slipping down the premiership ladder. It was all supposed to be a relatively easy match for Manly. Instead it was to explode into the most controversial and dramatic match of the season, generating huge headlines and resulting in fines of $10,000 being imposed by the NSWRL.

'I thought we could beat Manly. And we had to because of the situation we were in at the time,' Gould said. 'The players had performed a lot better than our record of four straight losses suggested. We had been in every match from the start to the finish. The players were not giving up and with a little bit of luck we could have won at least three of them against Canberra, Norths and Brisbane. But we didn't and that made the Manly match crucial. I think our record on paper of those four losses and our position on the table might have helped us against Manly. I know Bob Fulton would not have been fooled by the record. He would have seen the matches on video and known how well we were playing. But it was a matter of whether his players genuinely believed we were competitive and not another easy side to beat. In rugby league matches the difference in the result can be attributed to something as slight as key players only performing to say 85 per cent of their ability.'

Gould fine tuned Easts attack to take advantage of perceived deficiencies in Manly's defence. It was a daring manoeuvre. Manly's defence was the best in the premiership with the players conceding only 140 points in 15 games—an average of around nine a match. But Manly also had four players, Danny Moore, Geoff Toovey, Steve Menzies and David Gillespie backing up in the match just two days after completing a comprehensive 3–nil clean sweep of the Test series against New Zealand.

Easts played disciplined and extremely controlled football from the start and in the second half led 19–4. It was then that things started to go haywire. Gould had been sitting in the grandstand, slowly simmering about the performance of referee David Jay. He chose to move to the sideline for the second half—a move that is forbidden by ARL rules to prevent possibly inflammatory situations. As Manly started to make up ground in the second half Gould's temper rose like a ground-to-air missile. Easts 19–4 lead was cut back to 19–14 as Menzies crossed for two tries in four minutes. That was the

Good as GOULD

trigger for Gould to boil over. Gould was sitting in the grandstand when he was joined by James Packer.

Packer commented: 'You must feel like the bloke who had taken the same girl home six weeks in a row and all you get is a kiss good night at the door.'

Gould: 'What do you mean?'

Packer: 'Well you can't win a game. You've lost the three State of Origins, we've lost half a dozen games in the final minutes and it looks like it's going to happen again today.'

Gould: 'Bullshit!'

With the epitaph still floating in the air, Gould promptly walked from the grandstand to the sideline, followed by his mate Ross Seymour. There he walked up and down, arms flapping like a pelican trying to get airborne, yelling at his players.

Those closest to Gould's outburst have no doubt he was threatening to call his players from the field over the issue of the refereeing. Gould says the reports are exaggerated and it was just a theatrical stunt.

'My main objective was to let the players know I was with them and we could still win the match,' Gould says.

'I sent the trainer out to tell the players in earshot of the referee: "If this continues, we're coming off." But it was never going to happen. I wanted the crowd focusing on me and not the referee. They were giving him a real hard time and he was under pressure. Penalties also started going Manly's way and he sent one of our players to the sin bin. We were losing confidence and momentum. It was a game we just had to win because we had been going so close in other matches against good sides in the past few weeks.

'Tony Iro came up behind me from the bench and I looked at him and said: "What are you doing here?"

'He said: "You replaced me five minutes ago."

'I said: "Get back out there!"

FROM PLAYER TO COACH

' "Who for?"
' "I don't care. Just tell someone to get off." '

Gould's antics on the sideline were not missed. Thousands of people at the ground and tens of thousands of television viewers around the country watched the coach, his face contorted with anger, waving his arms and motioning towards the players.

Later Iro said he understood Gould to be telling the team to come from the field, but that was something he would never have even contemplated. 'That was unthinkable,' Iro said.

Sitting behind Gould in a Manly jumper on the interchange bench, Test prop David Gillespie watched with growing interest as the drama unfolded. 'David could see how enraged I was,' Gould laughs. 'I turned around and looked at him and he said: "What's up Gussie?" It was one of the funniest comments I've heard in my life.'

Gould suggests that the entire episode, still regarded as one of the most dramatic and tense in the recent history of the game because a team could have been called from the field, was over rated.

'It really wasn't the big thing that everyone thought it was. I was just trying to get the team to lift,' he said.

Gould eventually calmed down and left the sideline. Easts went on to win 21–16 in a result that produced even more controversy. After Gould had set nerves on edge, referee Jay disallowed two Manly tries in the final minutes that looked legitimate. Gould's histrionics would not go unnoticed or unpunished by the NSWRL. Easts were fined $10,000 for Gould's outburst—a decision critics felt was light in view of his previous run-ins with referees.

In the dressing room after the match, Gould was his usual affable self and in total control. The darker side of his temper was now locked securely away. There, he explained his actions away lightly, insisting he had never intended calling his players from the field.

'I would never call a side from the field,' he declared. Gould's case was helped by the fact that a touch judge and the referee had been too engrossed in their own duties to hear what he was saying. Run-ins with referees are nothing new to Gould. Refereeing standards are the dimension of rugby league he thinks is most in need of repair. In 1994 his celebrated row with leading referee Bill Harrigan had come to an ugly confrontation that had also captured the attention of the ARL in sensational circumstances. Gould was still coaching Penrith at that stage and they were playing Cronulla at Endeavour Field under referee Bill Harrigan. Gould had again moved his seat to the sideline for the match as he became infuriated with Harrigan's handling of the match. Harrigan had penalised Penrith 13–2 at the time when he caught sight of Gould sitting on the sideline. He came over and ordered him from the field. Gould left but returned a short time later and resumed his seat on the sideline. Gould's return was brought to Harrigan's attention by a touch judge. He again came over, and with play stopped and players from both sides watching with amazement, ordered Gould to retire permanently from the playing area. This time he did. When Harrigan walked through the tunnel to his dressing room after the match Gould was there—captured in full colour by the photographers—clapping.

Penrith were incensed by Harrigan's performance of a 13–2 penalty count plus sending two Penrith players to the sin bin in a match the club lost 32–nil. Harrigan actually awarded Cronulla 13 consecutive penalties before giving Penrith their first in the 73rd minute. It was as lop-sided a penalty count as anyone in rugby league could remember. Although Harrigan got a pass mark for his technical handling of the game, referees' officials were keen to quiz him on how Cronulla earned so

FROM PLAYER TO COACH

many penalties in a row and played for so long without committing a breach worthy of a penalty.

The furore erupted when Gould raised both of his arms in the air in feigned triumph when his Penrith side was finally awarded a penalty. He turned to a Penrith official and said in a loud voice that could have carried: 'At least we'll get the chance to practice one tap-kick move.' Two other Penrith officials on the sideline were openly and loudly critical of Harrigan's performance. A touch judge reported what they had said to Harrigan.

Queensland second-rower Trevor Gillmeister found himself in the sin bin at one stage leaving Penrith a man short. His blemish was to say to Harrigan: 'Can we have a penalty before the end of the game to practice our tap moves.' Penrith claimed it was a light-hearted quip to ease a tense situation.

Harrigan was an always controversial figure in the refereeing ranks whose image of a glamour identity in rugby league was viewed as outstripping his contribution as a referee. He was a member of the police SWAT team and also took up a career as a celebrity speaker until the ARL said he could not combine that with refereeing.

The aftermath of the Gould and Harrigan confrontation raged for days. There had been bad blood between the pair since the 1991 grand final. Gould was still critical of decisions Harrigan made in that match. Harrigan's performances in State of Origin matches involving Gould's NSW side had also added to the drama. In the 1991 grand final, Harrigan sent Penrith's star second-rower Mark Geyer to the sin bin for 10 minutes. It was a crucial decision and unjustifiably harsh according to Gould. Evidence was also presented by Gould at the hearing into the Cronulla sideline blow-up that Gould-coached teams had only won the penalty count under Harrigan four times in 19 matches since 1991. 'I had no problems with Harrigan but he has said publicly that he has a problem with me,' Gould said.

Good as GOULD

'Whether it was reflected in that game against Cronulla or not I do not know. I just know that I have never coached a side in my life that has been penalised 13–2 in a match. We were not that undisciplined a side. And Cronulla were not that perfect. I did not say anything to Harrigan from the sideline. He just stopped the game, came over to where I was sitting and told me leave. And I did. The second time I went out again it was to see our doctor about an injury to our prop Barry Walker. He again stopped the match and waved me off. I had no great problem with that. He obviously did not want me near the sideline. I didn't feel embarrassed by what happened one little bit.'

The ARL subsequently called Gould and Harrigan together for a special meeting with general manager John Quayle, which preceded a planned appearance by the pair before a judiciary panel. Harrigan had lodged complaints to the ARL about alleged comments he heard from Gould at the match.

The panel of Quayle, ARL solicitor Colin Love and referees' boss Mick Stone produced a masterpiece of diplomacy. Harrigan withdrew his complaint during a marathon two-and-a-half-hour sitting and Gould apologised. It was never really clear what Gould was apologising for if the complaint had been withdrawn. There was also a $4000 fine for Penrith for remarks made to Harrigan in the tunnel after the game. The key questions of what Gould allegedly said and Harrigan's actions were never revealed. Much of what followed was almost tongue-in-cheek as Harrigan and Gould went through a public kiss-and-make-up routine. Gould said he had never had any problems with Harrigan, who said he wanted to make a fresh start. More important was the fact that keeping the dispute 'in house' in front of a select panel was a better option than having the matter thrashed out in full before the nine man board, where much more of what was actually said would be made public. Quayle admitted he had encouraged Gould and

FROM PLAYER TO COACH

Harrigan to try and sort the matter out between themselves rather than have to ask the nine-man board to decide who was guilty and who was innocent.

'I did say something about Harrigan's refereeing on the night. What coach wouldn't say something if his team was down 13–2 in the penalties,' Gould admits. 'But it was said to another Penrith representative on the sideline with me. It was not directed at the referee but it was overheard by a touch judge who told him it was.'

The peace was as artificial as plastic. It is unlikely Gould and Harrigan send each other Christmas cards despite their public utterances of reconciliation after appearing before Quayle and Love. In reality nothing had changed. When Super League erupted Harrigan was among the first referees to change sides. 'It did not surprise me at all to see Bill switch sides for more money,' Gould said.

So Gould's eruption as Easts coach in the game against Manly was not a surprise. It was also not a moment Easts would boast about but it did produce two crucial premiership points to end a four week losing streak, boost team morale and move the team to within striking distance of a top eight position again.

Perhaps it was the dramatic circumstances of the win that left Easts mentally and physically drained but the advantage they gained was lost immediately. The week after beating Manly, Easts lost to Illawarra 28–6 at the Sydney Football Stadium. Ironically Illawarra half-back John Simon, the player signed by Easts for 1996, was the star player for the winning side. Easts already knew Simon was a good player. He picked an inopportune moment to underline his talents to his new bosses.

The loss left Easts on 16 competition points—four points out of the top eighth—and chasing eighth place with Norths, Penrith and the Western Reds, who were also on 16.

Good as GOULD

Gould got Easts back on track with a 26–20 win against Parramatta, a 25–6 win against the Reds in Perth and a 26–12 win against Newcastle at the Sydney Football Stadium but the momentum was stopped by a 16–4 loss to Cronulla at Caltex Field. Going into the final round of preliminary matches, the top eight was clear cut with Manly and Canberra on 38, Brisbane on 32, Cronulla and Newcastle on 30, Canterbury on 26 and St George and Auckland on 24. Sitting on the next level were Norths on 23 and Easts and the Western Reds on 22. It looked a forlorn hope for Easts to make the eight. They had to beat Balmain convincingly to improve their points for and against and then hope that Auckland lost to Brisbane in New Zealand, which was possible. But the second necessary scenario did not look so likely. Norths had to lose to the lowly rated Gold Coast. Even allowing for North Sydney's alarming drop in form in recent matches it seemed unlikely. Norths had been held to a 16–all draw with 17th-placed Souths at the Sydney Football Stadium the previous week. To expect Norths to lose to 18th placed Gold Coast the next week seemed frivolous.

'We approached the match against Balmain as if we *knew* it was the difference between us winning a place in the semi-finals,' Gould said. 'And it was not. Not in this second round game, but in the first round. Balmain were our very first opponents of the season and my first premiership opponents as Easts coach. The match was at Parramatta Stadium and it was incredible,' Gould says. 'We did everything pretty well. Just the way we had trained. We led 18–2 at half-time. Then we relaxed a bit in the second half and we lost 24–18. It was an embarrassing loss. I always felt it would be costly and that's the way it turned out. It was good luck for Balmain. They kept coming at us in that first round game and trying things. They scored three tries from chip kicks. You don't see that happen often in 40 minutes of football.'

FROM PLAYER TO COACH

In the last preliminary game of the season Easts would extract a fierce revenge on the Tigers, winning the game 44–6. Miraculously the other games also fell into place—at least momentarily. Brisbane crushed Auckland 44–6 and Norths had great trouble coping with Gold Coast. For 12 minutes late on the afternoon of Sunday August 27, Easts were actually in the semi-finals with Norths trailing 14–10. Then a late try earned Norths their second successive draw and the one competition point was enough to nudge them into eighth place on percentages after Norths, Easts and Auckland all finished on 24 points. In previous years there would have been a play-off for eighth place but with the expansion to eight semi-finalists, the ARL decided to decide positions on for and against.'

'We were still pretty happy with the way things turned out. We won 12 and lost 10 matches. We finished in equal eighth place on competition points and we unearthed some new talent,' said Gould. 'For a new coach at a new club it was a promising enough start. Peter Clarke had a good year. He started in reserve grade and quickly worked his way into first grade. He finished up as our leading try-scorer with 12 tries in 16 games. It was then a matter of going on with the job in 1996. If nothing else that first round loss to Balmain in 1995 will help focus the players' minds on competing for the full 80 minutes in every match.'

The 1995 season was also remarkable for the planned merger of Easts and St George into one juggernaut of a side, buoyed by money, history and talent. The genesis of the idea came to Gould and St George chief executive and NSW State of Origin team manager Geoff Carr during their lengthy bonding sessions before each of the matches against Queensland. It was a meeting of two similarly-minded people. Carr had long believed that St George was finished as a premiership contender because of the massive finance available to one-city teams like Canberra and particularly Brisbane. In conversation with then Canterbury chief executive and later Super League defector Peter Moore one night, Carr listened as the advantages enjoyed by Brisbane were detailed.

'Peter said that Brisbane's turnover was round nine or ten million dollars a season,' Carr said. 'I knew that St George's was around three million dollars. Canterbury's might have been a bit more. But neither club could match strides with Brisbane when it came to having money available to buy players.'

Realising how hopelessly lop-sided the situation was probably had an affect on both men. Moore found his solution with Super League. Carr pondered a merger with Easts. The plan had merit. Easts had plenty of money and a reasonable line-up of talent. St George was not spending as much on football as in past years but was a long way from being strapped for cash. Merging their forces would reduce their spending demands on both clubs and would also establish what would be the first merger of two inner-Sydney clubs into a very potent force that would serve two purposes. If Super League did get the upper hand in its battle with the ARL, St George-Easts would be a side it could not ignore in its competition. If the ARL maintained control, St George-Easts would be a high profile team that could compete against the big-spending Manlys and North Sydneys for players. A merger would also short circuit any plans by either Super League or the ARL to force a marriage between Easts and Souths or St George and Cronulla or Canterbury.

'It was an idea we thought had a lot of merit. And that is why it developed as far as it did,' Gould says. 'It would have meant St George and Easts deciding their own destinies instead of taking the risk of someone else deciding what they would do if amalgamations had to happen. We gave it a lot of thought and looked at all of the pros and cons. In the end we just decided it was too good an idea to let go.'

FROM PLAYER TO COACH

Initially the idea struck a chord with both St George and Easts. The boards were attentive to the idea, even though some members were reluctant to see two such venerable identities blend into one. St George supporters made most noise against the amalgamation and their momentum built. Meetings were held. Threats were made by a newly-formed Save our Saints movement to oppose sitting members at the next club general election. 'In the end St George's board pulled back under pressure from their supporters, who never really understood the full picture,' said Gould.

The aborted merger left Saints in turmoil for many months and the club was still struggling to come to grips with its individual status as the 1996 season kicked off. Carr parted company with St George as a consequence of the merger talks, unfairly blamed for trying to impose his will on the future of the club when his every move had been detailed to his board. Carr was subsequently snapped up by the ARL as its communication officer.

PHIL GOULD'S Reflections on
ROOSTER DAYS

I was never under any illusions about the task of trying to rescue Eastern Suburbs' rugby league fortunes.

The club had finished 14th in first grade and 15th in reserve grade in 1994.

Our recruitment in the off season was limited to what established players there were on the market.

There were a number of changes that had to be made to some attitudes around the place and some difficult decisions were made.

They culminated in what was an extremely good season for the club.

The 1995 season for the Roosters (by then 'Sydney City') saw the team established as the most dramatic improvers in the premiership.

They lifted to equal eighth and only missed the semi-finals on points for and against.

We were beaten four times very narrowly by the four top sides in the premiership.

Had we sneaked into the top eight I think we would have made our presence felt, given the style of football we were playing at the time.

The club and the people in it, like Nick Politis the club president, are tremendous, and if any man in rugby league deserves success, it is Nick.

It was a very important year for us. We had to improve even

though we had very few new players.

Without improvement we would not be able to attract the type of quality player we were seeking for the following year.

I knew the club wanted to sign Brad Fittler and I knew if I asked him to come and join Easts, he probably would have.

But I wanted to be fair to Brad as well and prove we had a side worthy of having a player of his calibre.

I did not want him making a detrimental career choice out of friendship with me so I asked him to wait until we had proved ourselves as a club.

I wanted a good work ethic, a solid foundation of improvement and a level of talent at the club so that he would be a bonus rather than a part of the foundation.

By the end of 1995 I could give Brad that assurance—which is why we were able to sign him.

Easts are, along with North Sydney, Balmain, Manly and the other loyal clubs, staunchly behind the Australian Rugby League and its battle with Super League.

Because of James Packer's involvement as a director of Easts, he found himself a target of a lot of the slanging emanating from the Super League side.

As a staunch supporter of the ARL actively involved in helping them maintain control of the game, I was also subjected to smear campaigns from various quarters.

Yet we were able to concentrate on our football and achieve success.

I'm just glad that the promises I made to the Eastern Suburbs' footballers in 1995 about their futures and the future of the club have been confirmed by the courts.

State against State, Mate against Mate

THE ORIGIN EXPERIENCE

Call to Arms: Origin Coach

Australian coach Bob Fulton is a prime example of how there can be a natural progression from one dimension of sport to another in a seamless and natural flow. Fulton went from great player to Test captain, to captain–coach, club coach, and finally Test coach, conquering each challenge as it came. For Phil Gould the transition from player to coach, then the next step from club coach to representative coach, required much more soul-searching, despite the premierships he won with Canterbury and Penrith. It also took an unprecedented and embarrassing (at least from NSW's point of view) domination of the State of Origin series by Queensland to catapult Gould into serious representative coaching.

By the end of the 1991 season the domestic representative scene was in disarray. The Test team under Fulton had continued to beat all comers in the international arena despite some close encounters. Fulton had taken the 1990 Kangaroos through England and France with the loss of only one game (the first Test against England) and he would do the same with the 1994 Kangaroos. France and New Zealand had also repeatedly fallen. In fact Australia had not lost a Test series against any country since France in 1978 when dubious refereeing displays saw the Aussies fall 2–0.

As commendable as the situation was on the international scene, domestically the power shift towards Queensland had been dramatic. After decades as the decisively lesser partner of

Good as GOULD

Australian rugby league, Queensland had risen from the dust to establish a stunning dominance in State of Origin matches. Trailing in the wake the Brisbane Broncos had emerged as a potent and glamorous premiership force.

Since the inaugural game in 1980, Queensland had made the State of Origin series its own, with wins in 1980, 1981 and 1982 (when the 'series' was in fact only one game) and 1983 and 1984 (when it was a genuine three-match series).

It was not until 1985 that NSW finally broke through for their first series win—under the inspirational leadership of half Steve Mortimer. A richly talented player, Mortimer was also a passionate and inspiring performer given to tears when emotion was heavy in the air. It was Mortimer who stopped the bus taking the team to Lang Park for the first match of the 1985 series through a throng of beer-drinking, jeering Queenslanders. 'Look at those bastards,' Mortimer said with passion. 'They want us to get beat. They hate us up here. Let's not make them happy.'

Prop Steve Roach still remembers it as the moment the NSW Blues united into a winning team.

The interruption to the Queensland march by Mortimer's side was brief. Of the 10 State of Origin matches played between 1980 and 1984, Queensland won eight against NSW sides that boasted impressive talent but failed to lift their desire and zeal to the same level as their opponents.

A rare win in 1990 under coach Jack Gibson, whose sides had been beaten 3–nil the previous year, gave NSW some brief breathing space, but Queensland's general domination seemed unstoppable.

NSW's failure was also taking a toll of coaches. Gibson declined to coach the side in 1991 after controversy during his tenure over the omission of then Test stars Steve Roach and Paul Sironen from the team. Gibson was followed in 1991 by

THE ORIGIN EXPERIENCE

Canberra's premiership-winning coach Tim Sheens, who was beaten two matches to one in the tightest of circumstances, 4–6, 14–12, 12–14. But more significantly Sheens' reign highlighted the undercurrent of frustration that existed among the NSW players about their continued losses. There were headlines involving Sheens and the NSW camp banning Sydney referee Bill Harrigan from the post-match party in Brisbane after a Lang Park loss. And there was also a celebrated clash between Sheens and NSW hooker Benny Elias over team tactics and performances in the final match of the series at Lang Park. Sheens was publicly critical of Elias' captaincy and performance. A State selector was quoted publicly but anonymously as praising Elias' involvement but was less happy with some of the options the hooker had taken at vital times.

Never a player to accept criticism he considered unfair, Elias said he had simply been following the coach's instructions to 'run as much as possible from dummy half to relieve some pressure on the forwards. He emphasised that for the three matches.'

A few days later on television Sheens hit back with: 'I didn't tell him (Elias) to throw flick passes in his own half. I didn't tell him to miss tackles or ignore calls for the ball to go out to the backs.'

In that same series giant second-rower Mark Geyer had been involved in the most colourful and controversial incident in State of Origin football since Queensland's much-loved legend Arthur Beetson had biffed his then Parramatta teammate and close friend Mick Cronin in the inaugural game in 1980, giving the concept immediate credibility.

In the second match of 1991, Geyer had erupted like a volcano at the Sydney Football Stadium. In driving rain Geyer, who had adopted an enforcer's role, was almost uncontrollably aggressive as he took the battle to Queensland's forwards in a match NSW had to win to keep the series alive. In the first 40 minutes there were several flare-ups. Then, almost right on half-time, Geyer hit Queensland fullback Paul Hauff with a high tackle. Players ran from all directions to throw punches. Geyer and Queensland captain Wally Lewis stood in the middle of the ground shouting abuse at each other in the rain and bumping chests as the half-time hooter sounded.

Geyer was later suspended for six weeks over the Hauff incident.

In the third match NSW winger Michael O'Connor suffered bruising of the brain, a gashed lip, black eye and a broken nose in a high tackle from Queensland's Mal Meninga.

It was a time of enormous turbulence and bitterness in relations between the two rugby league states.

NSW hated its drastically reduced status in the Australian domestic championship and carped at the cockiness of the Queenslanders and their claims to being able to generate more passion in matches. The Blues clearly needed a hero, a saviour who could rally the available forces, lift the yoke of Queensland domination and reinstate NSW to its perceived place as the major force in Australian rugby league.

But where was this bold man to be found? NSW had used Jack Gibson, Tim Sheens, Ron Willey, Frank Stanton, Ted Glossop and Terry Fearnley as coaches at different times with inconsistent success, even allowing for Fearnley, Willey and Gibson winning a series. There was also pressure on the NSWRL nine-man board to come up with a winning answer.

Repeatedly, at various stratas of rugby league's hierarchy, in almost any era, administrators under pressure to produce a winning team would deflect pressure from themselves by appointing a high-profile personality or former first grade player as coach. It was in that vein that Penrith appointed Royce Simmons, Balmain appointed Wayne Pearce, Wests appointed Tom Raudonikis and Parramatta appointed first Mick Cronin and then Ron Hilditch. If the coach succeeds, then the board has made a brilliant decision. If the chosen person proves unsatisfactory, well it wasn't the board's fault. They had worked hard to give members and supporters the best man available. It was a policy that had been fully explored by previous NSWRL boards as well as club management.

Gibson had two premierships with Easts and three with Parramatta and was arguably the highest-profile coach in the game when he was appointed NSW coach. Frank Stanton was an Ashes-winning Kangaroo coach. Tim Sheens was flavour of the month when he was appointed after two premierships in two years with Canberra. Queensland did something similar. Arthur Beetson was followed by Wayne Bennett as Queensland coach after his success with Brisbane in the premiership.

The policy is not a reflection on the commitment and ability of the men involved, but it does suggest the strong sense of self-preservation that exists among football administrators.

Into this remarkable imbroglio of wounded pride and self-serving interests, deceit, disappointment and frustration came Phil Gould. His record of two first grade premierships in three years with Canterbury and then Penrith guaranteed an invitation to the next coaching level—despite his youth. Gould, in more reflective moments when things have gone awry at representative level, turns to a rugby league writing mate of his and says: 'This is your fault. If it hadn't been for you I'd be coaching at club level.'

The fact of the matter is that the rugby league writer, impressed by Gould's record, *did* put his name forward to NSWRL boss Ken Arthurson for the job when it was obvious Sheens' chances of being retained were minimal. Arthurson was in immediate agreement, saying he had already considered Gould the obvious candidate. 'He had done such a good job winning two premierships that he obviously had the potential to move into the representative scene without a problem,' Arthurson said. 'Gould also seemed like the man who could calm the uproar in the side.'

For Gould the decision was harder to make. Club coaching is months of preparation. Months of getting to know the strengths and weaknesses of players. Months of building bridges between the coach and players about reliability, grace under pressure and commitment.

State of Origin is guerilla warfare. Three matches of hit-and-run football at three different venues under enormous pressure from officials and supporters to win. No time to build relationships. Just time to get in, hurl the grenades, get the job done and get out.

'I didn't see representative football as something I ever wanted to do or something that I would be capable of doing even though we had won a couple of premierships,' Gould said. 'Apart from the premierships I'd never been involved in representative football or played representative football. I'd played with a lot of players who had played representative football and I just didn't know if I could function in that environment. I didn't know if I had what it takes to coach at that level. I was still young and still learning. I was really nervous about the whole thing. I really didn't know if it was me. I saw it as a no-win situation. At the end of the day it was going to be the players who won it or the coach who lost it. The coach is just someone who's there to be blamed when something doesn't work out.'

Such self-analysis is common with Gould. Outwardly he reflects the confidence and knowledge of someone who knows and studies the game at great length. Inwardly he has to deal with the same demons as other coaches. Was the loss my fault? Was there something I could have done differently?

THE ORIGIN EXPERIENCE

Gould eventually agreed to have his name go forward after the NSWRL officially contacted his then club Penrith and formally sought his services. That should have been the end of the recruiting process. The NSWRL bureaucratic wheels, having started to move, should have continued to turn until Gould's appointment was officially gazetted.

Life though is never that simple. Although publicly agreeing to be considered for the NSW job, Gould still harboured a secret escape clause in his mind. He believed his old and bitter nemesis Peter Moore, the Canterbury chief executive and a member of the NSWRL board that would assess the NSW coaching nominations, would do all he could to thwart the appointment.

'One of the reasons I was reluctant to get involved with the NSW job was because I did not want to go through the whole Peter Moore thing again the way I had at Canterbury.'

Moore says Gould's fears were unfounded but there is no doubt that an unprecedented gauntlet of confusion, surprises and disenchantment lay ahead before the appointment was confirmed.

Bob Fulton emerged as one hurdle. There was a move to have him appointed NSW coach in defiance of a previous ruling that the NSW and Test coaching jobs be kept separate. The change followed the drama associated with Terry Fearnley being Test coach on a tour of New Zealand in 1985 after coaching the NSW team. In a controversial but justifiable move Fearnley dropped four Queenslanders for the third Test team. The team selected then lost 18–nil. He returned to wild controversy in Australia as NSW coach for the final match against Queensland. The fired-up Maroons won 20–6 and prop Greg Dowling took time out during the game to abuse Fearnley who was sitting in the NSW dug-out.

Stunned ARL officials quickly voted in a resolution to

divorce the two jobs so such a situation could not happen again.

The reality of Fulton's name being mentioned as NSW coach threatened that ruling. Fulton was a successful Test coach, had established close ties with senior administrators and was assured of widespread support—until ARL and NSWRL chairman Arthurson stepped into the flurry and said Gould would have the job.

It was a remarkable twist. The almost father and son relationship between Arthurson and Fulton is legendary in rugby league.

'I think it was Peter Moore who was behind the move to get Fulton appointed,' Gould said. 'It was a case of doing anything to stop me being appointed. When he realised his effort to stop me being appointed had failed, he turned around and nominated me for the job to the board. He came to me at the launch before the first State of Origin match and said: "Mate, congratulations. I'm happy you got the job. In fact I moved the motion to have you appointed."'

With the drama of his appointment finally settled after Fulton decided to withdraw, the scene should have been set for Gould to take over as coach of a combined team of players aching with ambition to wrest supremacy from Queensland. The fact is the scene from the outside is often more impressive than the situation inside. To an outsider looking in as Gould was, the NSW team had always appeared competitive enough in its approach to State of Origin matches. That proved deceptive.

Gould, like every other rugby league follower on the east coast of Australia, was addicted to State of Origin. He would watch matches on television, sometimes at the ground, and wonder what there was in the Queensland makeup that made them so desperately passionate about beating NSW. 'Tim Sheens had a great side in 1991 but to my mind they handled it very poorly,' Gould said. 'They lost the two Lang Park games by two points and they won in Sydney by two points and probably should have been beaten in that game in the rain. That year I really thought they should have won the series.

'I had an honest belief from watching the side play that there were some basic ingredients missing that had to be put in place if we were going to ever beat Queensland. And I thought that while knowing nothing about any other situation. The type of football NSW was playing was, to my mind, getting them beat. I thought there was a chance to improve the football. To change things.'

Re-inventing the Blues

The first thing Gould did as coach of the NSW team at his initial meeting with the team was produce two footballs. He kept one and threw the other to hooker Benny Elias.

'This is our ball,' he said pointing to the one under his arm. 'We play with that one. The other one is for Benny. He can play with that.'

It was said with good humour but the message was serious and pointed. Gould considered Elias too much of an individual player for his plans to turn the NSW side into winners. He would have to be more of a team player and cooperate more on the field or changes would be made.

Elias was at least up to handling the initial taunt. 'Thanks, Gus,' he said when he got the ball. 'You must have a crystal ball. They don't usually hand out the game ball to a player until after the match. This must mean you think I'm going to get it.'

It was a dramatic start to Gould's tenure as coach but as always he was determined to do things his way or not at all. No point in being the coach if you cannot call the shots, he reckoned. At least then if you get beaten, you know you gave it your best shot without outside interference.

There was a sprinkling of players in the team who had known or played under Gould and they did their best to convince their team-mates of his ability. Winger Graham Mackay, John Cartwright and Brad Fittler were from his then club

Penrith. Reserve forward David Gillespie was with Gould in the 1990 Canterbury premiership-winning side. The word had been conveyed to the team that Gould was something special as a coach. Young, remarkably astute, a gifted tactician and not averse to a drink, a bet or some fun. NSW's preparations under him would not take on the monastery-like climate generated by other coaches.

'When I met Phil for the first time in 1992, I didn't know him much at all except that he had won premierships with Canterbury and Penrith,' said team manager Geoff Carr. 'He was very impressive in everything he did with the team. He thought about what had to be done, the team tactics. He thought about the way Queensland played their football. And the big thing on his mind was that Queensland was being portrayed as having a mortgage on team spirit. In that first series he worked very hard on keeping everyone together.'

Gould made it clear that he regarded Elias as a key factor in team harmony. Elias' playing style though would have to be refined for the good of the team and morale. 'Gus had looked at the 1991 tapes of NSW playing,' Carr said. 'He said, "Benny's just playing for himself." It was something that convinced him that NSW did not have the same spirit as Queensland. When there were things on and Benny could also make 10 metres up the blind he was taking the option for himself, rather than the team.'

Gould did not disguise his disappointment with Elias' play in the 1991 series and said there had been no option but to confront him with his findings. 'In the game they lost in 1991, Benny had a shocker. He played very selfishly and Gus knew he had to front him about it,' Carr said.

'He didn't want to embarrass Benny either. So he decided on the ploy with the two balls. It worked. The players weren't blind. They were aware that Benny had to be told—they'd all played with him the previous year. They were all happier that Benny now knew the rules. In fact I think some of them were not all that confident about Benny being there. He had not played all that well the year before.'

It was not the first time that Elias' play at Origin level had been criticised by coaches but his skills were undeniable and his record of achievement and his doggedness were impressive. Despite his stature, Elias had held his own in the forward clashes for years with Balmain, had played State of Origin football for seven years, captained NSW, been vice-captain of the Kangaroos and elevated the hooking role to one of distinction with his unprecedented skills of kicking in general play, ability to kick field goals and his guile with the ball.

'I think Gus was always looking for someone to come into the team as hooker but when Benny played to the plan he was a very good player,' Carr said. 'But there were also question marks about his defence. At that stage with Balmain he was just playing second marker. He was a smart player and he was playing smart at Balmain. With NSW he would have to do more.'

In a controversial move, the NSWRL gave a more public face to what had been up until then a private matter—by replacing Elias as Blues captain after two years with Laurie Daley, who had led Country to a 17–10 win against City. The appointment coincided with Balmain's new coach Alan Jones saying prop Steve Roach would be his first grade captain because the job was adding to the pressure on Elias.

It added up to a turbulent beginning to the always difficult task of beating Queensland. Gould, his problems with the players' attitude settled, worked quietly and enthusiastically towards harmony and team spirit. Good tactics and the courage to implement them are the foundation of any football team, but not necessarily in State of Origin football where game plans from theoretically better sides have been blown away on the night by an opposition fuelled by pride and loyalty.

Coaching at the highest level can often involve emotions at a much lower level. It takes an alchemy of understanding and the ancient arts of male bonding and friendship as well as the right moves on the field.

'Gould was a very impressive coach,' Elias remembered. 'He was a players' coach. The relationship between a coach and a player is very important. He had the advantage of being young and it was not all that long before that he had been a player. He was the mentor of the side. The players could react to his way of thinking. He was at the same time very funny, very serious and very focused. You had good times with Gus but when it was time to settle down and start working, he let you know.'

Elias remembers the emphasis on bonding at that first Origin preparation and the difference it made to the team's attitude. 'There was a relaxed attitude about the camps and a lot of young blokes tended to stretch out and be laid-back about it. You can drift into that kind of attitude yourself. You're trying to look cool because you're overawed by the status of the players around you. The Canberra players for example might come into the camp late because of flights to Sydney. From then on it would be casual. Clyde might not have his training gear. For the first few days it would be pretty casual and I suppose it did get a little blase. New players would think, "Hey, if this is the way it's done, I better be the same." Gus got everyone together and reminded us just how important it was for all of us. He told us no-one is too cool in this game and no-one is too good. These blokes (the Queenslanders) had our measure from the previous year when they beat us. So we had to refocus. And we did.'

That first NSW camp also produced the first 'golf match'.

Good as GOULD

Daley and Stuart approached Gould about playing golf one of the days and got his immediate approval because he was a keen player himself. 'What about clubs? I'll get someone to organise a course we can use,' he said.

That would not be necessary, they said. Daley and Stuart had already mapped out the course that would be used. It included 18 hotels—this was the plan for the famous pub golfing match that caused more headaches than an entire State of Origin series ever has. In pub golf a course is drawn up of either nine or 18 holes. Each 'hole' is a pub and carries a pre-determined designation of being a par 3, par 4 or par 5. Players have to sink a corresponding number of beers to the par within a designated time period. The size of the beer glass, seven ounce (usually), middy (occasionally) or schooner (very rarely) is decided beforehand. At a par three hole, the players have to drink three beers in half an hour, at a par five it is five beers and so on. If you drink four beers at a par three, you've had a birdie, five, you've had an eagle. Only two beers is a bogey. One, a double bogey.

The great golfing challenge started in the Eastern Suburbs. To give the tournament greater authenticity, Craig Salvatori produced a gold jacket that Jack Gibson had once given him. It was to represent the coloured jackets worn by the leader in a bike race or a big golf tournament. It changed hands depending on who was leading after each hotel. The players also produced a leader board and everyone had to wear a golf hat. This first year Salvatori was a tearaway early leader. Memories are understandably hazy but Salvatori is estimated to have been anything up to 11 under par after half a dozen pubs and wearing the gold jacket. 'He dropped off the pace soon after that,' Gould said. 'Someone remembers him slumped in a chair at one stage, the jacket falling off his shoulders.'

The eventual winner was stalwart Chris Johns, an always

THE ORIGIN EXPERIENCE

formidable competitor and a man with a healthy thirst. The golf day was almost instantly elevated to legendary status within the team ranks.

Gould has finally confessed that although he has been linked to the golf day, he in fact missed it. He took the chance to return to Penrith and try to sort out the club's recurring problems. 'But I left Geoff Carr, who is a very good judge of a schooner, in charge,' Gould said. 'He chaperoned the whole day.'

Gould did not return to the team hotel at Coogee until the next morning and the first person he ran into was co-manager Bob Saunders from North Sydney who volunteered what a great success the golf tournament had been. 'It was a terrific day,' said Saunders. 'The good thing was that they were all home in bed by midnight because they had been drinking all day and were too crook to continue. In fact at 6 o'clock this morning when I came down to have breakfast there was David Gillespie already having his breakfast.' Gould listened attentively to Saunders without a trace of scepticism. 'Knowing David Gillespie better than Bob Saunders I went to David's room,' Gould remembered. Looking up, Gillespie could only mutter: 'Oh, Gus. I've had a shocker. They told me we were going to the Robin Hood Hotel. I jumped into a cab and fell asleep. When I woke up the cab had taken me to the Riverwood Hotel (about an hour out of Sydney). I didn't have any money so he took me to the police station and I got locked up. Jimmy Tuit had to come and bail me out. I got in about five to six and as I tried to sneak in, Bob Saunders came down. I jumped into the restaurant to pretend I was having breakfast.'

The performance of the NSW side that first year of Gould's coaching tenure in 1992 could directly be linked to the more open and more emotional approach introduced by

Good as GOULD

Gould. He made patriotism popular. He convinced the players that wanting to win for your State and being prepared to stand by a team-mate and the team no matter how tough the circumstances were commendable and praiseworthy attributes. His was not the new-age philosophy of the early 1980s but a welcome and winning move away from the forced and artificial scepticism and indifference that previous teams had affected when beaten by passion-driven Queenslanders. He wanted NSW to win—and to be in pain if they lost.

Gould was unsparing with the players and himself. 'The other thing that worked well with Gus is that although you might be out having a drink and having a good time, football was never very far away,' Carr said. 'We've had a million days and nights on the drink since we all started and it has always been the same. I remember Gus was concerned about Laurie Daley. He was concerned that Daley might be intimidated by Mal Meninga, who was Queensland captain and also Daley's club captain at Canberra. I can remember countless nights with us standing around with Laurie, telling him he was the best player in the world and didn't have to worry about Meninga, that Meninga was at the end of his career and going out. It might be four o'clock in the morning and Gus would be working. He was never off the job. We also decided that because Mal had been in the job so long as Queensland captain he had developed a real arrogance. So we decided to upset the toss of the coin. We would not let Daley go out and wait in the middle for Mal to come out. We'd keep Daley in the dressing room so Mal would have to wait for him in the middle. I noticed in the last series (1994) that Laurie has the same sort of arrogance now. When they come in to say it's time for the toss, he's more inclined to say: "All right, mate. I'll be with you in a minute." It's like, "I'm in no hurry. They can't do it without me and I'm not going to stand out there waiting. I'll come in my own good time." Gus put a lot of effort into that.'

If the conditioners were making the players fitter and the gymnasiums were making them stronger and team doctor Nathan Gibbs was keeping them healthy, Gould was making them mentally tougher and more focused. Part mind games, part taunting, part mockery, part seriousness, part psychology and part tactical, it was a successful mix—and all of it done in the social atmosphere of an Origin camp.

Gould pushed Ricky Stuart to the limit, provoking him into running more. Although Gould had a great opinion of Stuart's passing and kicking game in matches and his ability to sum up options and take the best one, he wanted him to run more. He believed Stuart had even more to offer in a game if he ran the ball and he would say so, especially around three or four in the morning. 'Don't you worry though, Sticky. Don't bother running it. If you can't handle it, just throw the ball to Laurie.' Stuart would get worked up about it and say, 'Fuck you. I'm going to run it.'

Carr says: 'There was a lot of that going on in the early days. We were having a good time but football was never forgotten.'

Gould was reshaping, redirecting and reworking his team so that the total sum of his team was more valuable than the individual parts. Elias was blending into the hooker he could always be in big games. Daley was over any paranoia he might have had about Meninga and Stuart was prepared to alter his game and run the ball. Gould's final contribution was to pinpoint the tactics that would beat Queensland and supervise training and rehearsal of the set plays.

'Gus' homework was always great,' says Elias. 'He did his homework very well. To him it was not practice makes perfect. It was *perfect* practice makes perfect. That's how our attitude was focused. He would show us video of Queenslanders and point out who the lazy defenders were. He'd say if we attack in this area and play to these patterns, we'd find them out.'

Pinpointing individual habits of opposition players has always been a strong point of Gould's as a player and a coach. His former lock at Canterbury, Paul Langmack, remembered attending a video session conducted by Warren Ryan before a big game against Balmain. Ryan mentioned the name Steve 'Blocker' Roach, the Balmain prop. Gould, who was a player then, instantly responded, 'Steve Roach. Always carries the ball in his left arm.' 'I thought to myself. Geezus. How clever is that?' said Langmack. 'And I started looking at opposition players myself to see what I could learn about the way they played.'

For Queensland in that first match in 1992, Gould prepared something special. He was convinced that Meninga's reduced lateral movement acrossfield in defence was a weakness in the Queensland side. He devised a set move that would isolate Meninga in defence and lead to lock Bradley Clyde scoring. 'If you do this, you will be one on one at Mal,' he told Clyde. And that was exactly how it happened.

'I remember it well,' said Elias. 'We attacked down the left-hand side of the Sydney Football Stadium and it worked perfectly. Clyde scored.'

The manoeuvre was widely praised by the NSW players for the 6–nil lead it established. The acclaim in the media, however, sounded a discordant chord with Warren Ryan, whose years with the Country Origin sides had failed to produce a win against City. Speaking on Channel 7's *Sportsworld* television program the Sunday after the first State of Origin match and in reply to a Dorothy Dixer from fellow panellist Roy Masters, Ryan dismissed the recognition for the move as unnecessary—because it was an old one he had devised.

It was a provocative response that touched a nerve with

THE ORIGIN EXPERIENCE

Gould, who viewed the remarks as an accusation of rugby league plagiarism and was deeply cut at the accusation. He hit back strongly in his weekly column in the Sydney *Daily Telegraph* at a time when Ryan was having trouble with refereeing interpretations and had surrendered the Country coaching job to Mick Cronin after failing to win a game in five years.

Gould wrote: 'I know Warren Ryan would prefer that everyone in the world bowed at the hip when they came into his presence and thanked him for creating the game of rugby league in his own image and letting the rest of us all be involved. That way Warren could take credit for everything good that has happened in the premiership since 1908 and let the rest of us take the blame for anything that has gone wrong. Frankly I don't care and I would guess that the rest of the premiership coaches don't care if Warren Ryan takes the credit for everything. It's not that important to us. But it obviously is to Warren. He showed that last Sunday on television when he accused me of "plagiarising" one of his moves to use in NSW's State of Origin win against Queensland. Since when has a simple run-around manoeuvre near the ruck been a patented move? I wasn't there but I think there is every chance Dally Messenger was using that trick back in 1908. And I certainly remember Jack Gibson using it back in the 1960s. Coincidentally that was around the time that Warren was playing. Perhaps the move subconsciously sneaked into his mind and has stayed there so long that he now thinks of it as his own. Warren would be aware of the debt a lot of coaches say they owe Jack Gibson so I know he won't mind being mentioned in the same paragraph. I'm just glad that Warren had the chance to get to see the State of Origin match. A lot of his time nowadays is taken up with appearing on television as a commentator, sitting beside people he had always sworn were his mortal enemies. Nothing like the lure of television to settle a feud. Nice to know there is such forgiveness in old Wok after all. For the record, Warren had nothing to do with the moves NSW used in the State of Origin game. It was a polished-up version of a very old ruse and owed its successful execution more to the skill of Bradley Clyde, who scored the try, and the lead-up work of Benny Elias and John Cartwright than anything the coach thought up. When you have players of their class in your side, scoring tries becomes a lot easier.

'Sorry to disillusion you, Warren, but we didn't steal your move. Next time you devise one that works without incurring the wrath of referees for decoy running, you can stamp it with your copyright. In the meantime anyone wanting to pick a move could do a lot worse than study Mick Cronin—the man who steered Country to an historic win against City at his first attempt.'

Ryan, with ready access to replying through his own column in the *Sydney Morning Herald*, let the matter drop. Driving to training with Western Suburbs and with his hooker Joe Thomas in the car for company, Ryan would at one stage comment, 'He really got me, didn't he?'

With a foundation built on Clyde's early try and another from replacement forward Craig Salvatori plus goals from winger Rod Wishart, NSW skipped to 14–6 with 10 minutes to play. It was always going to be enough in one of the tightest and fiercest matches seen in State of Origin. Clyde and Laurie Daley were lost during the game through injury and Elias went off for treatment to a deep head gash that pumped out blood like a Texas oil strike and needed 10 stitches to close. His face smeared with blood and a red-stained bandage around his head, Elias returned to the fray to help protect NSW's two-tries-to-one margin.

Elias was also swept into the most emotional family scene ever witnessed in State of Origin football and probably in any first grade football competition. When the final hooter sounded Elias' mother Barbara ran onto the field and started wiping the blood from her son's head and forehead. Ignoring photographers and TV cameras—with pictures of the scene being beamed live into millions of homes all over Australia—Mrs Elias worked hard mopping the blood from his face with a handkerchief.

It was a spontaneous reaction from a concerned mother. Although some blame was directed towards Elias for generating another 'grandstand' performance, it was an incident that gave rugby league and especially State of Origin football a human face. Cut or no cut, Elias had lived up to his pledge when Gould threw him his own personal football. He was named man of the match.

There was more emotion in the dressing room as players grabbed each other with excitement. The bonding and the hard work put in by Gould in uniting the players had produced an immediate dividend. At half-time Gould had told the players: 'We've heard about that Maroon jumper for years. Take a look at your own. It's time to stand up for it.'

It was probably the pivotal moment in the story of NSW's State of Origin success. Emotion was good. Indifference was bad. Loyalty and pride were the buzz words for the Blues rugby league side. The exuberance of the players and delight of Blues supporters in seeing the team take a one–nil lead overshadowed the quality of the football which had been brutal rather than brilliant. But a win was a win.

'The atmosphere in the dressing room was more like, "well, we did it",' Gould said. 'I think at that stage we all realised that we were on the right track in preparing for State of Origin matches and in beating those mongrels. I don't think Queensland gave us a chance, which was in our favour. It was a really fierce match and we had five new caps in the side.

Good as GOULD

Queensland thought it was just going to be like old times. The new faces would go to pieces. We did it tough. Bradley Clyde was injured after scoring the first try and left the game. We lost Laurie Daley just after half-time after he knocked himself out in the in-goal.' The injured Daley stumbled groggily into the dressing room and mumbled, 'Mate, you're in charge,' to Elias who was getting his head stitched before running back out.

The second match was set down for Lang Park, representing a new challenge for Gould and some of the players. He had been there as a coach of club sides but not for State of Origin although he was well aware of the madness that could occur in crowds—numbers of whom arrived full of drink and got steadily worse all night.

The momentum of the NSW win in the first game was also affected by players returning to play with their club and their coach returning to the rapidly deteriorating situation with his side, Penrith.

Gould's worry was that the attitude from the players might not be quite as sharp as in the first match. After all, there was always the third game at the Sydney Football Stadium to come for the series decider if the Lang Park match was lost.

'The preparation for Lang Park where we hadn't won for so long was different,' Gould said. 'I'm convinced that we played the right type of game on the night but we ran into some drizzly rain and we ran into a referee, Bill Harrigan, who would not penalise.' Gould's disenchantment with Harrigan was already picking up the speed that would lead to a head-on collision in later years.

Harrigan perhaps didn't referee to Gould's liking but he gave NSW a tremendous lift in the opening minutes when he sent Queenslanders Martin Bella and Peter Jackson to the sin bin for dissent leaving the Maroons with only 11 men. It was a brave call by a referee at Lang Park. The remaining players showed great courage to keep their line intact with only 11 men and it awakened a resolve to win the match that they never surrendered. 'I think the commitment we showed in those 10 minutes won us the match,' Queensland captain Mal Meninga said later. 'That fact that it happened early helped. We were all still full of hype.'

After trailing 4–nil, Queensland levelled the score at 4–all with a try by Billy Moore. It was wet and greasy in the second half and scoring chances were minimal because of the conditions and the impregnable defence. As the minutes ticked away Langer seized the initiative as he would so often in State matches. Discovered by NSW stalwart Tommy Raudonikis, Langer regularly made life a misery for the Blues.

This time, with only 65 seconds left on the clock, Langer kicked a field goal—the first of his first grade career. 'It was the first one since I was a kid,' he told pressmen later. 'It just left my boot so well. Normally something goes wrong.' The one point squeezed Queensland home 5–4 to level the series.

In a moment that later embarrassed him greatly NSWRL chief executive John Quayle let slip that he was disappointed with the quality of the play in both opening Origin matches of 1992. When Gould resigned at the end of the first series, Quayle's remarks would be blamed for the decision but the truth of it was they had not been a factor. Quayle had been as disappointed as anyone else by the loss and had spoken rashly out of frustration. 'I think it was down to a real rivalry thing with him against Queensland,' Gould said. 'He was just dirty that we had been beaten. It didn't worry me a bit. What I pointed out was that while NSW had not won at Lang Park in five years, we also hadn't won under a NSW-appointed referee for five years. I think the referees were intimidated by Lang Park crowds. The loss didn't worry me. If it had been a draw we would have still needed to win the third game to take the series. We were criticised after that game for being a little negative in our play but in the conditions it was difficult to risk everything on one match. If we went for it and lost, even though we had played well, we would have to get up again for the third game. It wasn't a do-or-die preparation for game two but I still thought we had done enough to win,' Gould said. 'Queensland stood up on us all night. The players walked off the field disappointed and to make it worse we could hear the celebrations going on outside. I got the players together and said, "Look, things didn't go our way tonight but I don't think they are a better side than us. We're better than them. If I stick with you blokes for the third game will you stick with me?" The answer was yes.'

Gould turned to the chairman of selectors, Don Furner, who was standing nearby and said, 'No changes.' 'Fine,' said Furner.

It was a switch for Gould to get himself so directly involved in the selection of a team. His preference had been to let the selectors pick the side with minimal intervention. Other coaches such as Test coach Bob Fulton preferred to be heavily involved in selecting the line-ups that he would have to handle. Fulton's policy has always been that as he is taking responsibility for the team's performance, he should have considerable say in who is chosen, to ensure the chosen players fit in with his tactical plans.

'All along I've allowed the selectors to pick their sides,' Gould said. 'I've had conversations with them but I've never really disagreed with anything they have done. In that first State of Origin side we had five new caps, which plenty of people thought made our mission impossible. Then we lost Ricky Stuart and replaced him with 19-year-old John Simon. Laurie Daley was our new captain for the first time. But they played well and won.'

THE ORIGIN EXPERIENCE

NSW walked out of Lang Park that night as a losing side, but already the process of rebirth was beginning. The team headed back to Gould's room at the team hotel and there the players slumped on the chairs, the bed, the floor, sharing some beers. They talked about what had gone wrong and what had worked. 'They were genuinely hurt to have been beaten,' Gould said. 'We had been confident of winning but we hadn't. It was an important step in the bonding. If you can overcome a little adversity, sometimes a setback is good for you.'

After the first game second-rower John Cartwright had undergone an arthroscope to have a piece of cartilage removed from a troublesome knee. He wanted it done quickly so he could fulfil an ambition to play three games for NSW. The mini-operation was done at Penrith Park and he rang Gould while still affected by the anaesthetic. 'Tell them I'll be right,' he slurred, so groggy he could hardly be understood.

Cartwright had barely trained for the second game so he was part of the overall package of circumstances that led to NSW's loss. Then came the lucky break that welded the side. Next day the team's plane back to Sydney was delayed for three hours, time that was spent drinking and relaxing and warming to each other's company. 'By the time we got out of that bar I was convinced that the third game was as good as over,' Gould said later. 'The players agreed. You could feel the steel in their resolution hardening.'

Bradley Clyde had missed the second game but was back for the third. It was a decisive occasion for Gould and his team. They had been trying to establish themselves as a side to be contended with at representative level. Winning the first game had helped. Losing the second had raised doubts. Losing the third on home turf at the Sydney Football Stadium would mean that for all of the promise, all of the ambition of the side, nothing had changed. Yes. It was a decisive moment.

Good as GOULD

The last man out of the dressing room after the prematch talk on the night of the decider was Clyde. 'How are they?' Gould asked him.

'They can't get us,' Clyde replied.

The result was never in doubt. NSW won 16–4 to take the series. Balmain utility back Tim Brasher, making his Origin debut as a 21-year-old, pulled off two try-saving tackles after replacing injured Rod Wishart. One was after he had left his wing and taken the giant Meninga ball and all. Throughout the game the Blues were full of enthusiasm and power. They scored the first of three tries early when Stuart went over from a rehearsed move in the 14th minute. It was Benny Elias who confirmed his value to the side and erased earlier doubts by starting the move that led to NSW's second try midway through the second half. Elias went to the blind side, passed to Daley who grubber-kicked. Centre Paul McGregor got to the ball first, stepped past a tackler and found Daley backing-up. Daley gave the ball to Ettingshausen who scored for 8–4. Stuart back at the scrum base, displacing Simon who had made such a favourable impression in his representative debut, had a sparkling game. His long kicking and long passing were too much for the Queenslanders.

The quest that had begun in such difficult circumstances had been successfully completed. NSW had won the series and seemed to have established a foundation for continued domination, by unearthing great players, an astute coach and a committed and professional back-up team of managers Geoff Carr and Bob Saunders, Dr Nathan Gibbs, the NSWRL's Paul Broughton and others. It was a team that worked as effectively off the field as the players did on it. Gould had overcome the difficulties of coping with new faces and new circumstances and the initial loss to Country.

'I know people reckon that it doesn't matter,' he said. 'But

THE ORIGIN EXPERIENCE

if it's your first game as a representative coach you want to do well and you want things to go all right. City–Country is a very rushed week. There are a couple of brief training sessions and there is really no genuine coaching possible. That year all happened very quickly for me. I was very frustrated going into that first representative game. In my own mind I knew we were under-prepared. But that's the way it goes.'

The City–Country game, however, produced some positives. Number one was Laurie Daley's captaincy of the Country side—a bonus because NSW was looking for a captain. Players like Paul Harragon, Paul McGregor, Clyde, Lazarus and Johnny Simon performed well that year. So did Newcastle's Robbie McCormack.

'Suddenly we had a very new, young group of players trying to force their way into representative football,' said Gould. 'NSW had in the previous years stuck with a number of the established and elite players. It was encouraging to me that with a younger and more refreshing outlook and a fresher start, it would make my job a little easier. So although it did not seem so at the time, Country winning that first match was good.'

In a single series Gould had turned around NSW's record of losses, put pride back in the blue jumper, had unearthed new players and connected with them emotionally and tactically and, from that mix, blended a winning formula. The future had never looked brighter for the NSW Blues. Except for one thing. The coach was quitting.

The Brotherhood

Gould had long harboured a suspicion that motivation and pride had been the missing ingredients in the NSW side. Commitment was there to a degree—no-one wanted to lose—but it was not the white-hot intensity needed to match Queensland's zeal.

To Queenslanders, pulling on a maroon jumper and beating NSW, preferably at Lang Park in front of 30,000 supporters, was rugby league utopia. No-one ever asked Queenslanders if playing in a winning State of Origin side surpassed playing Test football. Questioners might have been surprised by the answer. The mateship, patriotism and pride in playing for Queensland was as palpable as the energy Souths could generate when playing at Redfern Oval—an experience Gould had personally recognised.

New South Wales players had traditionally been sceptical of the blind Queensland enthusiasm and unabashed pride in playing for their State, even when stories emerged of Maroon players chanting 'Queenslander' to unite themselves in times of adversity in matches.

Journalists with access to both camps were aware of the disparity in approach to State of Origin football, but could not convey their impressions to NSW players who could not *experience* Queensland's attitude.

Gould's first experience with the NSW team confirmed his suspicions. Players were indifferent to training schedules and

THE ORIGIN EXPERIENCE

timetables. There was more emphasis on socialising, cracking jokes and reminiscing than concentrating on training.

'Even during the 1980s when Queensland were giving it to us, our side always seemed under-prepared. The players didn't seem to have any passion for it—certainly not enough to match the passion that was coming from the Queensland camp,' he said.

Although apprehensive, Gould was reluctant to start demanding immediate changes, preferring to hope the players' attitude would sort itself out and improve. 'You get together with players like Glenn Lazarus, Ben Elias, Andrew Ettingshausen and Chris Johns. There were blokes I'd never had anything to do with, people like Bradley Clyde, Laurie Daley. We'd have a meeting and they'd stroll down the stairs. They didn't worry if they were 10 minutes late. You'd ask them to meet in the foyer to go to training and half of them wouldn't have their boots on.

'We'd go down to the park and I'd try and get organised for a training session and they would just lumber around and joke. That sort of thing. For the first two or three days it was a real shock.'

Something had to give in what was an increasingly tense situation for Gould although the players were probably unaware of the impression their attitude was having on the new coach.

Gould puzzled why players he knew would not behave so irresponsibly at training sessions with their own clubs, suddenly became carefree when they made the next step to a representative team. 'I'm not using it as a reflection on anyone who had coached them in the past but it was obviously a situation that had been allowed to slide,' he said.

After three days Gould was ready for battle. Either do it his way or the team could get a new coach. He spoke to an old friend from his playing days at Newtown, Jim Tuite, then the conditioner with the NSW side, to get a perspective.

Good as **GOULD**

Gould told him: 'I'm not happy with this. I think they have to do it our way or I'm out of here. We'll leave and let them have it.'

Growing disillusionment and a series of poor training sessions with no enthusiasm or urgency finally made frankness the vital element. Calling the players together after another sloppy session Gould spoke with brutal honesty. 'The last three days have taught me the reason why Queensland blokes have been kicking our arse in this competition and why you blokes haven't been successful and why you *won't* be successful with your current attitudes. Now if that's the way you want to go, that's fine. But you can do it without me. I have enough problems back at Penrith and I'd rather be back there sorting them out if you blokes don't want to take this seriously.'

Gould considered some of the players at that stage to be more concerned with their own reputation and personal status than the good of the team and made it clear he would quit if attitudes did not improve.

It was Tuite who provided the emphasis. Running with the players out of Gould's earshot he said: 'I've known him too long. I know that he's fair dinkum. This is our first crack at this game and if you don't support him he'll walk out.'

Back at the hotel there was another team meeting and the barriers finally fell. Gould had never doubted that playing for their State was important to the players. He believed they were just embarrassed to make their feelings known to their teammates for fear of being ridiculed and thought soft. He told the team he genuinely believed they took their blazers home and were proud of having played for NSW—otherwise they would not be so complaining when they were omitted. They had to learn to be more professional about their feelings. It was all right to be passionate about representing NSW. It was an achievement of which to be proud.

THE ORIGIN EXPERIENCE

It was Bradley Clyde who broke the silence when Gould finished talking. 'Yeah, I'm like that. I'm really proud to play for NSW but I'm too scared to say anything when blokes muck up. I'm too scared to show how much it means to me and I fool around at training like everyone else.'

Gradually all of the players admitted to the same self-doubts. They had always come along to representative football camps, gone along with things and trusted in their ability to pull it out on the night. They knew that preparation and attitude had never been 100 per cent.

The building process having begun, the new emphasis would be on pride. Queensland had always melded players from Canberra, Brisbane, Canterbury or any number of sides into a fiercely competitive composite team for State of Origin. NSW had to do the same.

'Gus told us that the Queenslanders were just like spies pretending to be something they were not. They would play with us at club level and then go to Brisbane and reveal all they knew about our individual plays and habits to make it easier for Queensland,' one player recalled. 'We'd never thought of it that seriously before.'

International Ian Roberts said that the meeting with Gould ensured equality among the players. 'There are no egos. He makes sure of that from day one,' Roberts said of Gould's method. Roberts said he remembered clearly the team meeting with Gould back at the hotel and the effect it had on the players. The fundamental thing had to do with the Australian sportsman's philosophy. It's not that they are embarrassed to succeed. They are embarrassed to *acknowledge* that they have succeeded. Unfortunately players don't give themselves enough personal 'wraps' for the levels of achievement they reach.

'That's the Australian attitude. I don't know why. Whenever sportsmen achieve something they tend to play it down instead of enjoying it like the Yanks and the Pommies do. It's wrong. It did all change with us when Gus got there, I'll tell you that.'

Gould asked the players to name the essential ingredients they believed it took to produce a winning side and the players subsequently realised just how many of those components were missing from the NSW line-up. From then on information was pooled. The players were canvassed on what type of game they wanted to play and a tactical plan acceptable to everyone was devised.

'We agreed that if we were going to beat Queensland we had to be organised and we had to have something that would stand up under pressure and we had to be ready to go,' said one player.

The philosophy behind Gould's coaching has always been togetherness and fraternity built on a foundation of players' skills and astute tactical planning. The unit came from bonding sessions that could have found a place of honour at a Munich beer festival. Grouped around a piano singing songs in the lobby of their hotel, the players would stretch the festivities until the early morning light through the plate glass windows would reveal early surfers catching the first of the day's waves.

From time to time the players would be joined by a passing parade of notables, the occasional jockey, player–manager, chief executive and, on the odd occasion, NSWRL general manager John Quayle. 'The big thing on Gus' mind was that Queensland had a mortgage on mateship,' said NSW team manager Geoff Carr. 'He worked very hard on team spirit, especially in the first series in 1992. He worked hard on keeping everyone together. We would go into camp on Monday and the players would be together until Thursday when they would be sent home. They would return on Saturday morning ready for the Monday night game and that is when the hard work would start.

THE ORIGIN EXPERIENCE

'Everyone knew when they came back on Saturday morning that the party was over. It was the end of festivities. The end of bonding.'

It was an adaption of Queensland's policy of togetherness but done with more formal planning and cohesion. It might not have always seemed so to the casual onlooker, but there were firm guidelines. 'I think Queensland over the years haven't been able to cut off when the party finishes and the work starts,' Carr said. 'Because they were winning all those years, they were just partying through to the weekend. Our players knew that Monday, Tuesday and Wednesday, particularly Monday and Tuesday, they would have a good time. Wednesday was winding-down day. When they came back on Saturday it was strictly business.'

Now it was 1993, the first match of the series just 48 hours away. 1992 had been run and won and the hope was there for the turnaround, for the long-hoped-for period of NSW supremacy but what lay ahead was not without drama, controversy, Gould's resignation, and severed friendships . . .

MG's Crash

The fireworks that marked the 1993 representative season started a long while before the scheduled pyrotechnics to celebrate the start of the first game. After watching NSW reassert itself as the king of Australian rugby league the previous season with a tight 2–1 series win, it must have heartened Queensland to see the opposition seemingly intent on self-destruction. Once again it was the yin of Gould's personality against the yang of Mark Geyer's. Only Chinese philosophers, astrologers and stargazers could interpret the fatal alignment of the planets that kept propelling Gould and Geyer into each other's orbits with such headline-generating and emotionally draining force.

This time would be a clash like no other as they butted heads in the dressing room at Leichhardt Oval in their first meeting since the dramas of the previous year when Geyer had walked out of Penrith. Geyer had spent the rest of the 1992 season saying he was getting himself together and tossing up offers from half a dozen clubs. He chose Balmain after deciding that the club's then coach Alan Jones offered the stability and guidance he needed. As the 1993 season unfolded Geyer became more and more of a chance of forcing his way into the first representative game of the season, City–Country, even though he had missed three or four of the opening six rounds of the season. Geyer's selection was more an idea by selectors to have a look at him again in a representative match with a longer view to the State of Origin series.

THE ORIGIN EXPERIENCE

Geyer had played State of Origin and two Tests against New Zealand in 1991 and toured with the 1990 Kangaroos, returning voted as the most improved player and having played one Test against France. It was a record too full of potential to dismiss simply on the basis of a wickedly disrupted 1992. Loyalty towards a proven player is not rare but it is seldom duplicated if the performance is below par. With hindsight, the selectors might have been premature in rushing Geyer back into the representative teams in view of his delicate emotional state. He still had not recovered from the death of Ben Alexander the previous year and despite his claims to the contrary, he had not settled in as well as expected at Balmain. Geyer had continued to live and socialise at Penrith in an environment Balmain did not think was ideal. Eventually Balmain and Geyer were to part company the following season after new coach Wayne Pearce set about establishing a playing strength that contained only players in whom he had full confidence and trust.

Geyer's was a brief stay in the Tigers' den but memorable for one explosive Tuesday when unprecedented scenes of conflict erupted at the City team training session. Geyer had been chosen in the City Firsts side the previous Sunday night but had failed to attend training and the medical the next day at Leichhardt Oval.

Often a breach like that is enough to get a player dropped from a side because of the limited time available to prepare for the match the following Friday night. Luck was with Geyer. He rang Dr Nathan Gibbs, the team medical officer, to say he could not attend the session because he was in bed with a virus. Gibbs simply passed on the message at training to team managers Geoff Carr and Bob Saunders and coach Gould. Had Geyer contacted either manager he might have been ruled out immediately. By ringing Gibbs, Geyer managed to complicate the situation.

'We had a bit of a meeting there and then about whether he

should still be dropped,' Carr said. 'I told the NSWRL representative Paul Broughton that Geyer had to come to the session. Broughton rang Geyer's home but was unable to contact him. Instead he spoke to Mark's mother and told her Mark had to be at the next day's medical at 9am sharp or he would be dropped. He said he had impressed upon Mrs Geyer the absolute importance of Mark arriving on time because he was already getting a concession by not being ruled out that day.'

Carr was concerned that the circumstances were already worsening City Firsts' chances of beating Country and adding to the strain of being ready to meet Queensland. 'The medical has to be on Monday because of the time factor,' Carr said. 'Players who have been chosen from Brisbane have to fly to Sydney, we have to know who is in and who is out, training has to be organised, medicals completed, playing gear distributed, photographs taken and replacement players decided upon and then contacted—then brought to training if changes are made. You need to know on Monday who is in and who is out because you only really have Tuesday and Wednesday to prepare for a Friday night match.'

Gould had deliberately kept out of the situation involving Geyer's failure to attend training because of the animosity of the previous year at Penrith. The catalyst for that dispute had partly revolved around Geyer's perception that Gould had misled him about his chances of NSW selection if he dropped out of the City side. To Gould, it was not worth raking over old ashes by getting involved in more representative team drama the following year. If the management team had extended the deadline for Geyer, that was fine with Gould. He would just wait for the final decision. Gould was technically not even involved because Alan Fitzgibbon was coaching Geyer's City Firsts side. Gould was in charge of City Origin.

Gould, however, did confide his anxiety to Carr. 'Between

you and me,' he said, 'I'm not going to get involved in any of this. But I'm telling you he will let you down. I know him very well. He hasn't played for two or three weeks and he's suddenly back in representative football where he hasn't been for a while. He's not ready to play yet and he doesn't want to embarrass himself. So I'm sure he's going to let you down. But leave me out of it. I can't be seen to be involved and I won't be involved.'

Despite Gould's misgivings he kept them private apart from his talk with Carr. Geyer's fate was in his own hands. If he turned up for the 9am deadline and passed the medical, he was in the side without problems and would be treated the same as any other player. The gathering tension was probably only felt by Gould, Saunders and Carr as they watched the clock at Leichhardt Oval tick down the final minutes towards 9am the next day. 9am came and went. So did 9.05. Then 9.10 and finally 9.15 and no MG.

'That's it,' said Carr to Saunders. 'We said 9am and he's still not here. He's out.' At 9.20 Geyer walked in. He started shaking hands with team-mates as he made his way through the shed and walked up to Nathan Gibbs, who began looking at Geyer's thumb injury.

Carr walked over to intervene, telling Geyer there was possibly a problem about his inclusion in the side because of his late arrival. 'You were supposed to be here at 9am. By 9.15 we ruled you out,' Carr said. Geyer took the rebuke in his stride and almost it seemed with relief that the strain of playing had been taken from his shoulders. All he asked for was that Carr let him disappear quietly and not be embarrassed. Carr, trying to be fair, then offered a stay of execution if Geyer could explain his lateness.

Geyer told him he had started out from Penrith at 7.30am and had been caught in traffic. Carr responded: 'Is that it? You were caught in traffic?'

Good as GOULD

Geyer: 'Yes. I've taken an hour and 50 minutes to get here.'
Carr walked across to speak to Gould in a move that was interpreted by Geyer as a conference. In fact Carr simply asked Gould a couple of questions.
'Where do you live, Gus, in relation to MG?' Carr said.
Gould: 'I live about five minutes further west.'
Carr: 'How long did you take to get here?'
Gould: 'About 50 minutes or an hour.'
Carr: 'How was the traffic?'
Gould: 'Fine. I got here in plenty of time.'
The apparent scenario was that Gould, who lived further west than Geyer, had left later than him yet still arrived an hour earlier. It left Carr no choice. He consulted Saunders and then returned to Geyer's side to tell him he was out of the team.
Geyer, probably influenced by the fact that he had seen Carr confer with Gould, threw his training bag to the ground then picked it up and started walking towards Gould, convinced the coach was to blame for the decision. It was a remarkable turnabout from a player who, minutes earlier, had only been interested in departing as inconspicuously as possible from the ground if he were to be ruled out.
City Origin and City Firsts players, Saunders and Carr recounted the next exchange as Geyer eyeballed an equally determined Gould.
Geyer: 'I'm out of the side.'
Gould: 'Apparently.'
Geyer: 'You're a ____ .'
Gould: 'Have you got a problem?'
Geyer: 'I'll have you outside.'
Gould, delivering the line that was to become a classic: 'Well don't let fear hold you back.'
Geyer later denied that Gould had come out with the 'Don't

let fear hold you back' line, saying it would have pushed him over the edge in the agitated state he was already in.

But other onlookers are just as certain Gould had used the words. Years later when Gould joined 2UE as a commentator, veteran broadcaster Frank Hyde approached him at a station party, saying he thought 'Don't let fear hold you back' was one of the best quips he had ever heard in rugby league. 'I wish I'd thought of it!' Hyde added.

On Gould's response those in the dressing shed said Geyer momentarily hesitated before deciding to continue on his way to the exit.

Dr Gibbs later observed to Carr: 'You're a bigger fool than him'—and pointed at Gould. 'You stepped between them.'

After confronting Gould, Geyer stormed from the dressing room and headed for his car. Onlookers reckoned that Geyer had tears in his eyes as he drove away, a further indication of his emotional state.

'Geyer should have been there on Monday. Everyone else turned up. We brought players from Brisbane, Illawarra and Newcastle in time for the medical but we gave Geyer the benefit of the doubt,' Carr said. 'It was his second chance. He sacked himself.'

Geyer headed straight to the home of his coach Alan Jones, who chose to launch the most extraordinary defence of his player, going to elaborate lengths to excuse his error. At his best Jones can sell sump oil from the back of a ute and convince customers it's champagne. His ratings figures on radio underline his mental and verbal agility as well as his intelligence. He pulled out all the stops on this one. Geyer was suddenly discovered to have made the long journey from Penrith without any money, which forced him to use the slower public highway rather than the faster toll road. Geyer's impecunity had not been mentioned in the discussions with Carr.

Good as GOULD

Then NSWRL general manager John Quayle rang in terse mood, wanting to know what had happened, why he had not been consulted and demanding a full report. 'I hadn't told him because I was busy with the media,' Carr said.

'Jones held a press conference at 4 o'clock that afternoon to give MG's story. He's got his own radio show but he chose to give a press conference about what had happened to MG—without having MG there. I figured I would hear from Jones the next morning to talk about it on his radio show. I was up at 5.30am to go for a run. Then I sat by the phone but he never called. He wasn't interested in anything else but pushing his own version. The toll money story was never mentioned by MG. But someone had to come up with a reason why it would take him nearly two hours to get somewhere when it took everyone else only an hour.'

The man who benefited most from Geyer's departure was Canberra second-rower David Furner, the son of the chairman of selectors and former Kangaroo Don Furner. Illawarra's Neil Piccinelli took Geyer's place in the City Firsts pack. Furner became the new reserve forward, beginning a representative trip that would carry him into the 1994 Kangaroo side the following year.

When the dust settled after that fateful day, City Origin got on with the job they had been selected to do and beat Country 7–nil at Parramatta Stadium. City Firsts beat Country 40–4. It was sweet revenge for City sides that had been embarrassingly beaten the previous year and the first time since 1979 that City had beaten Country to nil in the main game.

No NSW side has ever got its campaign off to a more convincing start than the team of 1993. Ignoring the recent history of eight previous defeats at Lang Park, NSW confronted the Queenslanders in their most comfortable environment in Brisbane and came away courageous winners 14–10. There was a post-match controversy focused on Queensland captain Mal Meninga turning the air as blue as the colour of the NSW jumpers as he motivated his team with a speech in a huddle in the middle of the field. Unaware that television cameras had sneaked up behind him and were recording live sounds and pictures that were being beamed into millions of homes all around Australia, Meninga held nothing back. Although Meninga's words wouldn't raise an eyebrow in a dressing room and were accepted as motivational language, the flood of expletives brought a similar flood of complaints from viewers. The Australian Rugby League banned cameras from similar intrusions into team huddles in the future.

After the match Queensland had even more to swear about as they contemplated having to fight back in the series from one–nil down. New South Wales led 12–2 at half-time and then held on grimly in a dour second half, repelling waves of Queensland attackers.

Queensland, under new coach Wally Lewis who had replaced Graham Lowe, seemed superglued in NSW territory. At one stage Queensland had the ball for 21 consecutive tackles inside NSW's 10-metre line. In all NSW made 161 tackles in the second half as they defended their lead. The commitment was so intense that NSW forward Ian Roberts had to leave the field late in the game suffering from exhaustion.

The NSW camp knew the dangers of playing at Lang Park against a dedicated Queensland team and the players had sworn in the dressing room before the match not to be overwhelmed. It was a pledge that these days carries considerably more weight under Gould's coaching philosophy of deep loyalty among the players.

'It was the start we wanted. It gave us the chance to wrap up the series on our home ground, the Sydney Football Stadium, in the second match and to put pressure on

Good as GOULD

Queensland to try something different to win,' Gould said. 'If we were beaten in Sydney we still had a chance to take the series by winning the third match back at Lang Park. Obviously winning the second match was the preference.'

The second match in 1993 at the Sydney Football Stadium produced one of the greatest images in the history of the series. It came close to full-time with NSW clinging to a 16–12 lead. Queensland's hopes rose when Meninga came charging out of his own quarter and raced 40 metres before confronting NSW captain Laurie Daley, the sole defender. It was a State of Origin moment frozen in time, captain on captain and the match result resting on the winner of the confrontation. It was the Canberra captain Meninga being chased by his team-mate Daley. It was the face of the future chasing down the present. It was Daley who perhaps remembered the way Meninga had conned him years back in his first State of Origin match by saying it was not all that serious—then Meninga belting him all night in a painful introduction to the big-time. It was Gould watching from the sideline and wondering if those long nights spent drinking with Daley and lifting his commitment had worked. And it was Meninga, perhaps glancing across and seeing Father Time coming at him in a NSW jumper. For whatever reason Meninga chose to pass the ball to front-rower Mark Hohn, who dropped it as the bell sounded.

'It was a memorable image,' Gould recalled. 'Daley racing across field. The player who would go on to replace Mal as Australian captain coming to get the current Australian captain and the result of the match swinging on the result. Moments like that are what the game is all about.'

For all of the celebration that went with NSW's second series win, there was no doubt that the Queenslanders played without luck on the night. The Maroons led 6–nil at half-time and Gould produced a stirring speech in the break to get NSW refocused.

THE ORIGIN EXPERIENCE

'We were up against a good side, who were playing well,' he said. 'We were not treating them with the respect they deserved.' The result was two NSW tries in three minutes after half time.

But it was Queensland's own self-destruct mechanism that was the major contribution to the result. They missed at least three try-scoring chances in the first half and two more in the second. In the opening 40 minutes Willie Carne scored a fair try from a well-planned and well-executed cross-field kick from Allan Langer but referee Eddie Ward ruled Carne was off-side. Television replays showed he wasn't. In the 30th minute Meninga passed to winger Adrian Brunker who was tackled short of the line after Meninga looked as if he might have scored himself. Four minutes later Dale Shearer inexplicably lost the ball in the in-goal area when he should have scored.

Meninga made amends to some degree when he crashed over right on half-time for 6–nil. Squandering three try-scoring chances is a fatal weakness in State of Origin and Queensland wandered forlornly from the field looking at a 6–nil lead that could have been a commanding 24–nil.

New South Wales were too professional to let a second chance escape after Queensland's mistakes. Laurie Daley scored early in the second half and lock Brad Mackay was over three minutes later after a Ricky Stuart clearing kick was touched in flight putting NSW on-side and allowing Brad Fittler to regain possession. From having been under pressure and looking as if a loss was imminent, the Blues had bounced back for a four-point lead at 10–6.

Both sides scored again leaving the classic Daley chase on Meninga as the finale. Lewis was philosophical about the loss, realising it was a match his players had let slip. 'It was a magnificent game of football,' he said. 'It was a case of us having more opportunities. We should have led 18–nil. You don't get that many opportunities in State of Origin football.'

Good as GOULD

NSW went into the match with a new hooker, Newcastle's Robbie McCormack, because Benny Elias had been suspended for backchatting a touch judge. Knowing that a quick assimilation into team routine was essential, Gould had the players ring McCormack at home after news of his inclusion came through late in the night. They all congratulated him and insisted he make the long trek to Coogee from Newcastle immediately, despite the lateness of the hour so he could meet his team-mates and have a drink in convivial circumstances.

At Lang Park in the final game Queensland played with the intensity of a team chasing a win rather than a side just finishing a dead rubber. At the end of it they walked off Lang Park convincing 24–12 winners after scoring four tries to two. 'Queensland were hungrier and more settled. They deserved to win that game,' said Elias, who had been rushed back into the side for the final match.

Featuring strongly was a wild brawl in the 23rd minute that saw Steve Walters and Martin Bella from the Queensland side go to the sin bin with Paul Harragon and Elias. According to Elias the brawl started after a quick scrum that broke up with Harragon and Bella clinging to each other behind the play. Bella was doing plenty of talking and Paul Sironen, who was nearby and a great believer in cutting the red tape, yelled out to Harragon: 'Belt him. Just belt him.' Which Harragon did. Walters, an old and bitter rival of Elias, then clocked the NSW hooker.

It was an anticlimactic finish for New South Wales, series winners but their achievement overwhelmed on the night. It would have been the same problem if the situation had been reversed and Queensland was being acclaimed as series winners despite losing the third match at the Sydney Football Stadium. Perhaps the presentation to the side that wins the series after two matches should be made immediately. A further presentation could be made if the team goes through undefeated. That scheme would have meant NSW making a lap of honour around the Sydney Football Stadium in front of their supporters after winning the second game. If NSW had won the third game at Lang Park they could have been presented again for making a clean sweep of the series.

'It was disappointing to lose the third game but we had won the series. That was the important thing,' Gould said. For a coach who was going to quit after his first series in 1992, Gould had now steered NSW to the dizzy heights of an unprecedented three consecutive wins. At the celebrations that night there was no doubt in any NSW minds that the run of success would continue. Meninga was retiring at the end of the year and would not play in 1995. Several other Queenslanders were likely to be missing as well like Bella, Gillmeister and Shearer because of age. Nothing, it seemed, could stop NSW from making it four straight. Nothing, that was, except extraordinary and unprecedented events that lay a little further down the road.

Magic Night at the MCG

Bringing off back-to-back wins in State of Origin football is like hunting lions. It is nice to celebrate the success when you bag one but you must remember to be just as cautious the next time. NSW forgot that maxim in 1994 and it proved an incredibly costly blunder which led to one of the most dramatic escapes in the history of big-time football in Australia. It also gave the NSW players the chance to prove their mettle and fight back from being one-down after the extraordinary circumstances which marked their loss in the only game scheduled for their home ground, the Sydney Football Stadium.

Season 1994 dawned without incident. Players with their eyes on the Kangaroo tour were looking towards the representative season with enthusiasm. Only 28 players of the 50 or 60 candidates would make the historic trip and continue a tradition started in 1908. No-one suspected that the 1994 tour would be the last time a Kangaroo side would go away under the auspices of the Australian Rugby League because the Super League bomb was about to explode and England was on the verge of switching to summer football. The knowledge that the 1994 tourists might win a special place in history as the last of the breed probably would not have made any difference to the major candidates. Competition was, as always, razor keen. The outsiders for the tour kept plugging away week after week waiting for a miracle. The obvious choices hoped and prayed they could maintain their best form without running into serious injuries that would jeopardise their selection.

The first indication that the traditional series of representative matches was going to be extraordinary came with the first game of the year. It was City against Country in Newcastle. To the delight of the biased rural crowd, Country, coached by Canterbury's Chris Anderson, inflicted City's biggest loss in 67 years, winning 22–2.

It was a complete and unanswerable win by a Country side that overcame the loss of five-eighth Matthew Johns with injury the day before the game and then the absence of half Ricky Stuart on the day of the match. Stuart's withdrawal was met with some scepticism by Country supporters who thought he should have withdrawn earlier rather than disrupt the side. By dropping out, Stuart at least ensured his fitness for NSW selection. Country and Canberra lock Bradley Clyde was man of the match against a City side that was swamped on the night.

Except for City's loss to Country, life was proceeding along traditional lines. St George, Brisbane and Canberra were on top of the premiership; Nick Greiner was premier of NSW, Wayne Goss was in charge of Queensland; the sun was still rising in the east and setting in the west. And everything was pointing towards another NSW win—possibly even a clean sweep in the State of Origin series.

The back-to-back wins in 1992 and 1993 had been graciously accepted by NSW supporters. Now they wanted more. It was time to crush the upstart Queenslanders completely with a three–nil whitewash . . .

The Blues were certainly well on their way to making it happen when they led 12–4 with five minutes to play at the Sydney Football Stadium in the first match of the series. The trickle of supporters moving towards the exits in an effort to get an early start on the traffic that would be generated by the capacity crowd obviously thought Queensland could not win. Those who left missed one of the great rugby league miracles.

Queensland cut NSW's lead to 12–10 as the clock ticked into the final five minutes. Willie Carne scored for Queensland, reaching over his head to take a pass from centre Mark Coyne, whose contribution to the match had not yet ended. Queensland captain Mal Meninga kicked the conversion but a NSW side that had been clearly dominant all night with a polished display of professionalism was surely not in danger. The enthusiasm that followed Meninga's conversion kick gradually dissipated in the balmy air as the clock ticked towards the final minute and the floodlights showed Queensland pinned in their own quarter.

Then came the greatest escape in the history of State of Origin matches, more dramatic even than Mark McGaw's last-minute try to win the second at Lang Park. McGaw's try was memorable in a tight and tense match. But what happened at the Sydney Football Stadium on that fateful night from a side that had been outplayed for more than 70 minutes was a miracle worthy of Lourdes.

Newspaper headlines called it the try from hell—a superb (or sinful) 80-metre spectacular of commanding flamboyance and brilliance, made all the more incendiary by the pressure of the clock and the desperate circumstances.

Gould, sitting on the sideline with NSW manager Geoff Carr, will have the image etched on his subconscious for ever. 'When Queensland scored to get back to 12–10 there were three minutes left on the clock,' he said. 'I figured we would kick off and they would have two sets of six and we'd have one set of six. The last scrum packed down with one minute 38 seconds on the clock and I said to Geoff: 'This is it!' He said: 'Don't worry, we'll be all right.'

That epitaph rattled loosely to the floor of the Sydney Football Stadium as the unthinkable happened for NSW.

THE ORIGIN EXPERIENCE

The coaches, officials and spectators sit in special sections at the Stadium on tiers just above ground level and just metres from the sideline. So Gould had a clear view of the try. 'Queensland took the ball two plays across the field and on tackle three they spread the ball right across the field,' he said. 'Our centre Paul McGregor had been injured but he had to return to the game on the wing because we'd run out of replacements. He sort of limped up in the line in defence because he was struggling. I can still see it all in my mind although it was happening very quickly. The ball came along the line to Willie Carne and the next player who would get the ball was Steve Renouf.'

In the official box, NSW minds silently willed the great gods of rugby league to open up a hole and swallow the surging Queensland attack. The NSW tryline was still 60 metres away but its impregnability was eroding with each passing second. If Renouf got the ball NSW would suddenly be enormously and unexpectedly vulnerable.

'I remember thinking "don't pass it to him, don't pass it to him" as Carne looked at Renouf,' Gould said. 'Carne was sort of half-tackled and managed to float the ball over the top. I remember saying out loud: "Oh fuck!".'

Almost existentially, the scene turned from too fast to too slow, as if a giant hand had reversed the control button on the Football Stadium. 'As I saw Renouf take off down the sideline, all of a sudden there was a little bit of panic in our defence,' Gould remembered. 'I looked back and I could see the wave of Maroon jerseys getting into position to support. I think Renouf turned it inside to Hancock and he bumped his way acrossfield, beating a tackle where he was finally, sort of half-tackled 30 metres out by Andrew Ettingshausen.

'Darren Smith bumped a player and half got through a tackle and gave it to Alfie Langer. He stepped around Graham

Good as GOULD

Mackay and got the ball to Mal Meninga 15 metres out. I could hear Geoff Carr in the background going "Oh no, oh no" with every step and every half-tackle. Meninga threw the ball to Mark Coyne who stepped back inside Brad Fittler and reached out over the top of Ricky Stuart's outstretched arm and got the ball down in the last gasp.'

TRY!!!

'The minute they hit the line I looked at the clock and there were 32 seconds left,' Gould said. 'I turned around to Jimmy Tuit our trainer and said: "This one is over" and I walked down and went back to the dressing room. There was nothing anyone could do about it. It was just one of those tries from hell, and that's how it was described in the papers.'

The NSW contingent was an island of silence in the pandemonium that exploded. The build-up to the night had been coolly confident. There had been the accepted player bonding on one of the first nights in camp. The sing-a-long around the piano at the Holiday Inn, Coogee. The training sessions at nearby Coogee Oval and the resharpened ambition to again derail the once-powerful maroon express.

'We came into camp and things went pretty well for us,' Gould said. 'No excuses. When the time came to start the series, we were ready to play. We wanted to be one-up after Sydney and have the series won after Melbourne and not have to play the decider in Brisbane.'

Even Queensland players had difficulty accepting that they had won a game in which they had been outplayed from the opening whistle.

'I thought we were gone. I'll be honest,' said half-back Langer.

'We had to score two tries in the last five minutes to win. That was going to be tough. When we got the first one we were still not certainties.'

THE ORIGIN EXPERIENCE

The lead-up to the try is etched in Langer's mind as it is in Gould's.

Langer can relate the lead-up work with accuracy and economy even now. 'It was possibly the greatest try in State of Origin history,' he says. 'And we scored it to beat NSW on their own home ground. I didn't think the try was certain even when Coyne got the ball off Meninga. He still had a lot of work to do.

'There were three blokes defending. It was miraculous really that he got over the line. I was amazed when he got up and the referee awarded the try.'

In hindsight Gould remembered the match as being more important to both sides than people realised. 'At the end of the night we knew really that we had not played very well. We hadn't handled those last eight minutes very well. Had not given them the respect they deserved.'

Gould remembered a premonition that the game was not secure even when his team led 12–4. 'I was nervous on the bench. I sent out two messages. Our fellas celebrated when they scored their last try,' he said. 'I told our runner to tell them that it wasn't over yet and not to be negative and to keep moving forward. I was not convinced we had won . . . but even I couldn't believe what happened.'

Carr, sitting behind Gould, was equally stunned. 'I'd brought my 11-year-old son down from the back of the stand to sit with me for the final few minutes when NSW led 12–4 so he could enjoy the win like everyone else,' he said.

'So Queensland score two tries and Wally Lewis and "Tosser" Turner are on the big screen hugging each other. And the Queensland players are hugging each other and are all excited. It went on for about 30 seconds I suppose but it seemed forever. I looked behind at Scott and he was sitting with his head in his lap, bent right over.

Good as GOULD

'I said: "Don't worry, mate. It's only a game. Don't take it that seriously."

'He said: "I'm not, dad. I'm just copying what you were doing".'

Knowing he only had a few seconds before his stunned and shattered players would walk through the door looking for inspiration Gould grappled with his imagination and his own shredded confidence to pull something positive out of the debacle.

It was as delicate a manoeuvre to repair shattered egos as any heart transplant surgeon ever attempted. One slip of the scalpel and the build-up to games Two and Three would be irreparably damaged.

'I sat them down in the dressing room and it was very, very quiet. No-one said anything until I spoke,' Gould said. 'I told them: "I don't have to ask how you feel. I can't believe it. I just can't believe it. But out of this we've got to find something to hold onto. This gives us the chance to prove that we are the greatest NSW side of all time. If we can win in Melbourne and then go to Lang Park and win the decider, which NSW has never been able to do in the past, we will be the best".'

At that point Gould turned the psychological burner to high. 'You know, I'm *glad* we got beat because this gives us our greatest opportunity to show what we can do.'

There was the baited hook. Here, in the midst of the carnage of shattered dreams, was the coach talking confidently about a decider. Hell. Melbourne was not going to be a problem. Let's get that out of the way and get on with playing the match that really matters, he was saying. Let's play and WIN the decider at Lang Park.

Heads slowly lifted from chests. Losing the match was not the end of the world. Life could go on. The coach had the answers.

'I don't know if it sounded like false bravado or sounded genuine,' Gould said. 'What I was trying to convey was that out of this loss, out of this shock loss, came a chance to prove we were the best of all time and could win the series with the most dramatic comeback of all time.

'I said that when we won the third game, they would remember that try from the first match but no-one would remember that we lost the game. They would remember only that we won the series.'

Carr recalled that Gould's prematch talks had inadvertently provided an escape clause if the side was beaten in Sydney. 'He always said that the side that won in Melbourne would win the series,' the NSW manager said. 'He was obviously thinking that we should win in Sydney and then we had to concentrate on getting them in Melbourne because if we had to play the decider in Brisbane you never knew what might happen.

'Gus said before the Sydney game that whoever won in Melbourne would take the series. So when we got to Melbourne he simply said: "Nothing's changed".'

Having raised the flagging spirits of a devastated team, Gould left the subdued post-match function to drive home to Penrith and get his own perplexed thoughts in order.

That series was the first time Gould had coached against a Queensland side that contained a Penrith player—Queensland forward Trevor Gillmeister. After the match, Gillmeister approached Gould asking: 'Gus, can I get a lift back to Penrith?' At that stage Gould figured he had extended as much hospitality and generosity towards Queensland as he intended. His reply was succinct. 'Get fucked, Gilly,' he said and kept walking.

The full impact of the night did not hit Gould until he arrived home about 2am. 'My normal practice would have been to put the tape straight on and watch the game—but I just couldn't do it,' he said. 'I just couldn't watch it. I remember once reading a story about Wayne Bennett, who was then the Queensland coach, going through a similar thing after Mark McGaw scored his last-minute try for NSW. He walked the streets all night. I thought at the time "gee, that's a bit over the top". Now I understood exactly what he felt. It was tearing me apart.'

In desperation and to give some outlet to his frustration Gould ignored the lateness of the hour and called his father and in response to a sleepy 'hello' replied at the top of his voice: 'What about fucking that!' Later it became a catchcry with the players.

Gould kept in mind the repercussions that can follow a bizarre loss. He thought of Balmain beaten by Canberra in the grand final of 1989 after having the match won with seconds of normal time on the clock.

'I don't think Balmain have recovered *yet* from that match,' Gould said. 'But I've got to say that in 1994 from the moment we walked into camp for game two in Melbourne the players were ready to go.'

The Melbourne Cricket Ground is one of Australia's greatest sporting theatres. Used for the athletic events at the 1956 Olympics it has a proud record of drawing huge and enthusiastic crowds of sports lovers. It is a virtual sporting cathedral which had previously been out of bounds when overtures were made to play major rugby league matches on its hallowed turf. As a consequence Test matches billed as promotional vehicles for rugby league had been played at lesser grounds like Princes Park and Olympic Park.

Warming relations with the AFL and a growing confidence by ARL officials in the game's ability to draw a big crowd after Victorian appetites had been wetted by television exposure of

THE ORIGIN EXPERIENCE

Origin matches played in Brisbane and Sydney finally saw the historic agreement made.

Game two of the 1994 Origin series had the MCG as its home. The Rugby League's media machine was cranked into top gear for the occasion and locked in place.

The Victorian public, who had lived in almost blissful ignorance about the peculiarities and attraction of rugby league, suddenly found themselves bombarded on all side with news, views, opinions and promotions for the State of Origin match. In a city where kite-flying would draw a reasonable crowd, the sporting public's curiosity was tapped.

The thrust of the marketing was that they were to see the most exciting sporting contest since Ben Hur's chariot race. To miss it was to risk being an outsider in a sports-loving city. The hype worked—brilliantly. An Australian record crowd of 87,161 turned up on a balmy night, grateful of the chance to see a sporting event they would be able to discuss with their grandchildren.

But by half-time they were wondering what all the fuss could possibly have been about. State of Origin II turned out to be a fizzer. It was plodding. It was unimaginative. It was comatose. It was also preplanned by NSW and it proved a winning formula.

Giving nothing away and oblivious to the growing irritation of spectators, NSW continued with a tight, grinding approach that produced a 14–nil win.

Preferring to be methodical rather than magical, NSW ignored the festivity and sense of expectation in the air. They won with a deliberate and risk-free approach and Queensland could not slip the noose this time. Queensland offered about 15 minutes of sustained pressure to open the match and when no dividends came could produce little else.

Ben Elias laid on the first try, confusing Queensland with

some sleight of hand and picking up prop Glenn Lazarus on the burst. By half-time NSW led 8–nil after two goals from fullback Tim Brasher. The match wasn't fancy but it *was* ferocious. Lazarus and fellow prop Paul Harragon threw themselves into the fray with gusto, subduing Queensland. Unused to such callous disregard for personal safety the Victorian crowd gasped at some of the defence. Unlike the first match, NSW turned its dominance into points. With nine minutes to play half Ricky Stuart reversed a pass to centre Paul McGregor who scored next to the posts. To a Melbourne crowd raised on the nonstop drama and high points-scoring of Australian Rules, the match was rated on a par with birdwatching.

'We had to play it tight. We had to win,' said an unapologetic Gould. 'We could not afford to lose. We were one-down and the series would have been lost if we had been beaten. I thought we totally dominated Queensland this time in the match but Melbourne proved difficult. It was a huge crowd and great atmosphere but we had some early problems.'

Unbelievably, the driver of the bus bringing the players to the match got lost even though the hotel hosting the NSW team was about a kilometre's walking distance from the MCG. 'The driver went to the wrong entrance and we ended up having to walk further to get to the game than if we had strolled across the road from our hotel,' said Gould. 'The players had to cart all the gear and the equipment we use to the dressing rooms.'

Gould's philosophy for game two was to improve the speed of the NSW team's reaction. Perusal of the videotape of the first game showed that NSW were too slow to react, too slow to get going in attack and defence and they paid the price.

'When Queensland scored their try from hell we were about half a yard short on about five occasions in making the tackle that would have stopped the ball carrier,' Gould said. 'That was our call in game two: "make up that half yard".

'The other thing was that right through the past two series, every time we had scored or done something good, they would hit right back. So we made a vow that whenever we scored, we would also be the *next* to score as well.'

So as Gould had predicted, more in hope than with expectation, NSW was still alive and now facing the unprecedented task of trying to beat Queensland in a deciding match of a series at Lang Park.

NSW teams had found themselves facing this challenge before and walked away with deep wounds. Too often Queensland's patriotic fervour had manifested itself in ferocious waves of attacking brilliance coupled with impregnable defence. Queensland's record in important matches at Lang Park was overwhelming. The Maroons had beaten NSW in series-deciding matches at Lang Park in 1982, 1987 and 1991. Queensland had also turned things around in 1990 and 1993 by winning the game at Lang Park to prevent a clean sweep by NSW sides that had won the first game.

For NSW to win the final game at Lang Park would be to end a legend—the task was to slay a dragon in its own lair and escape unscathed.

As the day neared Gould talked to the team incessantly, stressing how far the players had come since the heartbreaking first loss in Sydney and emphasising that Queensland could be beaten at Lang Park provided NSW mustered the same level of intensity they had managed in Melbourne. The players listened as he detailed NSW's emergence as a State of Origin power and listed the players who had gone before this 1994 team and willingly and courageously spilled blood to beat Queensland in previous matches. The bonds of unity and mateship were extended well past the 15 players who had been

Good as GOULD

chosen for this final game. Players from previous teams were co-opted to tell of their experiences.

This was a NSW side drawing strength from past glories as well as its own ability. It was taking first advantage of the brotherhood that now existed in NSW ranks.

This time the ice cream—it was now a Gould tradition to take his squad for ice creams and a last reflective talk—was eaten high on Mt Coot-tha after sundown, with the lights of Brisbane stretched out below like a carpet of brilliant jewels. Centre Chris Johns had arranged the venue because a friend of his owned the shop and had generously agreed to open it up that night.

The chance to sit in serenity under a darkened sky, each man alone with his thoughts while wrapped in a cocoon of team camaraderie, was rare. The challenge of what lay ahead at a Lang Park sure to be filled to overflowing with fanatical and often drunken Queensland supporters cheering on their heroes was in stark contrast to the peace of the moment. The emotional mountain confronting the NSW team was almost as high as the one they were sitting on.

Two Queensland legends were emotionally involved in this one as well. Wally Lewis had been appointed coach after an unsurpassed record as a Queensland player. Devoted supporters had chipped in to have a life-size statue of Lewis erected on the grassy slopes of Lang Park, overlooking the playing field. Unless the Maroons could win this match and take the series, Lewis would have spent two years as coach without winning the prize. Even his lofty status in the game would not be able to deflect moves for a new coach. The other legend was Malcolm Meninga, the 'Colossus of Toads' playing a record 38th match. In 1994 Meninga's standing in the game had reached legendary proportions. He had waited in the shadow of Wally Lewis' arrogant and unsurpassed brilliant performances at State of Origin level and made his name elsewhere.

THE ORIGIN EXPERIENCE

A unique double beckoned Meninga. If things fell into place Meninga would become the first man ever to captain two Kangaroo teams and the first man ever to make four Kangaroo tours. With Canberra also in line to win the premiership and Queensland chasing a win on its home ground in a deciding State of Origin match, Meninga was on the verge of unprecedented greatness as a captain and player.

Riches *did* flow Meninga's way in a torrent that year. Canberra won the premiership and he made history by captaining the Kangaroos to retain the Ashes.

But the third State of Origin match was another matter ... the toughest challenge.

Gould realised the enormous emotional appeal that would be generated by Meninga's last appearance in a match at Lang Park. Queensland players were at the upper end of the Richter scale for passion in *normal* circumstances. Being urged to win this match and send Mal out a winner was going to be like throwing petrol on the already brightly burning emotions of Meninga's team-mates.

Gould used logic and emotion as he plumbed the depths of his own players. 'This might be important to Mal, but it's more important to us,' he said. 'This is three years' worth of effort. We've got to be able to say we were the best ever. When we bring our kids to look at the State of Origin Shield we can say: "Well, Queensland might have been winning all those years but for the three years we were there, they didn't win. We got the money".'

Gould's words were telling and hit a nerve. But it was NSW captain Laurie Daley who hit the Mal problem right out of sight. Having had his appointment as captain questioned when he was first chosen, Daley had developed into a leader of skill and compassion, blending media commitments, his own form and leadership into a neat bundle. Like all players at that level, he was constantly being tested and there was no doubting Daley's total commitment to the NSW cause—it was deep and absolute.

But he was also a team-mate of Meninga's in the Canberra side and had publicly expressed his respect and admiration for the big man on many occasions. Now Daley had to line up against Meninga again in a crucial match and his feelings were going to be the cornerstone to the NSW team's own thinking. If the captain was only half-hearted in his call for total commitment—then the game was probably lost before it started.

Daley's reply to the question on everyone's lips stunned the room and focused attention on the need for complete unity.

'Fuck Mal,' he said. 'Fuck him. He's had fucking everything. He's had Kangaroo tours, he's captained Australia. This isn't his benefit night. This is our fucking game!'

Maybe Daley's mind had gone back to his first game in 1989 when he felt Meninga had hit him with a sucker punch. Meninga had suggested at Canberra training sessions that the fact of he and Daley opposing each other in the centres in an Origin match was a lark. Meninga had then flattened him in the match, helping pave the way for Queensland's 36–6 win.

Whatever the reason, Daley's tirade was the catalyst NSW needed and the players soaked up his words. If the captain was prepared to go head to head with his friend and Test captain everyone else had better do the same. That might have been the night Daley convinced the team that he was a leader both on and off the field and that nothing—not friendship, mateship or club team affiliations—took precedence.

'You could see him emerge as a leader,' said Gould. 'He was saying: "I'll run at him all night".' It was volatile stuff and just what the team needed. 'No-one ever doubted that the Canberra blokes Ricky Stuart, Bradley Clyde and Daley were anything but committed to NSW winning,' Gould said. 'But

THE ORIGIN EXPERIENCE

Laurie's speech dispelled any lingering doubts where he stood. Players from both sides loved and respected Mal Meninga for what he had achieved in the game. But they were not going to let it get in the way of them winning. We all knew Mal wouldn't starve if Queensland lost.'

The match to decide the series turned out to be an anticlimax. NSW won it 27–12. Maybe it was the pressure of trying to 'win it for Mal' or maybe just the stress of trying to bounce back from the Melbourne loss that played on Queensland's mind. They were a pale shadow of what their fans had hoped for.

Nervousness took over and Queensland supplied two vital intercepts. The first was taken by hooker Benny Elias off Langer and quickly given to lock Bradley Clyde who scored. The second came when Steve Renouf threw a diabolical pass towards winger Willie Carne. NSW winger Brett Mullins, one of the fastest men in the game, swooped on the ball and raced 40 metres to score for 18–nil. Daley chipped in with his own gilt-edged contribution, a try in which he sidestepped and swerved his way past five would-be tacklers from 15 metres out. Queensland cut the leeway to 18–6 by half-time but an Elias field goal for 19–6 left the Maroons having to score twice to be in front after a Renouf try made the score 19–12 after 55 minutes.

Two minutes from full-time Elias kicked his second field goal in what was to be his final Origin match. He had begun his NSW career 19 games earlier in 1985. A long-time scourge of Queensland sides and a target for much spectator and player venom, Elias was now engineering his own private farewell to Lang Park. At least one champion would go out a winner.

Queensland was shattered by the loss—the third year in succession they had been beaten.

Good as GOULD

'We just didn't play as well in the second and third games after getting away with the first one,' Langer said. 'We had our chances, especially in the third one when we threw the intercepts. Winning the first game and knowing we only had to win one more and that the third game was in Brisbane made us pretty confident.'

It was a magical time for NSW in State of Origin football. Clinching the 1994 series in the most difficult way possible by winning the third game had given the Blues an almost superhuman status. Gould's words about the 1994 team having the chance to be the best ever NSW side, issued in such haste weeks before in the debris of the Sydney Football Stadium loss, had become prophetic.

By the end of 1994, Canberra were the rugby league champions and the Kangaroos were on their way, about to again establish their supremacy in England and France.

Domestically there was peace and harmony. NSW was again the deserved champion side at Origin level and had looked so convincing in winning that a successful sequence of five or six years looked possible. The calmness that embraced NSW was deceptive. It was to be the calm before the storm of Super League.

The Fatty Vautin Miracle

There has never been a State of Origin series to match the controversy of the 1995 matches as the reality of players jumping the fence to join Rupert Murdoch's Super League heavily depleted the players Queensland and New South Wales could call upon. There was bitterness and cries of 'foul' when Super League players were excluded from representative matches, leading eventually to legal action over the composition of Australia's World Cup team. There was also the overriding reality of a stirring Queensland performance that rewrote the definition of the words commitment and loyalty.

When Phil Gould and Bob Fulton sat down at League headquarters, Phillip Street, on March 31 to draw up lists of the players who were likely selections in, firstly, the Test team and, secondly, the Queensland and NSW sides, the State of Origin series was a lifetime away. But the problems were becoming obvious. With the Brisbane Broncos already under the Super League umbrella and the North Queensland Cowboys certain to defect as well, Queensland was going to struggle to produce a recognisable State of Origin side. That was a pity but there was no time then for too much concern. The onus in March and April was on keeping the ARL alive, not worrying about a series that might not even be played at all if Super League was not kept at bay.

The effect hit home some time later. NSW would be competitive despite the absence of Canberra stars Laurie Daley,

Good as GOULD

Bradley Clyde, Ricky Stuart, Brett Mullins and Jason Croker plus Canterbury's Dean Pay and Cronulla's Andrew Ettingshausen. Queensland, however, represented a major disaster.

The ARL had hit at Super League by deciding, although not on the record, that its players would not be eligible for selection in representative sides. With Brisbane in Super League there was no Allan Langer, no Kevin Walters, no Steve Renouf, no Michael Hancock, no Willie Carne, no Julian O'Neill and no Wendell Sailor. The forwards would not be as badly affected because Gary Larson and Billy Moore were with the ARL-aligned North Sydney and Trevor Gillmeister was with the South Queensland Crushers. After that it was SOS time.

Then the appointed Queensland coach Wayne Bennett quit as well, saying he would not coach if his club players were not eligible for selection. Bennett's decision amazed NSW and Gould. Here was a coach who had built his reputation on Queensland's achievements. He had won State of Origin series 3–nil in both 1987 and 1988 and premierships with the Broncos.

When Bennett was beaten 3–nil by NSW in 1986 and the threat of dismissal hung over him, it was the Queensland Rugby League which gave him a second chance. That time he steered Queensland to six wins in a row, justifying his reputation as one of the best coaches in the business and enabling him to step down from the job as a winner rather than a loser. Yet now he was abandoning a Queensland side of such limited proven ability that his guidance and experience would have been essential. 'He's getting out because the good players aren't available,' joked one NSW player.

Bennett believed he was caught in a crossfire and could not keep everyone happy no matter what decision he made. If he coached the Queensland side, it could be interpreted by his

Bronco players as an act of disloyalty because they were ineligible for selection. The Broncos had agreed to stick together no matter what. By withdrawing as Queensland coach, he risked being seen as disloyal to a QRL that had supported him so strongly in the past as a representative coach. Queensland supporters reckoned a team of tyros would be cannon fodder in the Origin series unless Bennett's experience and skill was behind them.

At that stage NSW confidence in not only winning the series but winning 3–nil was high enough to be orbiting earth like a satellite. Even with Super League players unavailable, NSW would still have access to internationals such as Tim Brasher, Rod Wishart, Terry Hill and Brad Fittler in the backs and Steve Menzies, Paul Harragon, Greg Florimo, David Fairleigh, Mark Carroll and Jim Sedaris in the forwards.

On paper it was as lopsided a contest as was ever put down in State of Origin football. Queensland was not only limited in its access to certain positions, but in some cases the cupboard was absolutely bare. There was no topline half-back and no hooker who qualified for Queensland. For years two of the best hookers in the premiership had been Queensland brothers Kerrod Walters from the Broncos and Steve Walters from Canberra, who were both with Super League. Another Bronco, Allan Langer, had been Queensland half whenever he was available. If he was injured Kevin Walters, his Broncos teammate, would take over.

NSW was as worried as Queensland about the pending series. A walkover by NSW in the existing climate of Super League intrusion would not be in the ARL's best interests and could be a public relations disaster. It would emphasise the success of Super League in stripping the premiership of so many talented players and jeopardise the chances of maintaining interest in the State of Origin both in 1995 and the future.

The matches would still draw well but television ratings would be the real arbiter and there was nothing that could be done to influence those. State of Origin matches had always dominated their timespots on Channel 9. Anything less than top ratings again would suggest the public was both disenchanted with the Super League and ARL battle or had lost interest in the series. That would damage the ARL's credibility and long-term financial bargaining power in the areas of sponsorship and television rights.

Super League was poised to generate as much propaganda as possible from any disaster. So it was that Queensland appointed a new coach, giving the job to former Test lock Paul Vautin, who had always been upfront about wanting to coach the side after his own career of 20 matches during the State's glittering period of dominance. Vautin was such a rush selection as coach that he was unfamiliar with the faces he would be guiding. At training he had to ask the identity of one player. 'That's Ben Ikin, the 18-year-old winger from the Gold Coast,' he was told.

'Oh,' Vautin said.

Being an afterthought as coach did not worry 'Fatty' Vautin. 'Of course I realised I only got the job because Wayne Bennett stepped down,' he said. 'Everyone knew there was no Langer, Walters brothers, Renouf, Hancock and the others. But I also knew that *with* those players Queensland had lost the past three series against NSW. I also knew what the Queensland spirit had achieved against the odds before and if we were underrated, just as certainly the Blues were overrated.'

In hindsight Vautin's claims are credible. At the time they seemed the errant rantings of someone living on a different planet. In fact, Queensland was so disregarded in the opening game, NSW started 9–1 on favourites.

Vautin had long been one of the champions in Queensland's

THE ORIGIN EXPERIENCE

Origin sides as a lock forward and vice-captain to Wally Lewis. Although he played 13 Tests for Australia, Vautin, like Wally Lewis to some degree, was better known for his heroics at State of Origin level and passionate love of being a Queenslander, especially when it came to playing and beating NSW. There had been Arthur Beetson as the archetypal Queenslander as captain of the first Maroons Origin side. Then Lewis. Now Queensland was looking for another rallying figure. And they had found Vautin.

Fatty Vautin was not everyone's idea of a hero. Despite a long career with Manly his contract with the club was not renewed and he finished the last couple of seasons with Easts where his former Queensland team-mate Mark Murray was coach, with Jack Gibson in the background. Vautin would eventually fade out of football at Easts after a fallout with Murray about his form. Vautin then moved into television where he found success as a quirky comedian prepared to do almost anything for a laugh. Along with that went a switch to rugby league commentary.

A complex character, Vautin's witty, outgoing persona masked a somewhat serious and subdued man. As master of ceremonies at an ARL announcement that focused on Cronulla prop Adam Ritson being interviewed by a large gathering of media after he had rejected a Super League contract, Vautin proved an insulting host. He objected to *Daily Telegraph* columnist Piers Ackerman's questions to Ritson, declaring the conference over.

Ackerman: 'Who says so?'

Vautin: 'Ah . . . I do . . . You *****!!!'

It was not the professional and responsible image ARL bosses Ken Arthurson and John Quayle, who were at the meeting, were trying to convey.

Former Queensland and NZ Test coach Graham Lowe also took public exception to Vautin's habit of referring to people

Good as GOULD

for whom he had no time as 'spastics'.

So it was a tense build-up to the 1995 representative season. The first of the teams was chosen on Sunday March 31 and no Super League players were included in the City and Origin sides. There were headlines, debate, vilification, endorsement and abuse on talk-back radio on the wrongs and rights of the decision.

Gould had long been aware of the situation—that his representative sides would be missing a lot of familiar names. With concern growing about the quality of the Queensland side, Gould was asked by ARL general manager John Quayle if selectors should be told to relent and choose Super League-aligned players in the State of Origin sides.

'You can do that if you want to,' Gould replied, 'but you'll have to get another coach.' It was not complacency because NSW looked the stronger side. Gould's answer was to do with loyalty. Having spent months talking to and negotiating with players to sign with the ARL, Gould was not going to turn his back on them now.

The first game came and went with Sydney Origin beating Country Origin 16-8 in a quagmire at Steelers Stadium in Wollongong. Both sides had new faces, which quickly became obscured by mud in shocking conditions as nonstop heavy rain left deep pools of water on the playing area.

Confronted by difficulties, and after a thorough exercise in soul-searching and perusal of players' records and birthplaces, Queensland eventually found an imaginative solution to the problem of half-back and hooker.

Gould helped out with the half-back nomination, saying his Easts player Adrian Lam could do the job. Lam was a New Guinea Test player at the time. The reasoning behind his suddenly being converted to a Queenslander do not stand up to much investigation but he got the job. Lam's selection had myriad ramifications. He was for example the only player in either State of Origin squad who knew he had no chance of Test selection against the New Zealand side that would tour Australia that year. As a New Guinea Test representative, he could not be chosen for Australia although there were suggestions at the time that as Super League had distorted the scene so much, anything was possible.

Finding a hooker for Queensland involved further imagination by selectors even if it did not threaten international propriety. The man chosen, at the suggestion of NSW manager Geoff Carr, was his St George lock Wayne Bartrim. Bartrim had played hooker in the past with his former club Gold Coast and was at least a genuine Queenslander and he kicked goals—an asset that would be priceless in the first game.

Sent in as ridiculously priced outsiders, Queensland defied every piece of logic to win 2–nil. It was the lowest-scoring game in State of Origin history, the only points coming from a Bartrim penalty goal in the 30th minute at the Sydney Football Stadium. Referee Eddie Ward penalised NSW captain Paul Harragon for a tackle on Queensland's Gary Larson and Bartrim kicked the goal from 25 metres out. At the time and with 50 minutes to play it was regarded as a minor event. By full-time the goal had assumed epic proportions. NSW did have their moments. They crossed Queensland's line twice and should have scored. First winger Rod Wishart stepped into touch after taking a cross-field kick from Andrew Johns. Then in the second half NSW centre Terry Hill was held up by Matt Sing over the line with 17 minutes to play.

Even those setbacks failed to set alarm bells ringing. They were regarded as carelessness that would be overcome by NSW. But as the minutes ticked by the Blues could not score and the pressure led to more mistakes. It was not a pretty game but intensity, commitment and courage were there in abundance.

Despite the fact that NSW had been beaten, there was no

real apprehension in the ranks. Embarrassment perhaps, but no thought that the greatest upset in Origin history was only two games away.

Officials were secretly relieved. A Queensland win in the opening game was more than they could possibly have hoped for. Their worst fear had been of a lopsided NSW win that would reduce the crowd for the second match and kill interest in the series.

Gould had harboured similar thoughts but had not let them affect his coaching of the side. The preparation had been as sharp as usual. There had been bonding, nights out and the trip for an ice cream. But, with so many new faces in the NSW side there had not been enough time to establish too many set moves. This year NSW might have to rely more on the individual ability of its players than usual to produce a win.

'Things just didn't go our way in the first game but it was impossible to fault the approach of the players,' Gould said. 'At 2–nil I didn't think we would lose by the same score 50 minutes later. We had chances but Queensland tackled too well.'

NSW now faced going to Melbourne for the second game because the MCG had been booked long before Super League had erupted. To transfer the match would have been awkward. To play it before a small MCG crowd after the previous year's game at the same venue had attracted an Australian attendance record of 87,161 could also cause a loss of face. In fact the match attracted a more than reasonable crowd of 52,994 but the numbers on the scoreboard were of much more interest. At fulltime they showed Queensland 20, NSW 12. The unlosable series had been lost. The sun had set in the east. Rivers were running uphill. Sitting on the sidelines that night, Gould watched stunned as the Queenslanders performed the impossible.

'I was always confident,' he said later. 'So were the players. We thought we would win and then play the decider in

Brisbane. I was so confident that NSW could turn things around that the score was not registering. It was only with 14 minutes to play with Queensland leading 14–6 that I realised what was happening. I remember thinking, 'Gees, we could lose this. And if we do, we lose the series'.'

NSW cut Queensland's lead to 14–12 with five minutes to play but Queensland winger Brett Dallas raced away in the last seconds for a final try. Again NSW had looked slightly the better attacking side and always threatening but without actually being able to score. In the final five minutes, referee Eddie Ward disallowed two NSW tries that would probably have won the match because the defence would have been more resolute than it was when Dallas dashed away from dummy half for his 80-metre try as the siren was sounding.

The match was tight and a wild brawl punctuated the first half with players from both sides running in to get involved. The potential for a brawling start to the match had been the worst-kept secret in football. Both sides had talked about it, saying publicly that they hoped it would not happen but taking precautions just in case. They talked of peace but prepared for war. Gould made last-minute changes to his side, bringing Greg Florimo and Dean Pay into the line-up after they had been named as interchange players. The move would enable NSW to match whatever firepower Queensland unleashed early and still have attacking players like Steve Menzies to come into the game from the interchange bench.

Pay and Jason Smith, who was in the Queensland side as five-eighth, had signed with Super League but later responded to an ARL counter-offer and became eligible for Origin selection. Smith, usually a lock or second-rower, was superb at five-eighth, using deft footwork and ball skills to get his team's attack rolling.

The final match at Lang Park had only pride at stake. And

Good as GOULD

again Queensland had more of that than NSW. Captain Trevor Gillmeister in an inspiring gesture that underlined the ferocity of feeling in the side signed himself out of hospital to take his place in the side. He had been admitted with an infected knee and placed on an intravenous drip. His chances of playing in the final game looked impossible. But he took his place as Queensland wrapped up the series whitewash 24–16 before a crowd of 40,589. NSW led twice at 10–6, after 35 minutes, and again 16–12 after 41 minutes, but Queensland had come too far, endured too much, to weaken now. Somehow, a combination of first graders whose use-by dates could be questioned, players with debatable geographical qualifications and fringe first graders had carried Queensland up the toughest rugby league mountain in the world. Fittingly Gold Coast winger Ben Ikin, the 18-year-old whose identity had been such a mystery to Vautin when the series started, scored the clinching try, touching down when NSW fullback Matt Seers dropped the ball with three minutes to play and put Queensland ahead 24–16 after Bartrim's conversion.

Before the series had started, Vautin received a telegram from a Maroons supporter in Central Queensland saying: 'Queensland is looking for 17 new heroes. You can be them.' By the time this remarkable series was over, they were.

'I won't say I can't believe what we've done because from the moment I first met these young guys, I knew there was something special about them,' said the proud coach. 'But when I took over as coach, all I wanted was for Queensland to become winners again after three successive series losses. To beat NSW 3–nil? That's something else again . . .'

The Super League Wars

TALES FROM THE PHILLIP STREET BUNKER

The April Fool's Day Massacre

Whether by design or coincidence Super League sprang threateningly to public life on April 1, the traditional day for practical jokes. For a long time the threat of Super League had hovered over the game like a malevolent wraith. It was a rumour that had swept through the game for months without settling long enough to be substantiated or denied.

It was like an old biblical curse bringing pestilence, treachery, suspicion and intrigue. When the full extent of the Super League invasion of rugby league's stronghold was revealed it would paint a picture of cowardice, lies, deceit and betrayal of principles and friendships on both sides on such a gigantic scale it was almost impossible to believe.

Friendships forged over decades at the rugby league coal face were bitterly broken, tens of millions of dollars were spent in a fight for players and control of the game. There were legal actions on any one of half a dozen fronts in two hemispheres.

Players found themselves swept into a financial whirlpool where those with quicker wits and quicker tongues than playing skills could sign contracts worth more than they had ever dreamed possible.

Balmain's journeyman prop Steve Edmed, 32, was one—a player who had toiled steadfastly with the club for around a decade without threatening to duplicate the representative achievements of his team-mates Wayne Pearce, Steve Roach, Benny Elias, Paul Sironen and Garry Jack.

Good as GOULD

At his best even Sironen was probably only worth around $130,000 by Balmain's (Sydney City Tigers) 1995 standards after sterling service to NSW and Australia in 18 Tests and two Kangaroo tours.

Super League, desperate for players, ignored Edmed's age, decade of service and minimal impression on the representative scene and paid him $50,000 immediately to join their ranks and then a further $225,000 a season for three years.

There were deals done of such magnitude by both Super League and the Australian Rugby League, that players who had retired as long as three years earlier, were doing stretch exercises and looking for their boots. It was a civil war of great brutality and stealth in which honour, ethics and truth were captured early and locked in a place where they would not be in the way.

Three men chose to resign from the nine man board of the NSWRL rather than continue to serve when their circumstances changed dramatically. Others like NSW coach Phil Gould, Test coach Bobby Fulton, ARL general manager John Quayle, Souths president George Piggins, Souths team manager and radio personality Alan Jones, St George's Geoff Carr and ARL president Ken Arthurson re-affirmed their allegiance to the game and began a strident, forceful, personal and unrelenting battle for its survival.

As events unfolded it became obvious that there had been two camps in rugby league for some time. One camp was almost blissfully unaware of the determination and working schedule of the other as the greatest upheaval the game had known since its birth in Yorkshire's George Hotel in Huddersfield in 1895 ran its course.

One hundred years on at the start of the 1995 season ARL chairman Ken Arthurson would idly chat to a rugby league writer during a trip from Townsville to Perth, mentioning that

TALES FROM THE PHILLIP STREET BUNKER

English Rugby League director Maurice Lindsay was investigating the idea of switching seasons.

Rugby League in England would become a summer sport, Arthurson explained, as the plane full of media representatives en route to see all four new clubs in action during the opening premiership round of the season, continued its hectic schedule to Perth.

'I wonder why he would even think of doing that,' puzzled Arthurson. 'It would mean the end of Kangaroo and British Lions tours as we know them. It probably won't happen.'

A few weeks later Super League paid more than $160 million to secure the English Rugby League and rescheduled its matches from winter to summer, with Lindsay as its boss. The timetable Arthurson had pondered about so quizzically was suddenly much more understandable.

Super League sympathisers, a group that included Canterbury's Peter Moore, Cronulla's Peter Gow, Brisbane's John Ribot and his chairman Paul 'Porky' Morgan, the Canberra club and its Test half Ricky Stuart seemed much more vitally aware of what was coming.

It was Stuart who first alerted his State of Origin coach and close friend Gould to the impending detonation of Super League. It was an inadvertent warning but it was nevertheless of great tactical value to an Australian Rugby League that had been unjustifiably and perhaps arrogantly proud of its ability to oppose any intrusion, never realising until much later the financial scope and muscle of the gathering forces, underwritten by the world wide media conglomerate of Rupert Murdoch's News Ltd.

Super League was to prove an unrelenting and rapacious opponent in its efforts to secure some access to rugby league for its pay TV outlet Foxtel, which was in its own battle with a rival outlet Optus.

Good as GOULD

One rich man Kerry Packer had the free-to-air television rights to rugby league. A richer man Rupert Murdoch wanted some component of rugby league to boost the saleability of his pay TV channel Foxtel. It was that simple. But the simplicity would not make finding a solution to the problem any less complex.

Gould, now a premiership-winning coach at both Canterbury and Penrith as well as boasting the record of steering NSW to a record three successive State of Origin series wins, was busy with his own schedule in 1995, focused on lifting the competitiveness of his new club Easts.

'When I first signed to coach Easts, Ricky Stuart rang me and said he wanted to come to the club. He said if there was a change in the salary cap or if Super League started, he would be a free agent,' Gould said. 'That had always been part of his contract at Canberra. This was way back before the Kangaroos went away in 1994. So it could have been June or July.'

The words 'Super League' puzzled Gould. What did they mean? Stuart would just keep insisting that the concept was being introduced but would not elaborate. Gould rang Stuart and another close friend Brad Fittler while they were on the Kangaroo tour in October-November 1994 to congratulate them after he had seen them on television playing well and also to ask about Super League. Fittler declared that he knew nothing about the concept. Neither did other players except those from Canberra and Brisbane, who were not saying much to outsiders.

Officials were equally perplexed. ARL boss Ken Arthurson sat in the International Hotel in Cardiff during the tour, contemplating the rumours he was hearing about Super League. He was so concerned he made plans to fly back to Australia to talk to News Ltd chairman Ken Cowley. 'I really don't know what is happening,' said Arthurson, who was still cautiously hopeful that his friend of more than two decades Peter Moore, the Canterbury chief executive and NSWRL board member,

TALES FROM THE PHILLIP STREET BUNKER

was above reproach despite being consistently linked with Super League speculation.

Arthurson at that stage was still hopeful, if not confident, that friendships forged over decades of close allegiances would withstand the pressure of Super League. He was hoping for a traditional 'wagons in a circle' philosophy from rugby league clubs that had served the game so well in the past when danger threatened.

The Kangaroos returned home in December 1994 to find Super League still a major topic of discussion and speculation. Gould sought some insight from Stuart.

Stuart told him that he was still anxious to join Easts. His girlfriend was from Sydney and wanted to return home. Stuart said he also wanted to play under Gould for a couple of years to learn what more he could for a future coaching career of his own.

'He'd been playing under Tim Sheens at Canberra for a long while and he wanted to get more experience,' Gould said. 'He was a little bored in Canberra playing the type of football he had been playing, even though it was winning football. It was just repetitive and he wanted to do different things.'

The final thrust came when Stuart came to Sydney and watched Easts in one of the team's early home games and finally elicited a guarantee of a meeting with club chairman and loyal sponsor Nick Politis and board member James Packer, the son of Kerry.

Despite Gould repeatedly and deliberately stressing to Stuart that his two year contract with Canberra ended any hope of him transferring elsewhere, the champion half-back was adamant that a bargain could be arranged. Stuart again insisted the coming emergence of Super League would end the old rules and make him a free agent.

Gould: 'How can you be so sure?'

Good as GOULD

Stuart: 'It's all in place and John Ribot is going to be the chief executive. Everyone is going to be in it, and I want to know what part Packer is playing.'

Stuart stayed in Sydney that night and spoke to Politis and Packer without any significant breakthrough. Easts had already signed Illawarra's John Simon to be the club's half-back but could not tell Stuart because of a confidentiality clause.

Stuart finally accepted that contrary to his earlier presumptions, Easts really did not know anything about Super League and were obviously not one of the elite clubs chosen to participate.

Stuart believed that the financial power base of a rich leagues club, two prominent benefactors like Politis and Packer, and a high profile coach like Gould would make Easts automatic inclusions in Super League. The very factors that Stuart saw as assets were in fact debits. Kerry Packer's Channel 9 network had the free-to-air rugby league television rights under contract until the year 2000. Gould was linked to the ARL as NSW coach and Politis was a close friend of ARL chief executive, John Quayle. Easts were far too close to the ARL heartbeat to be approached by a planned rebel competition.

Three days later Politis rang Gould to tell him he had it on good authority that Super League was real and that Canberra, Canterbury and Brisbane were about to defect.

The ARL was convinced that some of its clubs and prominent officials had been acting as double agents. Brisbane via Morgan and Ribot were obviously prime movers for Super League.

At Peter Moore's club Canterbury, the players were taken secretly away from training one night and rushed to a clandestine meeting with Ribot and signed to Super League contracts.

Moore admitted in an interview with 2UE's sports director

Ray Hadley that he had received prior knowledge of Super League's emergence but had not immediately told his fellow members of the NSWRL board. Moore said he had been given the information as a member of the board of directors of Canterbury Leagues Club.

Other ARL members found it difficult to comprehend how Moore, who was always being rated among the more astute of chief executives, could not have known that his son-in-law, close friend and first grade coach Chris Anderson had negotiated a contract for himself with Super League and had helped lure the first grade squad to similar deals.

They would suggest that any chief executive who found himself in the position of having his first grade team and coach secretly signed without his knowledge to a rival football competition would be forced to resign in embarrassment or be sacked for incompetence. Moore would do neither.

A friend rang Gould at home on Friday March 31 to say Canterbury players had signed Super League contracts the previous night. The players had been bundled into a bus and taken to an office where they were given enticing details of Super League's plans and offered vast amounts of money if they immediately signed contracts. Players were not allowed to take the contracts away for perusal by their managers or lawyers. It was sign it or lose it. The emphasis on secrecy was to backfire on Super League. Four players, Jason Smith, Jarrod McCracken, Dean Pay and Jim Dymock later used the secrecy and failure for full consideration of the contract with a manager as levers to have their Super League deals overturned by the Industrial Court.

All four players signed with ARL-aligned Parramatta after the Super League contracts were overturned, although News Ltd subsequently appealed the decision.

Super League foot soldiers headed for Townsville on Friday

Good as GOULD

March 31 and signed all Canberra players that same night. Gould received word the next morning from James Packer about Canberra's defection and the gathering momentum of Super League.

He rang Stuart in Townsville to get confirmation.

Gould: 'What's going on mate?'

Stuart: 'Nothing. We had the Super League people here last night offering contracts.'

As a ruse Gould said Packer was keen to have another talk about Stuart's future.

Stuart: 'I can't tell you a lie, mate. I've signed with Super League.'

Gould: 'Who?'

Stuart: 'News Ltd. I signed last night. They gave us an hour to sign. They met us and told us the story about what the new competition would mean and where it was headed. It sounds really good.'

'I always believed that Super League did not intend running a competition. It was all a matter of destabilisation to force the ARL to talk to them,' Gould says. 'Stuart told me that when he was offered his contract, he said to the Super League negotiator: "The Australian Rugby League is not going to take this lying down". He says the negotiator (Stuart didn't say who it was) said: "The ARL is going to run the game. We just need your signature".' 'They offered me $100,000 up front to sign and $600,000 a year for three years,' Stuart told Gould. 'They had the cheque here for me to sign within the hour and I signed. I couldn't pass up that sort of money.' Gould: 'What made you think that you could not get that sort of money anywhere you went. Who else signed?' Stuart: 'All of us. Tim (Sheens the coach), the players. They're all with Super League. It's a goer. You've got to get into it.'

It was the realisation of the ARL's worst fears. The bear

was out of its cage. It was also the most crucial time in the entire battle. The ARL had been ambushed in stunning and staggering fashion.

Super League had a decisive advantage and, left unchecked, would have taken over the game totally, decimating the ARL's involvement.

With the leading sides signing willingly, the theory was that it was only a matter of time before the lesser sides that Super League was chasing to make up its premiership of 12 teams would capitulate.

The ARL can take no real solace from the fact that it eventually would mount an effective defence. There had been ample warnings about the seriousness of the situation for more than six months but no real precautions had been taken. After initial scepticism about any media mogul, even one as powerful as Rupert Murdoch, being able to take over rugby league, the ARL had allowed itself to be fooled into a false sense of security.

The first public hint of Super League had come in 'Gladys Craven's' column in the *Sun Herald* of July 24, 1994. Its evolvement, and support from several leading clubs led to News Ltd's David Smith and Ken Cowley being given permission to address the 20 premiership clubs at a special meeting at the NSWRL on February 6.

The presentation was always going to be a hard sell. It basically called for the premiership clubs, some with close to 90 years of proud history, who were not wanted by Super League to not only die, but to fire the bullet themselves by voting to support the News Ltd proposal. It was always an unrealistic objective. ARL boss Ken Arthurson had already seen Super League's proposal and had spent days considering its implications and deciding if he could support its concept in front of a hostile chief executive's meeting.

Good as GOULD

Eventually on Sunday February 5, the day before the crucial meeting of the chief executives, he decided, after a long walk with his dog, that he could not endorse Super League. When he returned home he phoned Cowley with the news. 'What was the dog's name? Kerry.' Cowley would inquire, suggesting Kerry Packer had influenced Arthurson's thinking.

Cowley insisted that Smith be allowed to outline News Ltd's Super League plans the next day, February 6, even though he realised it was an exercise in futility. But Super League's plans suffered a further setback at the meeting. Cowley and Smith were kept waiting outside in a separate room while delegates gathered and discussed the issue without knowing full details of the plan. Cowley and Smith were also pre-empted by the unexpected appearance of Kerry Packer who was ushered into the meeting at the invitation of Arthurson and who spoke with his customary bluntness. Packer told the club representatives that he owned the complete rights to showing rugby league on free-to-air television until the year 2000 and would not be surrendering any of his arrangement. If clubs defected to a new competition he would sue them and the ARL. Packer's speech was endorsed by Souths president George Piggins who emphasised the morality of maintaining loyalty to contracts the NSWRL had already signed with Packer. Piggins, correctly identifying that the future of his beloved Souths club was fatally compromised if Super League eventuated, became the fiercest and most vocal supporter of the ARL's campaign to maintain control of the game.

Balmain's Keith Barnes, long regarded as one of the game's most astute and conventional administrators, broke mould by telling the meeting that any clubs wanting to go to Super league should be expelled.

The ARL also produced its own counter punch, producing five-year loyalty contracts, and demanding that all 20 clubs sign them and return them the following day by 9am. Brisbane showed initial reluctance, eventually taking a couple of days to return the document to the ARL and then only after a threat of expulsion.

Brisbane's signed contract would be put on hold while several minor points were worked out by the club and the NSWRL. It was obvious that the loyalty agreements were a master stroke at that stage. In time they would become the ARL's most significant legal argument against the introduction of Super League.

The agreements were developed in secret, their existence revealed only to the absolute minimum number of people. Quayle, Arthurson and legal advisers were the only people with a full knowledge of the loyalty agreement surprise that was to be sprung.

Aware that Moore, Ribot, Canberra and Cronulla were Super League sympathisers, the ARL wanted to keep the agreements in lead-lined secrecy. It was a surprise attack along the lines that Super League would develop in weeks to come when it secretly began signing clubs.

The loyalty agreements were a bloodless coup for the ARL, especially when Moore, Ribot, Canberra and Cronulla sat mutely through the entire meeting, ignoring the chance to state their case.

Not having spoken that day would haunt Ribot in the future. It was a confidential forum of all club chief executives and presidents. A persuasive and forthright speech at that time, supported by the clubs with similar feelings about Super League, could have been a pivotal event.

Ribot and his co-delegate Paul 'Porky' Morgan may well have been in a state of shock. Before the agreements were tabled the ARL announced that not only did Packer have the free-to-air television rights, he had also been in possession of the pay TV rights for some time, having paid a million dollars for them.

Good as GOULD

Morgan turned to Ribot as if to say: 'Why didn't you tell me that.' A stunned Ribot could only think in reply: 'Because I didn't know.'

Confirmation that the pay TV deal with Channel 9 was long-standing would later be offered by Arthurson, with the explanation that pay TV was a long way in the future when the contract had been signed and the ARL had accepted the best deal offered at the time.

He offered to send the details to Cowley. Channel 10 also confirmed that they had previously inquired about pay TV rights when the climate was calmer and Super League was not a topic, only to be told they had been sold to Channel 9.

The announcement of the pay TV rights deal with Packer was numbing for News Ltd. It meant that the very aspects of the game they were trying to acquire—pay TV and free-to-air—were *all* held by Packer.

It was after this meeting of club delegates proved so unrewarding for their ambitions that News Ltd decided to take off the white gloves of diplomacy and buckle on the gauntlet.

Super League struck fiercely, with the secrecy of a guerilla attack. Canterbury signed on Thursday night March 30 after training. Canberra signed in Townsville on the Saturday night of March 31. Brisbane were next . . .

The next three would be no surprise. Cronulla, Auckland, and the Cowboys in Townsville, whose defection would see former Test winger and ARL stalwart Kerry Boustead quit. Then Penrith and the Western Reds in Perth would also fall.

It was Super League's reply and like the ARL's loyalty agreement tactic, it was well disguised. After the chief executives' meeting on February 6, the ARL had prematurely been lulled into a false sense of their own immortality. With all 20 clubs signed on five year loyalty agreements, it seemed inconceivable that News Ltd could find a crack to infiltrate.

TALES FROM THE PHILLIP STREET BUNKER

Rupert Murdoch gave a hint it was not over when he appeared on Channel 9's current affairs program 60 Minutes. Interviewer Jana Wendt asked Murdoch if the battle had now been fought and won. He conceded that it was Packer 1 and Murdoch nil. 'But it's only half time,' he added cryptically.

News Ltd brilliantly diverted attention with one aspect of their tactical plan. They lodged an appeal in the Industrial Court against the validity of the loyalty agreements, specifically nominating Canberra, Brisbane, Canterbury and Cronulla among the plaintiffs.

The move focused legal and ARL attention on Super League's attempt to sign clubs. Instead News Ltd moved into overdrive to sign individual players, starting with Canterbury and then Canberra in Townsville.

The move shattered the fragile peace that existed between Super League and the ARL and generated widespread confusion. To Super League, signing Canberra, Brisbane and Canterbury was meant simply as a shot across the ARL's bows. A positive and intimidating display of the financial muscle and power it could generate.

The ARL, with an all-out assault on playing ranks, signed as many people as possible as quickly as possible. 'Gee,' said Cowley to Arthurson at one stage during their recurring attempts to find a solution. 'You overacted. We had only signed 50 or 60 players. Did you have to go and sign everyone who's ever worn a football jumper?'

The moment Gould read in the newspaper of April 1 that Super League had been signing clubs he started making inquiries among friends, players and managers, chasing answers and prising admissions from reluctant lips that had been sworn to secrecy.

It was hard. Super League's hit and run policy was one of extreme caution and separation of players, managers and advisers. Players were offered lucrative deals then subjected to pressure to sign on the spot because the money might not be available if they delayed.

'I am of the opinion that the contracts entered into by the players were induced by the conduct of Super League which was unfair and unconscionable,' Justice Hill would rule in the Industrial Court in upholding the appeal by the Canterbury quartet Jim Dymock, Jarrod McCracken, Dean Pay and Jason Smith against their Super League contracts.

'I got the managers of players to ring me. I spoke to Jimmy Dymock, Jim Sedaris and Brad Fittler to see if they had been approached,' Gould said. 'Dymock denied it but it was obvious from the tone of his voice that he had signed with Super League. He was sworn to secrecy but he couldn't hide the fact that he was in it. Brad Fittler said the chief executive of Canberra, Kevin Neil had pulled him aside the previous week after the club had played Penrith and said they wanted him. He told Brad that Super League was a reality and that he could offer him $500,000 a season. I said: "What authority does he have to do that?" Brad said Neill had tried to assure him that Super League would get up and running and the ARL would be the losers.'

Gould said to Fittler: 'Don't sign anything until you talk to me again.'

Fittler, with his customary laid-back style replied, 'Cool, dude.'

There were frantic and frequent phone calls between Gould, ARL general manager John Quayle, and James Packer. Players were ringing constantly to find out what was happening and what the intrusion by Super League meant to the premiership.

On Sunday morning April 2, St George chief executive Geoff Carr rang Gould's car phone to give him the news that Super League agents were going to be at the St George and Canterbury game at Kogarah Oval that afternoon and the

Newcastle and Sydney Tigers match at Parramatta Stadium. They would be in the dressing rooms, the leagues club and the car parks trying to sign players.

'It was the day after I had spoken to Ricky Stuart. It was obvious then that this exercise was being planned with military precision. I rang John Quayle and he said we should meet the next day. I told him my feelings were that it could be all over by tomorrow and that we should meet immediately,' said Gould. 'I said the first thing we had to was get a press release out urging players not to commit themselves to anything until they had heard from the Australian Rugby League. We didn't get a full press release out in time but I put the message over 2UE that players should not sign anything until they had heard both sides of the story.'

At that stage the ARL was tottering and tentative. Officials knew something had to be done but an exact defensive strategy was a long way from being formulated against the greatest offensive the game had ever known. The ARL administration, which had proved professional enough in peace time, was unprepared for war.

In an environment of such uncertainty, the future of the traditional ARL game and structure genuinely swung in the balance. If another couple of clubs had succumbed to Super League, the NSWRL game as it had been known since 1908 in Australia, would have been a hollow shell of minor clubs and nonentity players relegated to almost a park competition.

The rugby league's slowness to react to an attack from its own core of officials reflected the long respected code of loyalty above all and closing ranks in the face of adversity. There might be constant and often fierce internal bickering. Factions might form and dissolve as clubs fought for one advantage or another. But in the face of calamity, for the good of the game or often more importantly to protect their own positions and stature, they would link arms to keep intruders out.

Good as GOULD

This time the intruders trampled on the time-honoured defensive system with ease by working from within, using the NSWRL's own representatives as double agents and seemingly unlimited amounts of money that would bring total spending on rugby league's civil war to more than $200 million. The ARL would also tap into its own financial resources of around $12 million to help fund the legal fights. Reserves that had been accumulated with careful prudence since the early 1980s when the game was facing serious financial problems would be spent in a rush.

'We're saving the money for a rainy day,' was a quote attributed to both Quayle and Arthurson. 'Have you looked outside lately. It's bloody well pouring,' was the pragmatic reply from former Labor Party heavyweight Graham Richardson.

Richardson, then a columnist and adviser within the Packer media empire, was recruited to the ARL defence team along with Kerry's son James and Channel 9 general manager David Leckie as well as an additional $12 million dollars to boost the budget.

The wrangle between Super League and the ARL also pitted James Packer and News Ltd heir apparent Lachlan Murdoch against each other although there were indications that away from the battle front the two men enjoyed each other's company socially.

Super League had sprung to life from two remarkable coincidences: Firstly: the growing dissatisfaction of the Brisbane Broncos in particular—with at least tacit endorsement from Canberra, Canterbury and Cronulla—with the ARL's administration and future expansion plans. The only privately-owned club in the history of Australian rugby league, the Broncos had emerged as a golden financial waterfall for its directors. Massive crowds first at Lang Park and then at ANZ Stadium, coupled with extensive sponsorships, marketing and catering generated turnover as high as $10 million a year. Brisbane also exploited its early position as the only Brisbane-based club by imaginative ways of getting around the ARL salary cap. It was impossible to keep as many as 11 internationals financially content on expenditure of $1.5 million. Rather than be vulnerable to raids from other clubs, Brisbane diverted its many sponsorships into player benefits.

A player would be signed for say $100,00 and that contract would be forwarded to the ARL for registration. In reality that same player could finish with as much as an additional $200,000 a season from sponsorship—endorsements arranged by the club. These were ruled to be outside the salary cap.

Other Sydney-based clubs were doing the same thing, getting sponsors to provide benefits for players that could be hidden from the ARL and in some cases from the taxation department. One player's deal with his club included $50,000 worth of home renovations from a sponsor. Other players got paid overseas holidays for their families and whatever else would clinch a deal.

Brisbane was unhappy with the ARL's approach to marketing, branding it eccentric and sentiment driven. Of particular aggravation was the ARL's refusal to switch State of Origin and Queensland-based matches from Lang Park's capacity of around 40,000 to ANZ Stadium which held around 60,000.

It was an increasingly volatile situation that became tinder dry. Super League would be the match. Concerned about financial backing for its premiership following Government legislation banning cigarette sponsorship of sport which ended Winfield's long participation, Arthurson had approached Cowley with a deal for Ansett to have naming rights to the premiership for around $8 million a season—half of the deal to involve cash and half to comprise contra.

Arthurson knew it was significantly less than the Winfield

deal of around $12 million a year but he also knew it was about the best deal the ARL could manage in uncertain financial times.

Despite his preference for and genuine like of rugby league Cowley was reluctant and eventually commissioned a report to see if the ARL's claims could be validated. The report showed that despite its healthy image, the rugby league premiership was growing at a snail's pace and that only the high averages of out-of-town clubs like Canberra, Newcastle and especially Brisbane were keeping the season's crowd figures looking healthy.

Ribot and Morgan were the leading protagonists of the Super League assault. They had access to Cowley, whose News Ltd company was a direct sponsor of the Brisbane Broncos through its Brisbane broadsheet newspaper the *Courier-Mail*. When Cowley asked how a proposed new competition would work if the 20 teams were condensed into 10 or 12, Ribot would say confidently: 'It could be done without any trouble.'

Ribot constantly portrayed himself as a free thinker and a visionary whose one ambition was to ensure rugby league was lifted to a loftier plane both nationally and internationally. The ARL's belief was that Ribot's basic philosophy was that if it was good for the Broncos it was good for rugby league.

Ribot and the Broncos did not oppose expansion, provide it did not include a second team in Queensland, an area they regarded as their private domain. Ribot and his directors wanted representative matches in Brisbane shifted from their traditional venue of Lang Park to the Broncos' home ground of ANZ Stadium.

'Ribot's ideas on rugby league revolved around supporting anything that might help the Broncos,' says Quayle. Perhaps the supreme irony is that after opposing the introduction of another club in Brisbane with both the ARL and Super League, Ribot and the Broncos would have to sit and watch the ARL introduce the South Queensland Crushers and the North Queensland Cowboys in Townsville. Ribot would then be forced to go cap in hand to the ARL- and Queensland Rugby League-aligned Crushers at one stage and ask them to join Super League as the search for franchises became desperate. It would not have helped his disposition to have his request rejected.

The lack of enthusiasm for franchises staggered Super League and seriously jeopardised its future. The ARL's belief is that Super League's miscalculation about its expected impact—and arrogance about immediately becoming the driving force in the game, was a fatal flaw in the planning. With Canterbury, Canberra and Cronulla already under lock and key, Super League expected a domino effect with clubs rushing to leave the ARL ranks and humbly queuing for annointment to the ranks of the new competition.

Clubs progressively rejected proposals from a Super League hierarchy that worked its way through Wests, Balmain, North Sydney, Illawarra, Parramatta, Newcastle and St George without success. Eventually Super League was forced to establish its own franchises in Newcastle, despite overwhelming support for the ARL side in that city, and in the rugby league wilderness of Adelaide.

Quayle believes Super League lacked understanding of the game's structure in their attempted coup. 'Super League thought the answer was to sign up the coaches at clubs and the players would follow. Tim Sheens (Canberra), Wayne Bennett (Brisbane), Peter Mulholland (Perth), Grant Bell (Townsville), John Monie (Auckland), Chris Anderson (Canterbury) and Graham Murray (Illawarra) jumped on board straight away,' says Quayle. 'They went after Malcolm Reilly in Newcastle and couldn't get him. They thought with the coaches aboard the players would follow. They did not understand at all. The coaches were easy to get. Super League just doubled the wages they were getting at the time and the coaches queued up to take the money. Super League failed in two areas. They failed to use the managers of players and they did not realise the relationship Phil (Gould) and Bozo (Bob Fulton) had with the players they had coached at club and representative level. Super League kept saying they would not talk to players' managers and would only talk to players. The managers were annoyed by the attitude and that helped us because we were talking to them. Super League also chronically underestimated the vigour with which the ARL would defend. Super League only wanted three teams from Sydney initially and two of them were already established as Canterbury and Cronulla. The next move from Super League was amalgamation among the clubs that would miss out. They wanted to wipe Sydney out. Then as they kept getting knocked back by clubs they wanted to sign and getting their arrogant plans for self-imposed amalgamation ridiculed, Super League realised they would have to take whatever they could get.'

The ARL was also forced to dig deep to keep its players and coaches on side. Malcolm Reilly at Newcastle was signed for $2.3 million. Gould and Fulton also received a loyalty payment of up to half a million dollars over five years. The money was a two-fold payment. Primarily it was in exchange for their loyalty to the Australian Rugby League but there was undoubtedly a component of gratitude as well for the tireless work they performed in opposing Super League.

There was controversy over the selective payments to Gould, Fulton and Reilly ahead of other first grade coaches but the ARL believes they were justified by the circumstances. Reilly was a vital acquisition to stop Newcastle defecting to Super League.

Quayle says that the ARL had no option but to financially retaliate once Super League started throwing huge sums of money around, including the multi-million dollar contracts to Canberra players.

The obscene amounts of money offered to players and coaches in both camps were staggering. Super League's outlay was pre-conceived and deliberate. The ARL's represented a counter-move. Working in the dark and totally unaware of Super League's agenda and future projects, the ARL says it had no option but to act quickly and efficiently to sign players and clubs to protect its own position and form the foundation for a spirited defence.

'It was war. Simple as that,' says Quayle. 'We determined in conjunction with Channel 9 and Optus that we would need money to sign up a number of players. They provided $12 million on Saturday April 1. By Monday April 3 we knew that would not be enough and they increased it to 20 million dollars. The money was given to us on trust. We never signed anything.'

Arthurson and Quayle had already discussed the best way of signing players and decided on Gould and Fulton as the principal negotiators. 'Ken and I just did not have the knowledge to do it,' he said. 'I contacted them both and they were happy to work with us.'

To the ARL, conscripting Gould and Fulton as its banner carriers was either an inspired choice . . . or just lucky.

Either way it proved a winner. For all of the millions of dollars Super League expended in its recruitment drive, it had no players or officials who brought the negotiating skills, experience, authority and highly acceptable public profile to the battle that Gould and Fulton could offer. Had Super League had the foresight to make signing Gould and Fulton a priority and listened to and followed their tactics, the entire confrontation with the ARL would almost certainly have swung decisively their way.

PHIL GOULD'S Reflections on
FOOTBALL'S WAR

The vast majority of players who signed with Super League did so for one reason and one reason only. Money.

The proposition that Super League was about a brave new world of rugby league domination of global sporting markets was only a giant hook to cover News Ltd's real intention—that of trying to steal a share of the lucrative pay TV market.

As the Federal Court eventually established, News Ltd did not have any legal or lawful right to rugby league—but that truism did not stop Rupert Murdoch trying.

He saw his powerful media conglomerate and his organisation's vast wealth as a way to steamroll the Australian Rugby League while at the same time convincing the public through non-stop propaganda in his newspapers that Super League was a wonderful and exciting project that was legally sanctioned.

One early incident showed me just what sort of a propaganda war the Australian Rugby League would have to endure in the battle with Super League.

The *Daily Telegraph*'s Peter Frilingos, a senior rugby league writer, was working with me on 2UE on Sunday April 2—the day after news broke that clubs were defecting to Super League.

For the first two hours of our broadcast that day he was extremely supportive of the Australian Rugby League, as I had known him to be for the past 20 years. Sometimes I thought he had been *blindly* supportive of the ARL but at least his loyalty seemed assured.

TALES FROM THE PHILLIP STREET BUNKER

A phone call to 2UE on that afternoon between 1pm-2pm saw Frilingos return to the News Ltd offices immediately. By the next morning he was the Sydney journalist leading the drum-beating for Super League, his declarations on radio the previous day of supporting the ARL forgotten.

He continued in that role for the rest of the battle with Super League as the ARL struggled to make any headway at all in its attempt to get its point of view—and the truth—into any News Ltd newspaper.

That is how quickly and how much of a media and propaganda issue it became.

To have one person's opinion of 20 years seemingly changed in a couple of hours indicated just how determined News Ltd was to use every media outlet in its possession to push its message.

It was always going to be tough battling a news organisation. I don't know if John Quayle, myself and Bob Fulton realised how tough on the night of Sunday April 2 when we met at the ARL in Phillip St, Sydney to discuss a fightback.

News had broken the previous day about Canterbury and Canberra defecting. Quayle had rung on Sunday to meet with Fulton and me. At the start of the meeting we just sat there shaking our heads at the enormity of it all. It dawned on us that the enemy was very well hidden. We did not know who to talk to or who to trust.

I had already spoken to players over that week-end looking for information. Players I had known well for years, suddenly became short and abrupt in conversations. It was obvious that Super League people did not want them talking to ARL-friendly people.

The big mistake that Super League made was not talking to the player managers like Steve Gillis, Wayne Beavis and Sam Ayoub. They controlled the greatest number of players, especially in the Sydney area. I think advisers to Super League such as Peter Moore, had told News Ltd that these managers were friends of mine and therefore friends of the Australian Rugby League. It would be no good dealing with them because they might advise their players not to sign with Super League. That would have accounted for the intense secrecy that Super League attached to everything it did.

I rate the loyalty to the Australian Rugby League of Gillis, Beavis and Ayoub as a key factor in the ARL signing as many players as it did. The three managers did nothing unethical. It was just that they had a wide understanding of the issues involved because of frank discussions held with the ARL. They came to their own individual conclusions that supporting the ARL's stance was the most secure alternative for their clients.

It was a lot harder to get that point of view across to the players who had signed with Super League because we were not allowed any access to them. Penrith players were banned from talking to either me or Beavis, even though I had signed eight or ten of them to ARL contracts and Beavis was the manager of many of them.

Many of those players who were signed to the ARL subsequently signed contracts with Super League as well, without discussing it with me or Beavis. Those players never contacted Beavis or myself, simply because Super League said they could not do so. That is another aspect of how ridiculous things became.

As we sat in the NSWRL headquarters that Sunday night, one thing at least was obvious. We had to have something to announce the next morning to the media. Something big that would show the ARL was fighting back to try and stop Super League's momentum. We signed two internationals, Tim Brasher from the Sydney Tigers and Brad Fittler from Penrith. Ian Roberts from Manly agreed to terms over the phone but later changed his mind and went to Super League. It was the first step in a long journey to save the game.

Our other strategy that night was to make immediate plans to sign as many players as possible to the ARL and as quickly as possible. Bob Fulton and I sat down and picked the best of the players we believed had not gone to Super League as a potential World Cup team at the end of the year.

Then we worked out the players we would need for State of Origin squads for New South Wales and Queensland. Basically the State of Origin squads were picked that night. Then we listed the top 60 or 70 players we thought had not been signed to Super League and decided to get them under contract as quickly as possible.

The first day of the battle had come and gone but the ARL was still alive. Bleeding a bit. Well, actually, bleeding a lot. But a long way from being fatally wounded . . .

The Lolly Shop

For the scores of media representatives gathered on the stairs outside the NSW licensed Leagues Club in Sydney, the impact of Super League had been more puzzling than anything else. Super League had struck two days earlier, signing Canberra stars Brad Clyde, Laurie Daley and Ricky Stuart and others—and now the ARL was supposedly fighting back. But how? When? Using what methods?

All day on Monday April 3 a steady stream of players and their managers had filed into the Leagues Club and made their way to the fifth floor where negotiations had been taking place in a marathon session that stretched for more than 16 hours.

If those media representatives had been blessed with their fictional newspaper colleague Clark Kent's x-ray vision they could have looked through the brick walls and witnessed the scenes of chaos—organised only as much as was possible.

Players were turning up with their managers, some invited, some perhaps having picked up the scent on the wind of additional money for simply staying loyal to the game and ignoring offers from Super League.

For some it was a bonus that had been totally unexpected—and they were delighted. But sometimes the joy was short-lived. Penrith second-rower John Cartwright, a friend of Gould's from the glory days of Penrith but playing possibly his last year in the competition because of recurring injuries and age, was offered $75,000 as a loyalty payment.

He said: 'There's no need to do that. I'll be right. You know I'm going to stay with the ARL anyway. I'll probably only play for another year. Super League wouldn't want me.'

Much of what Cartwright said was correct but Gould insisted that as a loyal and staunch servant of the game for so long and as a former Kangaroo and 'personality' of rugby league he deserved to share in the ex gratia payments.

'I mentioned $75,000 a year for five years and Carty said: "You're kidding". I said: "No. You can have the money within seven days". Cartwright cried with happiness when the deal was done, partly at the magnitude of the payment, partly with pride that his years of service and loyalty had been recognised.'

Within days Cartwright would be back on the telephone to the ARL equally passionate—about getting out of his contract. Super League had stepped in with a massive offer of $225,000 a season for two years plus a $70,000 immediate bonus.

'That could set me up for life,' Cartwright pleaded. He was told that he was under contract to the ARL and any attempt to sign with Super League would result in legal action.

It was a trend that would be repeated over and over again. The ARL says Manly fullback Matthew Ridge agreed to terms and signed a contract. There are claims that he then smuggled the contract out of the room and left to speak to Super League, signing with them for $400,000 as a bonus plus $300,000 a season for seven years.

The ARL is also convinced that Manly prop Ian Roberts agreed to terms (he says he did not) before switching to Super League and a million dollar plus contract to be basically a public relations and recruitment officer. On the face of it by the time he had completed his contract with Manly, his career would be almost over as a player.

Roberts initially appeared positive about the ARL's offer

but was granted time at his own request to consider his future and talk to Super League.

Unlike some others, Roberts would have the character to return to the ARL and tell John Quayle personally that he would be joining Super League.

It was a fierce and unrelenting battle. News Ltd's initial foray had delivered quality players and teams in Canberra, Canterbury and Brisbane. The ARL's retaliation had been fiercer and more intense than Super League had expected.

In hindsight Super League's expensive signing of Canberra, including a contract for Bradley Clyde worth $4.3 million was intended to be more of a muscle flexing exercise designed to intimidate the ARL and underline the futility of trying to compete with the money being bandied around.

Instead the ARL, with the help of an amount varyingly quoted between $20–$45 million in funds from Optus boss Geoff Cousins and a lesser contribution from Channel 9, widened the battle front with an all-out assault on the premiership's playing strength eventually sending the entire recruiting battle into a new financial dimension of stunning player payments.

The previously little-known Cousins emerged as a life-saver for the Australian Rugby League. He was in Australia from America to head Optus' multi-million dollar battle for cable television rights against Foxtel and Galaxy. Like all cable TV operators Cousins realised the crucial role sport would play in the battle to sign subscribers.

He arrived in Australia under the impression that Optus, who were in partnership with Kerry Packer, already had the rights to rugby league. It came as a shock to discover on this first day in the job that the Super League chaos had erupted. Proving his mettle from the start, Cousins entered the fray with total commitment, opening up the Optus' coffers to the ARL for the fight.

It is impossible to overestimate the impact and contribution that Optus, through Cousins, provided.

'He was just magnificent,' Arthurson said. 'He made it clear from the start that he was never going to back away from the battle.'

Optus had the option of pulling away from the dispute without loss and letting victory go to the stronger.

'We decided to fight in the belief that no-one had the right to come along and steal something as they (News Ltd) were trying to do,' Cousins said. 'It was a tough call. If we had walked away the chances are the ARL would not be here today.'

For Gould the battle began with a telephone call on Sunday April 2 while he was at Kogarah Oval watching Canterbury play St George.

'He came up and said he had to go. He was going to the NSWRL because the Super League raids had begun,' remembers then St George chief executive Geoff Carr, now the premiership manager for the ARL. 'That morning Johnny Raper had rung me and said he had just spoken to his son Aaron, who was playing with Cronulla. Super League had started to sign Cronulla players. He said they were going to target St George next. Super League had decided it would be a combined franchise even if St George did not join in.'

Carr, as the 1994 Kangaroo team manager, had been smelling the smoke of Super League for some time after being approached to join the rebel group as an administrator. 'While I was on tour with the Kangaroos Peter Gow, the president of Cronulla, contacted me about Super League,' he said. 'When I got back the chairman and deputy chairman of St George had met with Gow and he had outlined the full picture. Because the St George officials were still uncertain Gow had put them in touch with News Ltd's David Smith. Gow said that Smith would verify that the ARL would be running Super League and that there would be four franchises. St George would have to amalgamate if they wanted to be in Super League or they would be out.'

Gow wanted Carr to be chief executive of the Cronulla-St George franchise and offered him the job in early February, giving him 24 hours to make up his mind. Carr delayed a decision and suddenly the February 6 meeting and the reality of the loyalty agreements signed by clubs looked to be the end of Super League.

'Then we played Cronulla in the second premiership round. Gow was in the club and he told me the matter we had been discussing (Super League) was not over,' said Carr.

'The next thing I knew was on April 1 when the papers revealed how Super League had been signing players,' Carr said.

James Packer rang Carr on April 5, trying to work out revised contracts to stop St George players defecting to Super League.

The day the story broke about Super League's recruiting drive in Townsville on April 1 to sign Canberra, Carr and Gould spoke more than a dozen times so the events of the next day at half-time in the St George and Canterbury match were not such a surprise. Gould told Carr he was going to the NSWRL to pick a couple of teams and work out which players were still available for selection and had not gone to Super League.

First priority was to chase some high profile representative players. Brad Fittler, Tim Brasher, Paul Harragon, Ian Roberts and Glenn Lazarus were among the first players contacted. Brasher and Fittler signed that night (to the ARL), both for $300,000 loyalty payments.

'We guaranteed Fittler and Brasher up-front payments for

five years and explained the whole situation to them. We got their managers in as well,' Gould said. 'Paul Harragon was in Newcastle but he agreed in principle on the telephone. Ian Roberts gave Bob Fulton a verbal assurance on the phone that he would stick to the ARL.'

With hindsight the ARL's loyalty payments to players, like Super League's, went wildly askew. Problem was, the ARL was working in a vacuum. There was no positive information about what Super League was doing or how much success it was having with recruitment. The only certain knowledge was that Super League had signed at least Canterbury, Brisbane, Canberra and probably Cronulla.

The ARL's focus was simply on counter-punching by signing players as quickly as possible to make up lost ground. The presence of Gould and Fulton as the ARL's easily recognised and successful representative and premiership coaches was an enormous boost for the establishment.

Ian Trent, the manager of Kangaroo lock Brad Mackay negotiated with Gould and walked away satisfied when the ARL signed his client for the amount he asked. Within days Trent was back at the NSWRL saying he had not realised the amount of money other players were receiving and asking that Mackay's contract be re-evaluated. It was.

The ARL defence strategies took on a more composed look on Monday April 2, 48 hours after the storm broke—when Channel 9 general manager David Leckie and James Packer told Gould and Fulton to simply sign as many players as they could as quickly as they could.

'It was a very interesting part of my life,' remembers Fulton. 'It was a tough time but I was with quality people who knew what they were doing. We had a plan and, although we ad libbed a fair bit along the way, we stuck basically to the outline we had decided at our first meeting on the Sunday night after the Super League story broke in the newspapers the previous day. Our advantage was that we had a plan and they didn't. That was obvious by the way they were going around employing people on the run. They didn't have a junior development officer so they went and got Barry Russell two weeks after the battle started. They didn't have recruitment officers so they got Michael O'Connor. Graham Lowe was involved and Ribot was doing some recruiting as well. That all happened because the ARL fought back. They had no basic plan and that's where we got under their guard. We went to England and we upped player payments over there. The reason we went to England was to erode the strength of their (Britain's) national side. And we did.'

Fulton said the plan was to sign England's Test players to contracts that prevented them playing against Super League sides. That was because the England Super League side would be further weakened in the international arena. Fulton said English Rugby League boss Maurice Lindsay was unaware that players he was losing to ARL contracts would not be able to play Super League—and was stunned when he realised he had been outsmarted.

Initially as many eligible players as possible were signed in almost any circumstances. Few players were rejected, although there were some exceptions when applicants with proven shortcomings or limited ability wanted exceptional money. 'One player came to us from Illawarra because he had heard about the recruiting drive,' Gould says. 'He had waited nearly all day and I didn't see him until very late. To be honest I didn't recognise him. But he introduced himself and we started talking. He said he had already been to see Super League because his contract ended that year. He told me he understood the issues involved and had been offered $30,000 sign on and $125,000 a year by Super League. I said: "How old are you?" He said: "Twenty-seven". I said "How much first grade have you played?" He said: "About 12 games." I said: "You're 27, you've played a dozen first grade games. Do you think Illawarra will pick you up?" He said he did not know. If they didn't he would go and play in the park. Then I said: "What are you doing here when you've been offered that much by Super League?" He said: "I just can't believe it is happening." I said: "Believe it mate. Get across to Super League and sign".'

As well as signing players en masse, the ARL, at Gould's request, also started tying up junior representative players in an effort to cut off the supply line of talent to Super League in the long term.

'We also had to target players who obviously were not first grade but were a little older than junior representative class players,' Gould said. 'To my way of thinking, the competition that signed up the most players would have the most viable premiership. It would come down to numbers. We had to sign high profile players first to ensure that people knew the ARL was alive and kicking. Then we had to sign quantity and then we had to sign juniors. That meant that at any stage of the debate, we could argue that we had a competition that would survive for at least the next three years because we had players of the present and players of the future.'

The chief executives of clubs known to be loyal to the ARL were called in and given budgets of $500,000 to sign their junior representative players and a further $350,000 to sign players in the club—excluding proven first graders—who would be prominent in the next five years.

The recognised rebel clubs at that stage in the ARL's eyes—Canterbury, Canberra, Brisbane and Cronulla—were not included. But Perth, Penrith and Newcastle, who were wavering were invited.

In fact the allocation of money to clubs to sign young players proved a remarkable boost to the ARL because it exposed clubs whose sympathies were with Super League. Newcastle chief executive Brad Mellen for example did not sign any players to the ARL. Neither did Auckland chief executive Ian Robson, whose club was already well on the way to joining Super League. Their reluctance to be involved was seen as inexpensive proof positive by the ARL that these clubs were defecting.

The ARL sweep on Monday April 3 after Super League's raids were exposed eventually included players of all nationalities in the Sydney premiership, Australians, New Zealanders, English and the Pacific Islanders.

In a day of mayhem as players jostled for positions in the long queues forming to talk terms, Manly's Kiwi Test fullback Matthew Ridge came into negotiate—and left, leaving a sour taste.

'Bobby Fulton brought in a number of Manly players to sign including Ridge,' Gould said. 'He shook hands on an ARL deal with Fulton which was worth a lot more than I thought he was worth compared to what some other players were getting. I think it was something like $250,000 to sign plus a package of around $300,000 a year. He said fine to the deal but then told Bozo he wanted another $50,000 added to his Manly contract. Fulton said that was a side issue that could be sorted out at Manly, that we were only negotiating ARL contracts at the time. Ridge insisted, saying he was happy with the terms, provided he got another $50,000 from Manly. Fulton rang his chief executive Frank Stanton on the spot and organised it straight away. I was in the office as Ridge was going through the contract. He suddenly looked up and said: "Where does it say about my $50,000 from Manly?" I said that the $50,000 was a side issue with Manly but that his coach had promised the money and it was secure. As soon as our backs were turned Ridge picked up his contract and ran down to Super League with it and signed with them that night for

TALES FROM THE PHILLIP STREET BUNKER

$300,000 sign on and $400,000 a year for seven years according to the figures revealed in the Federal Court. I felt sorry for Bob Fulton because one of his own players had done that to him. I just couldn't stomach what Ridge did that night and how he came to be so critical of the ARL.

'The next thing we knew was that Ridge was great friends with Rupert Murdoch's son Lachlan. I think that during the entire Super League battle, people like Ribot and Ridge and some chief executives got carried away simply because they were rubbing shoulders with people such as Ken Cowley and Rupert and Lachlan Murdoch. They were just star gazing. It affected their judgement.'

Gould remembered: 'You would speak to Joe Somebody in the morning and put a value on him of say $50,000. A teammate of Joe's would come in that afternoon after talking to Super League and we would have to give him say $75,000 or $80,000 to sign with the ARL. The first thing the team-mate would do was go back and tell Joe, "I got $80,000 and you only got $50,000". We had a real greed situation there for a couple of days. It made me sick. Certain players and managers were making their decisions solely on the cash being paid. I can't remember too many "thank yous" being offered by anyone, or someone actually saying "gee that's a bonus" when they were handed an extra $50,000 or $100,000. It was all just take.'

In the middle of the turmoil, Gould came face to face with one of the leading protagonists of the insurrection against the ARL, Paul Morgan, a stockbroker and the chairman of the Brisbane Broncos. Morgan made a sizeable component of his private fortune as a backer of the multi-million-dollar generating Paul Hogan films *Crocodile Dundee* and its sequel.

Easts president Nick Politis invited Gould to have a drink with Morgan and a couple of Brisbane Broncos directors who were in town for talks with Kerry Packer, in what could have been a move to find a solution to the battle with Super League. Morgan made it clear that there was no peace in sight and his club had no objection to a full scale war.

Gould remembers: 'I had never met Morgan before but I got the distinct impression that he and the other Broncos' directors had a real persecution complex about the ARL and John Quayle. It was obvious Brisbane had been seconded by News Ltd to fight its battle because they were so convinced that they had a genuine grievance against the ARL. The complaints they were making that night about the ARL had nothing to do with what the battle with Super League was all about. News Ltd had found a couple of disgruntled employees in Canberra and Brisbane and promised them the world to get them on side.'

Canberra's defection was probably driven by other factors. Canberra's winning of the 1989 and 1990 premierships was based on overspending in excess of the salary cap limit of $1.5 million. Canberra's spending for the 1989 season in which they beat Balmain in extra time, was closer to $5 million although full details would be not disclosed until two years later by an inquiring media headed by John Hogan of *The Australian*. There were calls for Canberra to be stripped of the premiership but the eventual penalties would have long-ranging effects and come back to haunt the ARL in 1995.

Canberra's chief executive in 1990 and the man whose approval was needed for the money to be spent was John McIntyre, son of the patriarch of rugby league in the Canberra and Queanbeyan area and chairman of the Leagues Club, Les McIntyre.

The ARL's edict that John McIntyre be replaced as Canberra's chief executive was not palatable to his father who would simmer on the decision for several years while working behind the scenes to have him reinstated. When ARL's Ken

Arthurson appealed to Les McIntyre for support in 1995 and asked him to reject Super League's overtures, the knockback would be uncompromising. Adding to Canberra's pique was the failure of its delegation to the ARL to raise its concerns about its star players being offered huge amounts of money to switch clubs, despite still being under contract.

'The answer from Quayle and Arthurson at the time was that their legal advice was that nothing could be done,' Les McIntyre said. McIntyre also vented his anger that a claimed promise from Arthurson to publicly exonerate his son from any wrong doing in the overspending scandal had not been fulfilled. 'All John did then was try and keep his team together,' said McIntyre. 'The same as we are trying to do now. In 1992 the clubs who were crying foul were doing the same thing. They were caught out in 1993. I said to the ARL: "What happened to them? You didn't ask *them* to resign."'

Canberra maintained it was propelled into Super League by reports that Easts were openly bragging that the club had six million dollars to spend on recruiting players from other clubs, including Ricky Stuart, Bradley Clyde and Laurie Daley.

Ironically Arthurson asked Canberra for help on March 31—the same night star Canberra players were signing with Super League, which was originally called Star League in those early days.

The intensity of the battle blurred the parameters for both Super League and the ARL. Super League was not expecting such solid resistance from the ARL. The ARL was equally taken by surprise by Super League's audacious manoeuvre in signing the NZRL, England, Wales, Papua New Guinea, France and the Pacific nations, effectively freezing Australia out of the international scene.

Australia in turn, launched its belated international fightback, sending former dual Kangaroo coach Frank Stanton to

England to sign players he Gould and Fulton hand picked as the best available. The net would bring former Great Britain coach and glamour players Ellery Hanley, Garry Connolly and Lee Jackson under the ARL umbrella.

Gould believes that Super League were spooked and panicked by the rapidly changing circumstances and lacked administrators with a combination of experience, high profile and recognition in rugby league recruitment to successfully sign players in such a frantic and unpredictable climate. Only Super League's chief executive John Ribot could truly be classed as experienced in negotiating with players after his successful years with the Broncos.

Peter Moore was more experienced but his association with Canterbury and the need for secrecy made it impossible for him to work outside the circle of delivering his own club to Super League.

Players such as former dual international Michael O'Connor, who was working in a T-shirt shop at Noosa Heads before joining Super League and former Kangaroo captain Mal Meninga were recruited by Super League mainly to provide a bridge to the current players for News Ltd's administrators.

Former international Ian Schubert, who had worked at two ARL clubs as a marketing officer without noteworthy success, was also to be recruited.

Meninga, Australia's retiring Test captain, added to the furore over Super League with his performance at an 'information night' at Cronulla Leagues Club—designed to let members know as much as possible about the rebel competition and its implications. Even though Ken Arthurson and John Quayle had been invited to speak, the general tone and direction of the meeting was much more sympathetic to Super League's ambitions than those of the ARL. In a heated moment former champion lock Johnny Raper, speaking from the floor queried the motivation of players who had received as much as four times Kangaroo tourist and Test captain Mal Meninga had from the ARL in electing to join a rebel competition.

In an explanation that caused considerable damage to his public image despite his attempts to play down its significance, Meninga replied with some feeling from the stage: 'What has the game ever done for me?'

It was around two or three weeks into the battle when morality, which was already rusting, stretched to breaking point.

The ARL started trying to lure players away from Super League, beginning with Canberra, NSW and Test half Ricky Stuart, even offering him the Australian captaincy and to cover his legal costs if he returned to the establishment.

Stuart and his manager John Fordham had made a shock appearance at the NSWRL on April 3. Ignoring the gathered media, Stuart made his way up the steps and into the building, returning about an hour later and refusing to comment on what negotiations had taken place. There was speculation that Stuart had been offered a contract of a million dollars a year and the Australian Test captaincy if he returned to the ARL.

Three days later James Packer and Fulton flew to Canberra for more talks with Stuart. The pressure from the ARL worried Super League. Ken Cowley re-entered the fray, having more talks with Stuart, who eventually decided to stay with Super League.

'I don't know about Stuart,' Gould would say. 'It seemed he wanted to come back to the ARL but because the Canberra players had agreed to stay together, he stayed with Super League.' The Lear Jet carrying Packer and Fulton moved on to Brisbane where the pair had talks with Bronco players about returning to the ARL. They had no success.

The always-sensitive Broncos took it as a slight that the

ARL had taken so long to get around to talking with them, saying it was another example of Sydney arrogance. It was in fact a smart move by the ARL. The Broncos had never been candidates for recruitment. They had been swept up in the Super League philosophy from the start.

Although the ARL failed to retrieve Stuart or any Broncos, it delivered a more damaging blow by luring Canterbury first grade grand final stars and internationals, Jim Dymock, Dean Pay, Jason Smith and Jarrod McCracken away from Super League and contracts they had signed worth in excess of $500,000 a season.

Super League initially signed McCracken for $350,000 sign-on and $100,000 a season for seven years. Jason Smith for $250,000 and $75,000 for five years, Dymock for $250,000 and $50,000 for four years and Pay for $250,000 and $75,000 for five years. All four players then agreed to ARL terms of McCracken ($340,000 and $300,000 a year for four years), Smith ($320,000 and $250,000 for four years), Pay ($310,000 and $250,000 for four years) and Dymock ($265,000 and $250,000 for four years).

The court upheld the claim made by the four players that they had signed with Super League under duress—and they were freed to take up their ARL commitments. A desperate Parramatta subsequently signed all four to contracts so lucrative that they exceeded the money guaranteed by Optus.

The lost court action would motivate 34-year-old Canterbury stalwart Terry Lamb to have one more season (his 17th) in 1996 after he originally had announced his retirement after leading the Bulldogs to a win against Manly in the 1995 grand final.

Newcastle and Illawarra clubs were priorities for both sides because of their immense value to pay-television. In cities of more than 100,000 households, each hosting a single first grade rugby league side, the pay TV outlet with sole coverage of the premiership involving Illawarra and Newcastle had a ready made and extremely lucrative market.

Newcastle captain and international Paul Harragon signed early with the ARL and used his considerable influence to convince the rest of the side to sign as well. Harragon ultimately was the ARL's most expensive signing, costing $650,000 to sign on and then $350,000 a year for four years. That meant a million dollar pay cheque for the first season. Newcastle's talented Andrew Johns was not far behind, getting $557,000 to sign on and $255,000 a season for four years. His brother Matthew got $525,000 and $230,000 for four years.

Given the critical circumstances and the vital importance of Newcastle to the ARL competition, it was a major coup to sign the club and on the night that happened Gould rang John Quayle in Sydney on his way back around 2am. 'That's tremendous news,' Quayle responded. What was he doing up so late? 'No-one slept much in those early couple of weeks,' Gould says.

The Newcastle venture was triumph pulled from potential disaster. On the way to Newcastle for talks with the players Gould had a call from Harragon on his car phone to let him know that News Ltd had already been in action and Super League officials had made massive offers to try and get the players to sign contracts.

'They were offering stunning money. I think it was something like $2.1 million each for three years—around $700,000 a year—after their contracts with Newcastle ended in 1996,' Gould recalls.

During the battle for Newcastle, Gould boarded a small aircraft at Mascot to find that he, Michael O'Connor and John Ribot were the only other passengers. They were going to present Super League's case.

'I said hello and they said hello,' Gould said. 'Ribot knew

we were all just doing what we thought was right. We chattered a bit. Ribot said: "The problem with John (Quayle) is that he takes it all personally".'

The importance of Newcastle and Illawarra to pay TV plans could never be underestimated. News Ltd made that perfectly clear when they started their own Newcastle club called the Mariners, once it was obvious the established side was staying with the ARL. Newcastle, always a rugby league stronghold and an inaugural club in the NSWRL premiership in 1908, proved impossible to lure to Super League despite its sometimes fragile financial state and absence of a big spending and profitable licensed club to back its recruitment.

Feelings became so heated in the city that a public meeting attracting thousands of people was held at one stage to oppose Super League.

Illawarra was in a similarly geographically appealing situation to Super League as Newcastle and similar financial inducements were offered before the players mostly agreed to stay with the ARL.

'Illawarra was a prime target. We had a busload of young players come up from Wollongong and I signed some of them for probably more than they were worth and more than what I had signed players with similar qualifications from at other clubs. It was just important that we get Illawarra,' Gould said.

NSWRL General Manager and ARL Chief Executive John Quayle was a target for much Super League venom as the fight became personal. A former World Cup lock for Australia and highly-regarded first grade lock with Easts and Parramatta, he had joined the NSWRL as chief executive when the administration was restructured in 1983. For more than a decade he had proved his expertise, honesty and skill as rugby league reshaped itself into Australia's premier sport.

The Broncos in particular disliked Quayle, blaming him for

problems they had with the NSWRL. It was more a case of the Broncos believing in shooting the messenger—the man who was merely relaying the decisions of the NSWRL board.

When the Super League and ARL battle started Quayle could not always keep in check his intense feelings about the ethics of actions by News Ltd.

His relations with Ribot, Canberra chief executive Kevin Neil and Cowley became increasingly hostile. When Super League was steam-rolling along its path to taking over game, it was made perfectly clear that nothing less than Quayle's head on a platter would appease the rebel clubs in any truce.

At the height of the battle Arthurson called Quayle into his office to discuss the latest development in the peace talks. Quayle said: 'If my being here is stopping the chance of a peace being negotiated I will go. There won't be a problem. But I want you to do it. I don't want it to be Neil or Ribot.'

Arthurson assured Quayle his job was not in jeopardy—but it was common knowledge that it *was*. Quayle's pay-off would be a 'truckload of money in severance pay,' one official said.

Resolution to ensure Quayle's safety came from two unexpected sources. The 12 clubs who stood by their allegiance to the ARL's loyalty contracts made it clear Quayle would not be a scapegoat.

Sydney Tigers' president and former first grade hooker and captain Neil Whittaker stood up at a meeting of the loyal clubs and said: 'Mr Chairman, we want to make it clear that John Quayle's position as chief executive of the Australian Rugby League is not negotiable. We have complete confidence in him and he is not to be a scapegoat.'

Quayle was also supported by former chairman of the NSW and Australian Rugby Leagues, Kevin Humphreys who had resigned in 1983. Humphreys spoke to Quayle at the Sydney Football Stadium on the day of the International

Sevens tournament on February 4, saying he had the full support of previous administrators and the public and the battle for control had to be fought fearlessly.

Arthurson joined the conversation and Humphreys repeated the message adding that it was imperative Quayle was fully supported. Putting his arm around Arthurson, Humphreys, an old colleague and friend, insisted resistance to Super League be unrelenting. Quayle and Arthurson did not know that Humphreys had also been contacted by a Super League agent, looking for his support. He heatedly rejected the offer.

As the fight continued the casualties started to become public. Illawarra coach Graham Murray was sacked as first grade coach by his club because of his sympathy for Super League. Former great Test winger Kerry Boustead resigned as chief executive of the North Queensland Cowboys because of the club's move to Super League.

On April 16 Canterbury coach Chris Anderson was sacked as NSW Country coach because of his allegiance to Super League. Western Suburbs coach Tom Raudonikis replaced Anderson for the match—won 16–8 by City in Wollongong in torrential ran.

Ken Arthurson identifies a turning point as the moment giant young prop Adam Ritson stood on the steps leading into the NSW Leagues Club before a battery of media representatives and announced that he was rejecting his Super League offer and returning to the ARL.

Ritson had signed with Super League on the proviso that he could change his mind after he had consulted with his parents. Because he was only 19, Super League allowed him leniency and Ritson subsequently signed with the ARL.

The significance of his decision for the ARL meant that it had some good news and an improved public relations image. Not that the harassed ARL took full advantage.

Ritson's decision was announced on April 3, the day of the frantic scramble by media outside the Leagues Club and players traipsing in and out for hours to talk to Gould and Fulton.

A priceless chance for the ARL to get some much needed good publicity and show it was fighting backing looked like being lost until Ritson, at the urging of his manager Steve Gillis, slowed his departure and spoke to the media.

'I have decided to sign with the ARL because I believe they are the future of the game,' he said. 'I have always wanted to play with the ARL and I have decided to stay with them.'

To see his young face on television that night and in newspapers publicly pledging his future to the ARL at a time when so many were defecting had a stabilising affect, checking the impact Super League was making.

'I remember seeing Ritson on television that night standing up and declaring his loyalty to the ARL and I was very moved,' said Arthurson. 'We knew we were making headway upstairs with signing players, but Ritson was the first player who had stood up and declared his support so publicly. I still remember that night.'

The ARL's fightback steadily gathered momentum. The NSWRL nine man board met on Saturday April 1 and it was at that meeting that Peter Moore was sacked because of his public admittance to his club's participation in Super League. Moore arrived at the meeting after it had started and was intercepted by Arthurson in the corridor outside the meeting room. Moore left Phillip St headquarters immediately, telling the media he had resigned his position. 'Moore was sacked,' says John Quayle. 'He decided to tell people he had resigned.'

Sacking Moore might have *technically* been beyond the immediate jurisdiction of the nine-man board meeting that day. It would probably have had to be referred back to the full committee for approval. But the fact that the board chose to dismiss him was an indication of its feeling towards Moore. Prolonging the matter by going before the full general committee would assuredly have produced the same result.

Graham Lovett, another member of the NSWRL nine-man board and a News Ltd consultant, had stepped down from his position on the nine-man board on December 12 because of a conflict of interest as Super League rumours grew and did not seek re-appointment.

It was Lovett who was the first of the nine-man NSWRL to see the outline for Super League. Ken Cowley showed Lovett the plan in September 1994. Lovett reportedly said he would have to tell the NSWRL what he had seen. Cowley said: 'That's fine.' Lovett told Arthurson of the situation and offered his resignation from the nine-man board. It was also Lovett, en route through London when the Kangaroos were playing the first test of the 1994 tour, who warned Arthurson about Super League's growing strength and who advised him to return to Sydney for talks with Cowley.

Arthurson followed that advice.

Gould and Fulton met at Phillip St on Sunday April 2 and began the fightback campaign. Initially they drew up a list of names of all players who were known to have not signed with Super League. Two potential sides for NSW and Queensland were drawn up. Then came a possible World Cup squad.

Quayle contacted 2UE radio commentator Alan Jones to put down a commercial urging players not to make a decision on their futures until they had spoken to the ARL. It was revealed during subsequent Federal Court hearings that Jones, fellow 2UE broadcaster John Laws and the *Sydney Morning Herald*'s coach-turned-commentator and chief rugby league writer Roy Masters had been nominated as essential recruits to Super League because of their influence on large sections of the public. All three in fact refused to become advocates of Super League.

Ironically Super League and News Ltd were on a similar course of action in regard to condensing the competition. The difference was that Super League was in a Ferrari. The ARL in a horse and buggy. Quayle says the ARL always knew that 20 teams was too many in the competition and 'rationalisation' was scheduled to take place gradually in the years toward 2000. 'Our agenda was always to expand and then start rationalising from 1998,' he said. 'Our charter was to have as many people as possible playing the game. Super League's charter was profit. That is why they only wanted 10 or a maximum of 12 teams. Anymore than that and it stopped being profitable.'

Life in the bunker for the ARL was hectic. Gould became so exhausted by the endless hours of negotiating and signing players at Phillip Street that he pulled over in his car one night on his way home and went to sleep even though he was only driving the few kilometres from the city to Bondi Junction.

The Chinese restaurant on the second floor of the NSWRL maintained a constant delivery service to the fifth floor where negotiations with players were taking place. Sandwiches were delivered from a shop in a nearby arcade. 'We must have gone through a tonne of dim sims, satays and spring rolls,' says Quayle. 'For a while we all thought that if we ever saw another one of any of them it would be too soon. Every decision we made had to be made on the run. Gus and Bozo were committed 24 hours a day. Bozo's Manly team was winning but Gus' Easts side wasn't. He was in Newcastle doing things for us when he should have been with Easts. James Packer also played a major role.'

Quayle's personal private secretary Micki Braithwaite and the rest of the ARL staff were swept into the drama. 'People were packed into every crevice of the rooms,' Braithwaite said. 'It was absolute madness. People were all over my desk whenever I looked. James Packer, Phil Gould and Bob Fulton were always negotiating with someone. Players were lined up just everywhere.'

Good as GOULD

Gould worked close to 18 hours some days between April 1 and Easter, driving back and forth across the city to personally talk to players and officials, trying to counteract the lack of ARL views presented in newspapers. 'I didn't see my own team Easts that first week. We then went to Darwin and were belted by Western Suburbs. I felt sorry for my players because they were aligned to the Packer organisation and the ARL. They were very, very confused about their situation at that stage and still had doubts about having done the right thing by rejecting Super League. Losing to Wests and playing very badly just added to the pressure and stress of the week.'

Even now Gould is uncertain of how his role in the fightback grew so dramatically until he became a major figure. He had started with the ARL simply because he believed it was right and that Super League's approach was morally wrong. Within the blink of an eye he was addressing the chief executives at NSWRL meetings and executives of Channel 9, Optus, even Kerry Packer himself, after planning most of the fightback strategy with Fulton.

'It all came from nowhere. I found myself on the *Footy Show* on television and radio stations expounding the virtues of the ARL. Suddenly it got to the point where I was perceived as a crusader for the ARL. My beliefs were simple. I thought that the majority, the very high majority of players who signed with Super League did so for the money. And that the majority of those who were prepared to leave the ARL were doing so for money. I had no reason to be loyal to anyone else other than the ARL. That's how I got swept into the early part of it all. As time went by it became more and more obvious that this was a corporate takeover of a sporting body. It was a company attempting to buy our game purely for money for the television rights.'

Gould and Fulton were risking more than money. A convincing win by Super League would effectively have ended their involvement with rugby league. Super League could hardly be expected to be sympathetic and generous in awarding coaching appointments to two men who had been such successful and high profile opponents of its introduction. 'It didn't matter to me,' said Gould. 'I just didn't want to be associated with these people who had been so greedy and so stupid and so jealous as to join Super League.'

Gould's efforts certainly made an impression on the Packer camp. There was almost daily contact with James Packer and often Kerry Packer. Gould was offered the role of controller of the fightback program, which would have freed Quayle and Arthurson to keep the important day-to-day workings of the ARL functioning. The appointment would have meant Gould stepping down as Easts coach. He considered it carefully, but finally rejected the idea at the urging of Easts president Nick Politis, who pleaded with him to stay and look after the side.

Gould says an essential but very difficult aspect of the ARL's fightback plan was the difficulty of getting its message out to the public and the players that Super League had not taken over the game and trampled any opposition in its path.

The News Ltd newspapers slashed any available space for the ARL's point of view to minimal space, if they ran anything at all, while emphasising Super League's successes. 'Super League was ringing clubs and telling them they would pay them $4 million a year,' said Gould. 'They were ringing players who had signed with the ARL and offering to double their contracts if they came to Super League.'

Penrith in fact had initially agreed to stay with the ARL but later decided to swap sides and join Super League. It led to key players Brad Fittler and Matt Sing going to Easts and Gary Freeman joining Parramatta. All three wanted to stay with the ARL contracts they had signed.

Quayle concedes the Super League strike against other

Good as GOULD

rugby league playing nations like England and New Zealand—and eventually France and Papua New Guinea as well as Pacific nations like Fiji and Tonga—was a shock. 'They all sold us out,' he said. We understood England's decision a little. They were offered 87 million pounds. But New Zealand went for a song although their chief executive Graham Carden was looked after by News Ltd with a job as we understand,' Quayle said.

Gould says that at no stage of his negotiations with any player was the prospect of assured representative team selection raised. However the unfolding reality of the season was that players in Super League teams were not chosen in City-Country, NSW and Queensland or Australian Test teams.

The ARL held that line despite legal action from Canberra players after they were omitted from the Test teams that played New Zealand and before Australia's World Cup team was chosen.

Justice Barrie Hungerford in the Industrial Court on September 19, 1995, found that the Canberra players had been discriminated against and ordered the ARL to consider their achievements for future teams. But the court ruling stopped short of ordering that the Canberra players be included in the World Cup team and their names were missing when the squad was announced five days later. With no Super League players included, News Limited had the opportunity to pursue the apparent discrimination through the courts, but declined.

On September 25 the Super League and the ARL moved into a new and less emotional arena with its hearing before Justice James Burchett in the Federal Court in Sydney.

After 51 days of testimony from both sides that converted into 8000 pages of transcript, the preliminary hearing was over on November 15, 1995. There was initial speculation that a decision could even be handed down before Christmas.

In fact Christmas, New Year and January passed and there was still be no sign of a decision. Super League and the ARL were both scheduled to start their competitions on March 1 and as the days ticked by in February there was increasing concern about the need for Justice Burchett to make up his mind. Secretly legal representatives of Super League and the ARL spoke to Justice Burchett, gently indicating the seriousness of the situation with the dual premierships due to start in about eight days.

Justice Burchett heard the submissions and thanked both Super League and the ARL for their time, without in any way indicating the direction of his thinking. The announcement of the decision was finally set down for February 23 at 3.30pm in Federal Court (20a) in Sydney. The media throng was akin to an army with a dozen television camera crews from NSW, interstate and overseas, another 30 print media journalists and half a dozen radio commentators as well as dozens of members of the public and supporters.

The crowd was so big that the hearing was moved to the bigger court 21. Quayle had spent a nervous night, saying the tension was greater than when he played for Australia or in a grand final.

Justice Burchett added to the drama by delaying his appearance until 3.55pm, sending out a court official to apologise for the delay.

PHIL GOULD'S Reflections on the
NEWCASTLE COUP

On Monday (day two) of the scramble for players' signatures Newcastle's international forward Paul Harragon drove a mini-bus containing around a dozen team-mates to Sydney to talk with the ARL.

They sat in the NSWRL committee room while I explained the issues involved in the Super League struggle and why their Newcastle club was so important.

It had been explained to me that when laying (Pay TV) cable down the east coast of Australia, there were certain pockets of influence that had to be addressed like Newcastle and Illawarra.

I had signed a number of Illawarra juniors in quick fashion and so did the club's chief executive Bob Millward, which gave us a strong foothold in the club. Illawarra had been under pressure from Super League for some time from both outside and inside. The club's coach Graham Murray had been sacked for his association with Super League, which had extended to driving players to a meeting with rebel league organisers.

Newcastle's signing was vital. Club figurehead Paul Harragon had already signed with the ARL—he was one of the first. Now it was time to get his team-mates to come under the same umbrella.

The Newcastle players admitted as we sat there that they had been under pressure from their club officials to join Super League but they were waiting until they were absolutely certain which way was the best way to jump. I have to give the Newcastle players a huge wrap. They were totally committed to each other over the issue. They wanted to decide what was best for themselves as a group and as a club. The players were determined to put personal preferences to one side.

I was so impressed by the Newcastle squad that I decided to take a gamble. Rather than sign the dozen or so players who had come to Sydney, I offered to go to Newcastle and speak to the club as a unit. It was a risk sending the players back into Super League territory but I wanted to be as open and honest as I could possibly be. I wanted the whole club to fully understand the issues behind the fight. After Newcastle left, the hours flew by and it was not until around 6pm that someone said, 'Hey. Weren't you going to Newcastle?'

I grabbed my things, linked with managers Wayne Beavis and Steve Gillis and we set out on the two hour drive. All the way there the mobile phones were ringing non-stop with players ringing checking in to find out what was going on and what were the latest developments. We were swapping the phones around like pass-the-parcel. The managers would talk to players and then they would hand me the phone to talk to them as well.

It was all quite amiable until we got about 15 minutes away from Newcastle and my phone rang. It was Paul Harragon. He said he was calling with bad news: the Super League people had been in Newcastle and had made huge offers to the stars of the side, the Johns brothers—Andrew and Matthew—of around $700,000 a season each. The other leading players had also received offers and the Newcastle management was pushing them to abandon the ARL and join Super League.

I was so shocked I pulled over to the side of the road. It was a three-year deal for the Johns' boys. Around $2.1 million each. I could not believe it.

Harragon said the Johns boys were on contract for two more years and would not be free to take up the deal with Super League until 1998.

I rang James Packer and told him the latest development. He was as stunned as I had been to hear about the offer to the Johns' boys and asked what we should do. I said Newcastle was very important to the overall scheme of things and it was essential the area stayed with the ARL. I went so far as to say that I regarded Newcastle as the swinging seat in the whole battle. Whoever signed the Knights would certainly have increased bargaining power and would probably win the fight to own the game.

I said to James, 'Whatever I do you'll have to trust me.' He said, 'Do what you have to do.'

We got to Newcastle and I spoke to the players for about an hour by themselves and said how sympathetic I was to their dilemma. The players indicated that they were virtually being pushed towards signing with Super League by factions in the club headed by chief executive Brad Mellen and Robert Finch the reserve grade coach—both of whom subsequently signed with Super League.

I called Mellen into the room and said to him in front of the players: 'I've just explained to the team the ARL's point of view and the advantages of signing with the League. Can you tell these blokes why you're pushing them towards Super League.' He squirmed and said that was not the case. He said that whatever decision the players' made the club would accept. If they wanted to go to Super League, so would the club. Similarly if the players wanted to stay with the ARL, that would also be the club's decision.

There had been suspicions about Mellen's loyalty to the ARL for some time and it was no shock when he eventually went public with his sympathy for Super League and joined Perth.

TALES FROM THE PHILLIP STREET BUNKER

That night in Newcastle he must have bitten his tongue as he told the players that the club was indifferent to their preference between Super League and the ARL.

When he could not confess to the players that he actively supported Super League, I took up the slack and said: 'There you are fellas. The chief executive of your club says it's up to you.'

I knew there were Super League executives down the road waiting for answers to offers they had made to Newcastle players and waiting to speak to more players. There was not much time.

I came to terms with Adam Muir and Darren Treacey while the Johns brothers spoke to their manager and fellow first grader Tony Butterfield about the ARL offer.

The only way I could make any impact on the Super League contract was to allocate the money to the Johns' brothers over five years. I was told later that in between talking to me about finances and coming and going from the room to talk to Butterfield, the Johns brothers and other players were threatened by Super League sympathisers not to sign with the ARL. No names were mentioned but I imagine Finch might have been involved, knowing his devotion to the Super League cause.

Finally they came back and said they would sign with the ARL. From there on it was the Domino Effect. I signed 12 or 13 Newcastle players as the clock moved on towards 1am.

The players wanted to go home because they had a big game coming up that weekend. I told the rest of the squad that if they wanted to go home, we could complete negotiations by them coming to Sydney or I would come back to Newcastle.

We all left Newcastle for the return trip to Sydney around 2am feeling happy with a good night's work. On the way home I rang John Quayle, Ken Arthurson and James Packer to tell them the good news and they were delighted.

Good as GOULD

It was about then that Beavis, Gillis and I realised we had not eaten all day, so we pulled into an all night garage-restaurant on the freeway. We had mixed grills and chocolate milkshakes and stood there feeling content. It was not until the cashier rang up $38 and offered the bill that alarm set in. No one had any money! We had spent around three or four million dollars that night on players but could not pay for our meal. A few kilometres back up the track there were Newcastle players sleeping with dreams of dollar notes running through their minds. And here we were searching our pockets in embarrassment trying to find enough cash, or a credit card—things we had forgotten because we had left Sydney in such a rush.

Luckily I remembered I had $50 emergency money in my golf bag in the car and the bill was paid. It was a satisfactory end to a day of achievement and purpose for the ARL.

Earlier that day the chief executives of the loyal clubs had been into the ARL and Bob Fulton and I had explained what was going on, what our immediate plans were and what long term goals we were setting.

There were only about four defecting clubs at that stage I think—Canterbury, Cronulla, Canberra and Brisbane. Auckland had not gone, Newcastle was under pressure and Townsville was just about gone.

Fulton and I were asked by the clubs to continue to supervise the signing of players to the ARL. Later there would be criticism of us being so involved in such sensitive work. But it seemed a sensible and necessary plan at the time. It was essential that our fightback plan gather momentum quickly and there was no time for lengthy meetings. We were also representative coaches which means we knew the players well and we had both been in the game for a long time. We knew the players' managers and more importantly, we knew the issues. We could explain the complex situation without embellishment and show how it was in the best interest of players' to stay with the ARL and that the ARL had to remain in control of the game. We could also point out the pitfalls in Super League's contracts.

That morning, also confirmed my idea of how big this entire procedure was going to be. The big boys started to gather at the ARL. James Packer came in. So did David Leckie from Channel 9 and the big gun who would turn out to be a cannon, Geoff Cousins from Optus. They sat down and virtually asked Bozo and I the best way to handle the problems. We told them that there were a number of issues. The first was to sign as many of the bigger names in the game as we could and get our quota of top players up to similar levels to the opposition. Then we could start to work on Super League's weakness. For all the attention Super League gave to the present, they seemed to give little thought to the future and to replenishing their supply of players. This ignoring of the long term was another example of Super League's managerial weaknesses. I told Leckie, Cousins and Packer that if the ARL could run its competition for five years and keep replenishing it with junior talent we would have the numbers and the longevity to finish Super League. Even if Super League did get up and running in five years, they would be dead in the water because of the age of the players they had signed and their failure to immediately implement a youth program.

Eventually Super League was forced into another embarrassing compromise when it brought its starting date forward from 1997 to 1996 because it was losing the battle. When the dust finally settled, they did not have the players to run a competition or enough clubs. The original plan to steamroller the administration and take immediate charge of the game in about eight or ten days, buckled badly.

It became obvious to both parties that Super League lacked players and franchises. All they had was propaganda through

Good as GOULD

the *Daily Telegraph* and constant attempts at destabilisation by talking of compromise.

A look at the facts convinced Super League that they were holding a losing hand and that was why they constantly talked of a need for compromise. With each passing day the ARL's situation became stronger.

The propaganda did make some impact. When Super League first arrived I rang the Canberra coach Tim Sheens and tried to tell him that he was being manipulated and misinformed. He thought the whole thing revolved around Easts trying to buy Ricky Stuart and Bradley Clyde. I said he could not be further from the truth. He screamed down the phone that I had tried to buy Ricky Stuart. It was a desperate reaction to try and put the entire evolution of Super League down to Easts talking to Stuart. It was also absolutely ridiculous.

Here is what happened. Ricky did approach us but because he was under contract we told him there was not much point in talking. It was Stuart who kept insisting that there was a clause in his contract that made him a free agent if the salary cap ended. We told him to come and see us at that time but that basically he was under contract to Canberra and that is where he should be playing. We had also signed John Simon the Illawarra half-back, but we were prevented from telling Stuart, or anyone else for that matter, because of confidential commitments.

Bradley Clyde's manager George Mimis, who eventually turned out to be very sympathetic to Super League, contacted us to see if we were interested in his client. Nimis said that Clyde was off contract and would James Packer and Nick Politis like to meet him? Naturally we said yes as any responsible club trying to improve its playing strength would do. But James Packer was sceptical from the start. He told Brad that the chances of Canberra letting him go were minimal. Clyde said he would leave for the right money. James asked if

TALES FROM THE PHILLIP STREET BUNKER

$100,000 more than he was getting at Canberra would make him leave. Clyde said it would. James said he should go back to Canberra and then contact Easts again. Two days later Mimis rang and said it would cost us $800,000 a season to sign Clyde. We just laughed. We also knew then that Super League money was heavily involved.

Down For the Count

There was a cathedral silence in the stylishly designed Federal Court 21a when Justice Burchett made his way to his chair to begin proceedings.

Months earlier former world boxing champion Mike Tyson had returned to the ring after completing a gaol sentence on a rape charge and taken on challenger Peter McNeeley in a gross mismatch that lasted just 89 seconds before his corner threw in the towel.

If it is any consolation to McNeeley, he lasted longer and threw more punches than Super League in Justice Burchett's report in the Federal Court in Sydney. In four and a half minutes, reading in a monotone, Justice Burchett knee-capped Super League so effectively that the thought hung heavy in the air that it would never surely walk again.

When he had finished what was left of Super League was being wrapped in a body bag, with morticians hoping there were enough pieces left for relatives to recognise.

Super League had lost, and lost catastrophically, on every point it had contested, although further appeals, and especially the major one to the full bench, meant that the winner's hand had not yet been raised.

The credibility of its major witnesses such as John Ribot, Broncos director Barry Maranta and Peter Moore had been savaged.

Burchett dismissed Super League's claims that, under the

Trade Practices Act, clubs such as Canterbury, Cronulla, Canberra and Brisbane had been forced to sign the loyalty agreements under duress.

In a 218-page report, Justice Burchett found little to like about Super League, its aims, its principles, its morality or its ethics. He said News Limited had acted dishonestly and unlawfully in trying to capture rugby league.

'The evidence makes it clear that News Limited and Super League companies acted, in the relevant sense, with dishonesty,' Justice Burchett said.

He said News Limited had acted 'unlawfully' by inducing the rebel clubs to breach their contracts by releasing their players to sign with the rival Super League competition.

'The judge said publicly what the ARL had been saying all along,' Gould said. 'And that was that Super League was built on lies and total deceit about its aims and ambitions.

'There was never any doubt about the ARL winning as long as morality and principles stood for anything in society.

'Super League continually showed its contempt for the players it had signed by feeding them lies and more lies.

'Super League kept saying their competition was going to get up and running when they knew it couldn't and wouldn't.

'Super League players were continually used as propaganda tools.

'They signed documents of support that Super League had dictated and sent them to newspaper and media outlets to try and show that their support was solid.

'The support was always far from widespread among Super League players.'

Peter Moore became a headline figure when Burchett's full report was released. Moore was 'completely corrupted', Burchett found. He had 'shut his eyes to his obligations to the club and to the Australian Rugby League'. Burchett said Moore and other

Super League officials knew they were asking coaches to break their contracts in joining Super League but were 'overwhelmed by the amount of money offered by News Limited'. The judge said Moore had a duty not only to the Bulldogs club, where he was chief executive, but also to the Australian Rugby League, where he was a director. These were duties 'he sought to evade'.

'The connivance of some club board members cannot justify what occurred,' Justice Burchett said. 'That connivance had been obtained and given in disregard of their obligations. Mr Moore of Canterbury is a case in point. Not only did he owe fiduciary duties to his club as its chief executive, but he owed similar duties to the League as a director, duties he sought to evade (but only succeeded in implicitly acknowledging) by a resignation which came after the event (on April 1, 1995). Mr Moore had not less than an ordinary appreciation of right and wrong. He knew his duty. But stripped of all pretence in cross-examination, he was revealed as a man who had been overwhelmed by the magnitude of his temptation. He could not imagine the money offered to his son-in-law, the Canterbury coach—not to himself—being refused.

'He was completely corrupted and shut his eyes to his obligations to the club and to the League. But those who suborned the coach, and at least indirectly Mr Moore, were acting with their eyes open. They knew they were asking officials of clubs to break their contracts (in the case of coaches and other employees) and their duty of fidelity. They were using the financial power of News Limited to corrupt targeted individuals.'

Moore was not the only Super League identity to be criticised in Justice Burchett's decision. The judge also lashed organisers of Super League for their clandestine approach—especially after initial assurances that all approaches would be face to face.

'The secrecy, deceit and suddenness that were intended to

be the hallmarks of this assault upon the League are apparent at every turn in the evidence,' the judgement says. 'An example is the preparation of sample questions and answers, to be suggested to players who signed contracts with companies controlled by News Limited. The object was plainly to prolong deception. Players were to be encouraged to dissemble their involvement with Super League. If asked by a journalist: 'Are you in negotiations with News Limited?' it was urged that the answer be given: 'There is no point in that, when I have a current contract which I am obliged to honour'.'

Justice Burchett's rulings paralleled the thinking and attitude of Gould and the rest of the ARL team that had worked so hard to protect rugby league's heritage.

'We had always said that Super League was never interested in controlling their game. They wanted the ARL to do it while Super League did the easy part of just taking the profits from the competition,' Gould said. 'They could not believe we could fight for so long. They thought we would die early when they launched their first all out attack.'

Justice Burchett observed: 'It is not in doubt that the objective of signing up so many players, at very great expense, together with coaches and the making of secret arrangements with senior officials of clubs, was to put the clubs, and the League itself, in a position where there would be nothing they could do but capitulate.

'The evidence of Mr Arthurson was unchallenged that Mr Cowley later said to him: "We thought that after we had bought your players, that it would have such an effect on you, that we would be better able to negotiate with you and come through the front door". The theory seems to have been precisely that espoused with some pride by President Nixon in the infamous statement: "When you have them by the balls, their hearts and minds will follow".'

Good as GOULD

Ron McLean from North Queensland, who claimed to have heard Ken Arthurson threatening clubs with expulsion if they did not sign the loyalty agreements, was not believed by the judge. 'I think it is likely Mr McLean was mistaken,' the judge said.

Barry Maranta was described as 'engaged in a deliberate exercise in deception.' He had told the November meeting of the clubs that the Broncos were not involved in talks with Super League. 'What we're trying to do is find out what is going on,' Maranta had said.

Justice Burchett saw it differently. He was satisfied that the Broncos 'in fact knew very well what was going on and were intimately involved with it. Mr Maranta was engaged in a deliberate exercise in deception.'

About Cronulla president Peter Gow, Justice Burchett said: '(He) was one of the witnesses who appears to be unreliable in cross-examination.'

Of John Ribot, Justice Burchett said: 'Mr Ribot did not emerge from cross-examination as a reliable witness and I accept his version of events only where it accords with my view of the probabilities.'

The judge later thought that 'Ribot was apt to colour his evidence to suit the contentions he was supporting. He arranged in advance that officials of a number of the clubs would embrace such a coup, and would align themselves with Super League.'

Justice Burchett said he regarded the Super League assault as 'extraordinary'. He said there was obvious 'connivance' by some board members. He said many players, including those at the Bulldogs on March 30, had been asked to sign complex contracts without the chance to get legal advice and with the active encouragement or involvement of their coaches.

'The evidence makes it plain that News Limited and the

Super League companies acted, in the relevant sense, with dishonesty. The failure of Messrs Cowley and (former News Limited executive) David Smith to give evidence again enables the inferences to be drawn the more confidently. The secrecy, suddenness and deceit that were intended to be the hallmarks of this assault upon the League are apparent at every turn in the evidence.'

In contrast, ARL leaders John Quayle and Ken Arthurson were regarded as believable during their days in the witness box.

'I should make it clear that generally I accept the evidence of each of them,' he said.

'They were extremely able men and I accept that each was endeavouring to give truthful evidence. Obviously in a matter involving a great deal of detail and involving events that occurred over a period of years, my acceptance of them as truthful and capable witnesses does not mean that I think their memories were never at fault on any matter. But it does mean that I accept them on essentials.'

It was a complete legal rout for Super League but the news took a little while to sink in at the ARL table. Justice Burchett's brief condensation of his 218-page report did not immediately strike a chord with anyone unfamiliar with legalspeak.

There was silence when the judge had finished reading. The highly paid legal advisers on either side, although realising which side had won, gave no indication. For a moment Arthurson was equally mystified. 'Then I looked at our solicitor Colin Love and he was smiling. I knew we had won,' he said.

Quayle simply looked enormously relieved as it sank in that the first major battle in what could prove to be a long campaign was over. The ARL party retired victorious to the second floor of the NSW Leagues Club across the road from the Federal Court for a celebration that would last until the early hours of Saturday morning.

Good as GOULD

'It was a terrific night,' Gould said. 'It was the chance for everyone who had done so much to keep Super League at bay to let down their hair and have a breather.' A receptionist at the NSWRL, in a moment of emotion, serenaded Arthurson and Quayle with a rendition of *Wind beneath my wings*, with its appropriate first line of: Did you ever know that you're our heroes.

Before the celebrations began commitments were fulfilled first. Representatives of the 12 loyal clubs were briefed in the committee room. There was a full-scale press conference at which Arthurson extended the hand of peace to the eight rebel clubs who had joined Super League. Clubs and players who had joined Super League would be welcomed back to the ARL without recrimination and without penalty, he said. 'It is a time for repairing the game, not causing more fragmentation.'

This first offer of peace fell on barren ground. News Limited and Super League were determined to stonewall until the exact legal position was explained.

On Monday February 26, again in the Federal Court in front of Justice Burchett, Super League's worst fears were realised. Super League was forbidden to start a competition as scheduled on Friday March 1. The players were also forbidden to train together as Super League clubs. The rebel competition was also expressly forbidden to take its game to another country and televise matches into Australia.

Tampering with the rules to produce a hybrid game similar to rugby league was also vetoed by Justice Burchett. Two proposed peace conferences had to be cancelled when the eight Super League clubs refused to attend. Eventually the ARL decided to cancel its scheduled Challenge Cup series to start the season and deferred the kick-off date for at least a fortnight. It was, Arthurson said, a chance for all clubs to prepare for the premiership. Clubs that were not available for the premiership's opening round would risk being in contempt of court.

Ken Arthurson said the attitude of some people during the dispute had been remarkable. 'There were people I thought would stick forever, who ran at the first sign of danger,' he said. 'There were others who showed real steel that might not have been suspected and fought every inch of the way.'

The fear of News Limited rising Hydra-like yet again despite the lopsidedness of the court decision still consumed some people. Gould had a discussion with a journalist that went along these lines:

Journo: 'I just want to tell you that News Limited has plan B ready to go now that they have lost the first court case.'

Gould: 'It can't be plan B unless they are going through the alphabet a second time. It has got to be plan L, M or N.'

Journo: 'I'm serious. This plan B is foolproof.'

Gould: 'Well the Super League contracts were supposed to be nuclear-proof and they weren't. Plan A was supposed to be unbeatable and it wasn't. What they should have done in that case is swapped over and made plan B plan A in the first place!'

The conversation ended.

On March 11 in the Federal Court, Justice Burchett handed down his final orders in the Super League v. ARL case. Again it was an overwhelming win for the ARL. A total of 33 of 34 orders sought by the ARL were granted including the highly contentious ones of having News Ltd pay Super League players their full contracts if they returned to the ARL and also banning Super League from starting until the year 2000. Super League was also ordered to hand over its merchandising gear to the ARL and prevented from even hiring a ground.

Arthurson sat anxiously in the front row of the court room desks reserved for principals in legal matters and watched the QC's from both sides file in. 'When Manly played grand finals I would look at the opposition and think: "Gee, they look good." Then I would look at our side and think: "But we've got Bobby Fulton". Our lead counsel Bob Ellicott (QC) is our Bobby Fulton.'

Back at the ARL rooms on the fifth floor of the NSW Leagues Club, celebrations were soon underway. In the wake of the orders there was to be yet another calm before yet another storm.

A subsequent hearing before the full panel of the Federal Court changed a significant point in Justice Burchett's rulings, which had tied the players to the clubs and, by extension, to the ARL.

The full panel released the players from that bondage, saying they were not compelled to play in the ARL premiership. The rebel players subsequently refused to rejoin their former clubs and set about declaring their intentions of starting their own competition called 'Global League', which had astonishing similarities to Super League. English Rugby League chairman Maurice Lindsay, who had been deeply involved in the Super League was designated to run Global League. Because of the orders preventing News Ltd being involved with any competition not approved by the ARL, the company could not be a party to Global League without risking contempt of court charges.

Lindsay's attempt to start a competition without sponsors, without money, without a television contract and on a knife edge of contempt proceedings was an intriguing move.

He negotiated an agreement with airline company Ansett, which was partly owned by News Ltd, to at least fly the players to and from interstate matches.

Remarkably, after the leader of the rebel players Chris Johns, had bitterly renounced the ARL saying publicly that none of his players would ever want to play under its banner again, there was a sudden move from the players for peace.

TALES FROM THE PHILLIP STREET BUNKER

Provided the ARL agreed to 15 points put forward by the players and coaches of Super League, a compromise could be reached for 1996.

The letter was signed by Chris Johns (as players' representative) and Wayne Bennett (as the coaches' representative). The 15 points the players' demanded were:

1) *This proposal applies only for the duration of the 1996 premiership season.*

2) *In the interests of the game of rugby league and its supporters, all Super League contracted players and coaches will, subject to any necessary approval, participate in a 1996 premiership competition under the auspices of the ARL, regardless of, and without prejudice to, the outcome of the current court proceedings.*

3) *Players and coaches will participate under the terms and conditions of their existing Super League contracts and will not be required to sign new agreements (with the exception of player registration forms).*

4) *The competition is to be administered solely by the ARL and/or the NSWRL.*

5) *The competition will comprise 22 teams, including all current ARL based teams and all Super League contracted teams, including the Hunter Mariners and the Adelaide Rams.*

6) *All referees and other match officials contracted to Super League will be invited to officiate in the competition.*

7) *The New Zealand Rugby League has indicated that it is prepared to participate in a Test series between Australia and New Zealand. Only non-Super League contracted players will be considered for this series. Selection of players to represent New Zealand will be a matter for the New Zealand Rugby Football League.*

8) *Star League contracted players will not be available for the 1996 State of Origin series between New South Wales and Queensland.*

9) *A new three-way international competition will be staged* involving teams from Queensland, New South Wales and New Zealand. Only players contracted to Super League will be eligible for selection in this series.

10) At the conclusion of the 1996 premiership season, Super League contracted players and coaches will be free to participate in any Test or international club matches not involving the ARL, pending the completion of any court proceedings.

11) Any players currently in dispute with clubs as a result of the Super League issue will be permitted to play for a club of their choice, including an ARL club, for the 1996 season.

12) Super League contracted under-17 and under-19 teams will compete in the equivalent ARL sanctioned competitions (Jersey Flegg and President's Cup) for the 1996 season or a national competition as sanctioned by the ARL.

13) No Super League contracted players will be forced to participate in any promotional activities related to the ARL competition.

14) Super League contracted teams will wear their own Nike Super League jerseys including the Super League numbering system.

15) In recognition of the past support given to the players and coaches by News Ltd, we expect that Foxtel be allowed to broadcast certain games.

It was a demand stunning in its audacity. Here was a proposed organisation, listening to the sound of its own death rattle and making demands that would have been rejected if both sides were still waging an *even* battle.

It was all ARL officials could do to stop their chairman Ken Arthurson rejecting the offer the moment he had read the demands. Arthurson was persuaded to hold the line until the following day when an urgent meeting of the 12 loyal clubs would consider the proposal.

'We haven't come this far and been so successful in the

courts and spent all this money to surrender now,' Arthurson said. 'It would be total surrender to accept all of this.'

Expanding the premiership to 22 clubs by admitting the Newcastle Mariners and the Adelaide Rams was a particularly sore point. One of the reasons Super League clubs used for breaking away was the claim that there were too many teams. Now they wanted to extend to 22 clubs.

The 12 loyal clubs rejected the demands out of hand. The stillborn Super League promptly retaliated by re-creating itself as Global League. With the rebel players clinging desperately to Global League like drowning men in a life raft, the opening round of the premiership, which had become the Optus Cup after the sealing of a five-year six-million dollar a year sponsorship from the pay TV operator, was a shambles. Seven of the eight rebel clubs rejected overtures to return to the ARL for the opening round. Only the Auckland Warriors offered to field a side, but warned it would be of minor strength because all Super League players with the club had declined to play.

The initial orders from Justice Burchett had ruled that players be compelled to return to the ARL competition with their clubs. A subsequent appeal by News Ltd had that order reversed. It was a minor success and effectively News Ltd's only win in the courts during legal action that stretched over six months and three major hearings.

With players not having to play for their clubs, the Brisbane Broncos, Canberra Raiders, Cronulla, Penrith, Western Reds and Townsville Cowboys forfeited their matches. Auckland's effort to field a team proved immaterial because they were drawn to play another Super League club.

It was the first player's strike in Australian Rugby League since 1917 when Glebe players stood out. Before that the most famous of all 'no-shows' was when Balmain refused to play Souths in the 1909 grand final. Souths were awarded the game and the premiership on forfeit. Behind Balmain's no-show was a supposed agreement by both sides to boycott the game because it was scheduled to be a curtain-raiser to the fourth Kangaroos and Wallabies match. Balmain insist that Souths welshed on the deal. Souths say the deal was never in place.

After a season of such dislocation it was not surprising that crowds were down for the four games that were scheduled. Wests beat Illawarra in the opening game on March 22 at Steelers Stadium 17–8 before a Friday night crowd of 7944, on Saturday afternoon Easts beat Balmain 38–10 at the Sydney Football Stadium before a crowd of 5631, on Saturday night at their new ground at Carrara, the Gold Coast Chargers lost to North Sydney before a dramatically reduced crowd. In the last of the four matches Manly beat Souths 44–6 at Brookvale Oval before another lower than usual crowd.

Super League's impact and disenchantment had cut the opening round crowds by a drop of 50 per cent on the corresponding games of 1995 when the same teams played each other but at reverse home grounds.

On Monday March 24, the ARL was in the Federal Court—and in a triumphant day, had the orders freeing players from their clubs reversed. By a ruling of 2–1 the Federal Court ruled that the players could only be paid their contract money from News Ltd if they returned to the ARL premiership.

At an afternoon hearing, Global League conceded defeat and gave an undertaking not to proceed with plans to start a rebel competition. By mid-afternoon, their resistance crushed, the rebel clubs started trickling back to the ARL, led by Canterbury, followed by Penrith and the Western Reds. That night Brisbane Broncos met and voted to go back to the ARL. Here and there some star players indicated they would stay on strike.

Eventually almost all players—even the recalcitrant ones

like Laurie Daley and Chris Johns returned, and well into the season only Gordon Tallis (St George signed but determined to play with the Broncos) was hanging out.

On March 25, almost a year to the day after Super League exploded so violently on the Sydney Rugby League scene, the rebellion was seemingly quashed and life got back to something like normal—at least until Super League's appeal started on May 23.

If there was one standout double winner in the battle it was veteran half-back Craig Coleman. He was signed by Super League but when he could not be placed with a club, he was released with a goodly percentage of his $25,000 sign on and $100,000 a season for two years. Coleman told Super League that it would be in breach of his contract unless its financial terms were settled as well. More money changed hands. Then Western Suburbs offered Coleman a new contract which coincided with Super League boss John Ribot ringing to ensure that the tough little half-back was not upset about the entire episode.

'How would I be dirty on Super League, John?' Coleman asked. 'I want to kiss you and Rupert Murdoch.'

Coleman's extensions to his house included a new bar. The overhead sign reads: *The Rupert Murdoch Bar*.

PHIL GOULD'S Reflections on
THE AFTERMATH

As the last futile shots were being fired, well before the last gasp May 23 appeal, by Super League in the final days of its troubled existence, I rang Chris Johns, the spokesman for rebel players. I have a lot of respect for Chris and as soon as he came to the phone it was as if nothing had happened even though we were on opposite sides of the battle.

I had always had plenty of time for Chris, both as a player in the NSW State of Origin sides I'd coached and also a man.

I had no objections to his support of Super League. Everyone had to make their own decision and take a stand. What had alarmed me was the apparent hatred of the ARL that was coming across in his public statements. It was the same with Laurie Daley. Both Laurie and Chris were obviously enraged by something they perceived to be wrong with the ARL.

Despite their status as leaders of the Super League brigade, I did not think Laurie and Chris represented the opinion of the masses. Certainly the ones I was talking to were not in agreement with Daley and Johns. To my mind Daley and Johns were being primed by a sales pitch they must have been receiving every day from News Ltd either in person or in the newspapers.

I rang Chris to basically say you're making a fool of yourself because you don't understand all of the facts. To hear our phone conversation would suggest that it was between two old mates.

He rang me back and said: 'Gus? Johnsey.' Me: 'How are

things going.' Chris: 'I haven't slept for a week.' Me: 'I haven't slept for a year.' He said they were up and running with Global League that week and the players were confident of finally playing a match. I said: 'For what it's worth Chris, Global League cannot possibly happen.' Chris: 'Yes it can. We've had good legal advice.' Me: 'Johnsey, how's your legal advice been so far?' Silence then: 'I know it hasn't been good. In fact they've had a bag over our head.'

I told Chris he needed to spend an hour with me to get the full picture and that I could not understand his hostility. Opposition yes. Hostility no. I told him that his problem was with News Limited and not the ARL. He said we would spend an hour together but he was concerned that if he returned to the ARL, the 300 Super League players would lynch him. I told him that would not happen because Super League players were desperately looking for a way to start playing games again. I said the ARL had proved its bona fides by insisting that News Ltd pay Super League players their full contract money even though the rebel competition had been stopped. Chris said he would ring me the next day for a talk because he was going home to Brisbane that night to see his family. He didn't go home. He went to New Zealand to bolster support within the Warriors in Auckland.

Three or four days later the injunction was handed down in court and Global League was finished. I rang Chris back again and he sounded shattered. You could tell on the phone. He said he did not know what he was going to do next. It was a short conversation because he was so distraught. I simply said that I was there if he wanted to talk.

Our paths crossed again at Brisbane Airport on the weekend of the second premiership round when I was on my way to Townsville for our (Easts') game against the Cowboys. Chris was with Brisbane Broncos coach Wayne Bennett and major shareholder Paul 'Porky' Morgan. I was with Roosters president

Good as GOULD

Nick Politis. Nick and Porky had seen each other just a few days before in a luxury Sydney Hotel from where Super League seemed to be operating. ARL communications manager Geoff Carr was there as well trying to mend broken fences with Super League officials.

Morgan had floated his company which held the majority of shares in the Brisbane Broncos as well as owning the Brisbane Bullets basketball side and other sporting teams. Nick also held shares in Porky's company, which was suffering during the Super League war because its major asset was the Brisbane Broncos rugby league and it was not playing.

In his inimitable fashion, Nick walked up to Porky and asked him about the company in a compassionate manner. Then he suggested that other shareholders—certainly not him—might be worried enough to start complaining to government agencies because the company's major asset was not in action. It subtly got the message across.

So when we all met up at Brisbane Airport, everyone certainly knew each other. Wayne Bennett even said hello to me. It was the first time that had happened in eight years so it was a monumental breakthrough. I asked Johns if he was going to resume playing—he was the last of the stop-outs—and he said he did not know. I said, 'You should play. You're a long time retired. If you retire because of this issue, you'll be bitter in a few years time.'

I don't think I was the overwhelming influence and other people must have told him the same thing. Anyway he announced later that week that he would resume playing.

Through the whole battle, it was the players I mostly felt sorry for—especially the ones who stayed with the ARL because the News Ltd papers always made it look as if Super League was well on top and would invariably win. I was constantly ringing chief executives to shore up support and they were ringing me because they thought I might have known more about what was going on than what they had been told. That was never the case. We shared the information totally to the loyal clubs. We had no secret agendas.

Everything News Ltd could dream up they would turn into a headline. It became laughable. In the end even the most ardent Super League supporters among the public and players were starting to squirm with embarrassment at News Ltd's antics in Sydney and Brisbane.

The media bombardment had some effect of course. That was unavoidable. We would all be hit by bouts of depression, wondering if this war would ever end and whether we were just being stupid in continuing to fight. Someone would ring me to lift my spirits. Another time I might ring someone else. Looking back I'm glad we didn't all get the blues at the same time. I don't know what would have happened.

Australia's win in the World Cup was a tremendous boost to morale for us. Seeing Brad Fittler raise the Cup high brought tears to my eyes. John Quayle rang me at full-time and he was emotional as well. The win strengthened our resolve. Time confirmed, at least to me, that Super League had never intended to run its own competition. They never intended that because of the way they handled themselves. They never intended having to defend themselves in court. That's why they were so brutal, so secretive and so misleading and illegal.

Once the battle reached court, absolutely desperate offers were made by Super League to prevent some of their people having to go into the witness box. Had News Ltd boss Ken Cowley given evidence, who knows what affect it would have had on the result?

Short Passes

My life has just gone with the flow. I have taken it very much day-to-day. I don't plan a lot. And I probably see myself as a late developer in finding my real role in life. I always thought that when my real life began I'd be doing something that wouldn't involve football coaching or sport.

There will come a time when I won't be able to play kids games any more, although being around young players is what keeps you young at heart. A lot of things in my life have suffered because of my involvement with football, especially since I have been coaching. A lot of people believe I've had a stormy career in rugby league but mostly my emotional outbursts come as a result of me not releasing the pressure built up from other incidents. Because I kept the lid on my feelings about things I often seem to explode over something that is totally unrelated. There have been things in my life I would like to have stood up and told the truth about when they happened but instead of ranting and raving I've kept them inside. Sometimes the release comes in an explosion about something of far less importance—something that I laugh about later.

The turmoil that I have been through personally in the past four or five years has definitely left its scars. There are a lot of things I have sacrificed because of my involvement in sport and rugby league. My education was sacrificed. My first marriage was sacrificed. My parents who have been loyal, loving and tremendously supportive through the whole thing have probably borne the brunt of the tragedies I have known, more than I have. They know what I'm feeling and they know the truth. It is my parents who feel the need to get up and scream sometimes because of the unjust way they perceive their son is being treated. I know it has all been very hard on them as well. That is a darker side of football we all have to live with.

There is no escaping the fact that the headlines any footballer or coach generates on and off the field, good and bad will affect his family. I have lived my life for football, as a player and now a coach. There were things I should have done better but overall I see my involvement in football as having been great. Coaching is not as simple as some people might think. It is not just being with your players and turning up on Sunday and playing. I put a lot more into it than that. Therefore the rewards are greater and the pains are greater as well. Unless you take an interest in people personally it is hard to be a successful coach. It is a very big part of the picture. I do not want to paint an image of myself as someone who has been hard done by or someone beset with misgivings about what they have done with their life. Nothing could be farther from the truth. I view myself as extremely lucky to have become involved in rugby league the way I have. I have also worked hard and put in long hours to achieve any success that has come my way. Coaching and playing rugby league in the top echelon requires the same dedication and determination needed to be a success in any walk of life. I've gone beyond the realms of what a coach might do in order to get to know people and to help people and to achieve. It has been done not looking for reward. I love people and I love being with people.

After the death of Ben Alexander I questioned whether I should allow myself to get so close to the players. For a period of time I questioned whether my ideas were right in being so closely associated with the team and the players and their individual personalities. I wondered if it would be preferable to adopt a more clinical approach. A case of: I'm the coach and you're the players—and never the twain shall meet. I decided to continue as I had always done. But only after a lot of soul searching. My usual attitude to a situation like that is to bite my tongue and say nothing. I don't show I'm reacting even though inwardly I'm boiling. That frustration will come out some day, somewhere else. People say to me, 'you must hate referees'. I don't. For me it's just an outlet—to go to the footy and yell at the footy, the same as the bloke who pays for his ticket.

Here are some observations on things and people in and around my life:

GAMBLING:
I wish I had done a tenth of the things people say I have as a gambler. I do love it. But a lot of the stories and rumours about my gambling were instigated as part of a smear campaign by Canterbury. I'm certainly no angel. I've gambled since I was seven years of age. And I'll gamble until I'm 107. I used to go to the dogs with dad as a kid. I've wagged school to go to the races. The punt has been a big part of my life and like every punter I have great stories of success and great stories of near misses and great stories of failures. I've run the whole gambit. I had a difficult period after Ben Alexander died where I lost a few dollars. But gambling has never been a problem for me. It's always been just a release. Every year after the grand final when the last game of football is played, I can't wait to get to the race course. Then, come January 24 every year—my birthday—I stop going to the races and concentrate on football. I've done that for years.

I go hard during the summer, I don't miss too much. I love the anominity of the race track. Everywhere I go I'm Phil

Gould rugby league coach. When you go to the races you can have the prime minister standing 100 metres away from some crim. The track is somewhere I can go and get away from everything that is a problem in my life.

I've had some big wins. I once picked up $165,000 on a Melbourne Cup trifecta. I've held tickets for more than that, but that was the biggest win.

Punting has been good to me. I bought my first house from money I won at the races. I bought my first car out of money I won gambling.

I think gambling is the only real chance in life for the man in the street. For the fellow who goes to work every day and comes home with his $300–$400 every week, gambling gives him his shot at the title. Whether it is Lotto, lottery tickets, gambling on the horses or whatever it is a chance to get ahead. It is the light at the end of the tunnel. It's often the incentive to keep going. I've never been a saver. I just wait for the day when I have a win and then I get things done.

INFLUENCES IN MY LIFE:
My father Bruce has been a solid supporter of mine all my life, even when he was not totally convinced I was going in the right direction. He has always been there for me when the going was tough. He deserves to share whatever success I have achieved in rugby league because without his backing, it might not have occured.

When ever I've had trouble, dad is the first person I've contacted. I'll never forget the sight of him using his police pass to get me out of the eye hospital before they could perform an operation that would have prevented me ever playing again.

My mother, as all mothers are to their sons, has been a constant source of support. I worry sometimes about the headlines of the seasons past and the effect they had on her. I always knew they worried and hurt her a lot more than they did me, but she never said much.

The headlines and bad press generated through the dramas at Canterbury in 1989 were particularly hurtful for her.

My mother would not hurt a fly but when Justice Burchett handed down his damning report on Peter Moore she uttered harsh words for one of the few times in her life. She said: 'Now I can die happy.'

South Sydney coach George Piggins was always very generous about my contribution to the team. But I can tell you I learned as much from George as he did from me—not so much about football but about people and how to treat them.

He was and is also a genuinely tough guy, with a great attitude to the game and to life.

KERRY PACKER:
I have not had a lot to do with Kerry but I find him a very relaxed bloke at this stage of his life. I've been a great admirer of his achievements. And I can confirm he is a fanatical sports lover. He absolutely loves watching sport and talking sport and participating in sport.

In my view he's a great Australian but with that he's the kind of man that we ordinary blokes identify with quite easily. We don't see him as the high-flier who lives in a different world to us. We see him as someone who likes the things we like and does the things we do. He just happens to have a lot more money than us.

JAMES PACKER:
James is a great bloke, with two sides to his life. The first James Packer is a man I could never identify with because he travels the world on business, has great responsibilities, has an important job involving thousands of employees. When he calls it

might be from India, America or England. And that might all be in the one week. It's a busy lifestyle but he loves the competitiveness of it all and he is very, very good at it.

The James Packer I know better through his life with us at the Roosters is a similar man to his father. He is a great sports lover and a great bloke. He's a very, very normal 28 or 29-year-old who loves sport and is trying his utmost to make the Roosters a competitive force in the premiership. His life as a businessman does not overflow into his life as a director and supporter of the Roosters' football club. He has a great ability to keep both worlds separate.

James is unfairly criticised at times for his involvement with Easts. He was invited onto the board of the licensed club because of his expertise in business and he has played a significant role in re-establishing Easts Leagues' Club as a viable concern after some tough years. At the football club he just gets his ticket and comes and watches games. He has very little to do with recruiting players.

WARREN RYAN:
To my mind Warren is undoubtedly the greatest coach of all rugby league coaches. When they talk about 'Supercoach'—and it should be singular not plural—there is only one. Warren Ryan. He was a true visionary of the game and without doubt has been the greatest influence on both my playing days and my coaching career.

Ryan was ahead of his time in the early 1980s—and his record speaks for itself. His only Achilles Heel was his constant paranoia about the media and what people might be saying about him. Towards the end it was that attitude and those relationships with different sections of the media that took their toll. I think they diluted his enthusiasm for the job he was born to do—to coach rugby league teams.

Warren believes administrators had to change the rules of rugby league because of his influence—and he could be right. He used to recall how officials had changed the laws of billiards to check Walter Lindrum and say they were doing the same thing in rugby league. They were changing the rules of the game to undermine the way he coached, he reckoned.

Warren's tactics and the way he coached players to perform were well known. He was of the belief that Peter Moore was instrumental in having those aspects of rugby league eased out of the game—such things as the 10 metre rule, the downtown kick play, catching the bomb in your own in-goal resulting in a 20 metre tap instead of a line-drop out and increased scrutiny of head high tackles. All of them were pointed toward the kind of football Warren had used to dominate the premiership in the middle 1980s.

I have no doubt Warren was more than capable of adjusting his tactics to suit the changes but I think his priorities altered and rugby league went on the backburner. One thing I do know is if Warren Ryan had a football team to coach today and concentrated solely on tactics and match plans and nothing else, that team would be a force in the premiership. The hardest thing about coaching is trying to marry all the other aspects of the job together—the media, the club, the spectators, the committee, relationships with the management, and the rest.

If anything did, it was those 'other aspects' that beat Warren. A coach of hard, tough football teams he had much deserved success.

PETER MOORE:
I didn't need Justice Burchett to tell me about Peter Moore's character. I learned about that first hand. The man known as 'Bullfrog' is an odd contrast in character. But there are times when he can be disarming and even charming.

If I saw him today I would not mind having a drink with him. He can be very funny and good company. I often wondered about the relationship between Peter Moore and his former coach Warren Ryan. Moore's apparent single-mindedness in trying to put Ryan out of the game was wrong.

What amazed me during the Super League war was to hear players like Simon Gillies and even Terry Lamb say they did not want to go back and play for 'THAT' ARL considering the way it was run—when the fact was it was very much Peter Moore running the ARL. Via his influence and power over the media, which he used for his own self-interest and power and to push his club and his family, his influence over the game were significant.

I do not regret Peter Moore's departure from the (ARL) game. In my view if there was one good aspect of the Super League intrusion—and this is definitely the only one—it was the end of Peter Moore as a powerbroker in the ARL. I believe that had Peter Moore remained loyal to the ARL, to the game and to his friend of 40 years Ken Arthurson, Super League would not have found a footing. Peter Moore has been quoted as saying Ken Arthurson was his best friend in life. To do what he did to Arthurson says enough about Peter Moore without the need for any further embellishment.

ROSS SEYMOUR:
Few people know much about Ross. He's been reported as being a lot of things to me. He's been identified as my manager, my bodyguard, my spy. In fact Ross just happens to be a bloke who is awake at 3 o'clock in the morning when I am, and I can ring him and talk football.

He is a good mate and has been for a long time, going back to the days when I played at Newtown. He is always there when needed. Ross always manages to bring some lightheartedness into the most serious of situations. He has the ability to keep feet on the ground and heads from getting too big.

Here is one story. I was Penrith coach in 1992 at a time when we were scheduled to play Canterbury the next weekend. First up there was my first Origin match to get through and the NSW team was leading 8–6 with about 15 minutes to go. The situation was tense. Brad Clyde was off the field injured, so was Laurie Daley and we were running out of replacements. I looked at the clock and then across at Ross and I said: 'Do you think we can hang on?' He glanced back: 'Can we just get this over so we can start planning to play the Bulldogs on Sunday? I'm sick of this.' I just shook my head. I thought here's the one bloke in the Stadium who doesn't care a bit about what's going on. He's only here because I am. Everyone's got him down as the brains of the outfit and he couldn't care less. He brings levity into my life and it works. He is the most carefree, unflappable and nonchalant person you could meet. A hot dog, a pie and a game of footy to watch and he is content. Over the years people who speculated about his role with me were so wide of the mark, we used to read what they wrote and laugh out loud.

JACK GIBSON:
He's held in particularly high regard at Eastern Suburbs after his wins in the 1974 and 1975 premierships. He has been back to the club on various occasions and done things. You've got to admire someone who has the aura he has and respect of so many people within the game about what he does.

He has been less than kind to me for some reason. I fail to understand why but it does not make any real impression on me. It does not occur to me to think about Jack's opinion of me. I'm at Easts trying to do a job. I'm just like him. I live and die by what I do and I'm trying hard all the time. As for worrying about his criticism of me it doesn't make one iota of difference to me what he says or thinks.

BOBBY FULTON:
I like Bob. I didn't know him all that well before the Super League drama started. I find him super competitive at everything he does. He can open himself up to having a lot of enemies because he can be less than caring with most people he meets (laughs). You ask people what they think about Bozo and they say: 'Well. Bozo's just Bozo.'

That's usually just the best way to describe him. You've only got to look at his record and you can see he's a winner. He might not have always played strictly by the rules to get there. But he's a winner. If, at the end of the day, winning is what counts, then he's a winner in just about everything he tries to do.

And he's another one who can see the lighter side of life. His philosophy is basically: 'Life's a gee-up and then you die.' That's the way he lives.

JOHN QUAYLE:
If you were picking sides for toughness, he would be the first one selected. What he has withstood in the past 15 months of the ARL–Super League battle is astonishing. While everyone I knew who was closely involved in the battle tried to get away for a break at some stage, John stayed at his post for every minute of the drama. He bore the brunt of the attack superbly from Super League and News Limited and just turned up smiling every day. Justice has now prevailed and he is still in charge.

I don't know what his plans are for the future but I know he will be successful at whatever he attempts. He has come out of this drama as very strong and very resilient and a very, very capable administrator at any level.

Away from the public eye, and in the company of people he

knows and trusts, he lets his hair down (or what is left of it). He is a real good bloke. I said to him before the result of the Super League and ARL court case that, whichever way it went, he had nothing to regret.

GREAT PLAYERS:
The first ever game of rugby league I ever remember seeing was between St George and Newtown at Kogarah Oval. My father used to work at Newtown Police Station with Brian 'Chicka' Moore, the Kangaroo and Newtown centre. We went to watch the Blues play, Dad had me in the Newtown team outfit and I was a keen supporter. St George beat us something like 44–3 and from that moment I was a St George supporter and very much a Johnny Raper fan. He and Billy Smith and Graeme Langlands were the ones who started my interest in rugby league and made me want to play the game.

The best players I played against were mostly the ones who could do something. You know, scare you because they could do something phenomenal with the ball—players such as Arthur Beetson, Eric Grothe, Brett Kenny or Greg Alexander. They were the ones in the opposition side who could do things by themselves that would hurt you on the scoreboard.

The best player I played with was Terry Lamb by a long way. He's also one of the best blokes I've ever known.

The most gifted player I ever coached was Greg Alexander, by a long, long, way. He had stunning individual skills. Some of the things he could do were never seen by spectators. They might have happened at training. But he had unbelievable athleticism. Greg always had an inferiority complex which we worked hard to erase. I love Greg—we are good mates. I know what he did in his career and he does not have to answer to anyone. He captained a grand final winning side and he played Test football and he was a Kangaroo.

MARK GEYER:
I know he has caused a lot of heartache to a lot of people—me included—but he is very difficult to dislike. He's just one of those loveable rogue type blokes. He is someone you could always go and have a drink and a laugh with. He's a very funny fellow.

BRAD FITTLER:
I've been involved with Brad for most of his career and I think he will end up as one of the all time greats. He is a tremendous talent and a personality. To withstand what he had to endure at Penrith when his best friend in life Ben Alexander was killed, and for him to then go on and achieve what he has done, is a sign of his great inner strength and composure.

Comparing what he has done with the careers of other players who were at the Penrith club at the time, is a testimony to his own determination and his mother's guidance, illustrating the kind of person he is as a footballer and man. I'm very proud of him and very proud for him. I love him like a brother. We are very close.

Last year when Freddie picked up the World Cup at Wembley after Australia won the final, I was watching it all unfold on television in my lounge room and I shed a tear. It was just a magnificent achievement knowing who Brad was and where he had come from. At 24-years-of-age, he still has a lot of great football ahead of him.

TOP THREE MOMENTS IN MY CAREER:
Running onto the Sydney Cricket Ground for the 1981 grand final with Newtown in front of 60,000 people. It was my dad's favourite club and he was there as a spectator. We lost but no-one really expected to win.

Winning the 1991 grand final with Penrith.

Good as GOULD

Watching Brad Fittler pick up the World Cup in 1994. Brad was very heavily targetted by Super League but he stuck with the ARL, probably through his association with me. I was just glad that everything I had told him would happen, did happen and his trust in me was vindicated. He has repaid me a million times over for anything I have done for him.

THE MEDIA:
You love them when they say nice things and you hate them when they say bad things. You can become very, very sensitive to it all. My attitude over the years has been to ignore it all and read as little as possible. Things are never as good as the media says or as bad as they say.

I do dislike the way the media takes sides on every issue. There is never as much truth as you might like. The media is not necessarily after the truth, it is chasing what someone wants to say.

Media people can be motivated and influenced by other people into writing and presenting stories. There is often a lot of spite and vindictiveness that comes through. A lot of the time it is someone else's vindictiveness and spite they use in a story, depending on how powerful in the game the person they are quoting happens to be.

I won't forget some of the spite, the ill-will and the lies that were created in News Limited newspapers during the Super League war. Some journalists—one in particular—in this town willingly surrendered credibility for reasons known only to themselves and wrote whatever they were told to write. They proved the old saying you cannot let the facts stand in the way of a good yarn.

I've had tremendous press over the years. But I have never believed life was as good as they were saying or as bad as they were saying when they wrote less flattering things.

Tony Adams of the *Daily Telegraph* is one journalist for

whom I have no time. I have made that clear to him. I am also aware of his antics in press boxes—along with another journalist from the same paper—of bellowing out deriding and demeaning remarks at players, knowing they will not be heard, remarks like: 'Get him up here with us.' and 'Get the hook out for this bloke.' These blokes are only brave in the press box.

In my case, I worry more about what my family thinks about what is said in the newspapers than I do myself. If I can ever convince my mum to stop reading the papers life will be a lot more peaceful.

I see the introduction of so many more former players into the media—especially television—as a good sign. It's what people want. They want to see fun in the game. That is why people like Paul Vautin, Steve Roach and Peter Jackson are so successful. For a lot of people rugby league is the core of their family entertainment. They rely on television, radio and newspapers for their information. That is why it annoys me when people write articles that are misleading.

Epilogue

On the morning of Thursday 23 May, 1996 rugby league's battlefield was once again in the courtroom as the travelling legal circus moved into 21A, Federal Court Sydney to continue the fight that had long since become known as the 'Super League War'. For Gould the season was shaping very nicely indeed. Now a man thoroughly on top of the job at Easts (Sydney City Roosters), Gould was getting great enjoyment out of the old club's best start to a season ever. With the days shortening and winter pressing in, the Roosters still hadn't lost a game. Old timers at the club were starting to pinch themselves. Was this really happening? (Easts hadn't won a competitive competition since 1975 . . . and before that, 1945!) The State of Origin series mid season brought sweet revenge for coach Gould and his committed NSW Blues after the shock defeat of '95.

Seemingly thoroughly in control of the many facets of his challenging life in football, Gould was looking like a coach at the height of his powers. Street smart and classically intelligent at the same time, he was matching his coaching prowess with the skillful handling of his many and varied media commitments. The kid from Penrith had come a long, long way, even though he was only 60 kilometres from 'home'.

With Phil Gould, the sailing would assuredly never be smooth, and the stormy days that arrived at irregular intervals would add seasoning to the tale of his pilgrimage through rugby league's 1980s and '90s.

Good as Gould? As the successes pile up season upon season, the phrase is taking on a new meaning.